Clear and concise, this textbook is an introduction to phonology for students which assumes no prior knowledge of this area of linguistics and provides an overall view of the field which can be covered within one year. The book does not confine itself to any specific theoretical approach and can therefore be used for study within any framework and also to prepare students for work in more specialised frameworks such as Optimality Theory, Government, Dependency and Declarative Phonology. Each chapter focuses on a particular set of theoretical issues including segments, syllables, feet and phonological processing. Gussmann explores these areas using data drawn from a variety of languages including English, Icelandic, Russian, Irish, Finnish, Turkish and others. Suggestions for further reading and summaries at the end of each chapter enable students to find their way to more advanced phonological work.

EDMUND GUSSMANN is Professor of General Linguistics at the University of Gdańsk, Poland. His books include *Introduction to Phonological Analysis* (1980), *Studies in Abstract Phonology* (1980), *Phono-Morphology* (ed., 1985), *Licensing in Syntax and Phonology* (ed., 1995) and (with A. Doyle) *Reverse Dictionary of Modern Irish* (1996).

Phonology
Analysis and Theory

EDMUND GUSSMANN
University of Gdańsk

CAMBRIDGE
UNIVERSITY PRESS

PUBLISHED BY THE PRESS SYNDICATE OF THE UNIVERSITY OF CAMBRIDGE
The Pitt Building, Trumpington Street, Cambridge, United Kingdom

CAMBRIDGE UNIVERSITY PRESS
The Edinburgh Building, Cambridge CB2 2RU, UK
40 West 20th Street, New York, NY 10011-4211, USA
477 Williamstown Road, Port Melbourne, VIC 3207, Australia
Ruiz de Alarcón 13, 28014 Madrid, Spain
Dock House, The Waterfront, Cape Town 8001, South Africa

http://www.cambridge.org

© Edmund Gussmann 2002

This book is in copyright. Subject to statutory exception
and to the provisions of relevant collective licensing agreements,
no reproduction of any part may take place without
the written permission of Cambridge University Press.

First published 2002
Reprinted 2002

Printed in the United Kingdom at the University Press, Cambridge

Typefaces Times 10/13 pt. and Formata   *System* LATEX 2_ε [TB]

A catalogue record for this book is available from the British Library.

ISBN 0 521 57409 9 hardback
ISBN 0 521 57428 5 paperback

Contents

Preface	*page*	ix
List of abbreviations		xiii

1 Sounds and segments — 1
1.1 Introduction — 1
1.2 Aspiration of plosives in English — 4
1.3 The Muskerry Irish [ɑ – a] alternation — 7
1.4 *Dark* and *clear l* in RP English — 11
1.5 Voicedness of fricatives in Old and Modern English — 12
1.6 Summary — 16
1.7 Suggested further reading — 17

2 The melody and the skeleton — 19
2.1 Introduction — 19
2.2 Equivalence of long vowels and diphthongs in English — 20
2.3 Germanic and Finnish nuclear simplifications — 23
2.4 Compensatory lengthening in Germanic and Turkish — 28
2.5 The phonology of English inflectional morphology — 31
2.6 English *linking r* and the unassociated melody — 40
2.7 Summary — 43
2.8 Suggested further reading — 44

3 Domains and phonological regularities — 45
3.1 Introduction — 45
3.2 The velar nasal consonant in English — 46
3.3 Preaspiration in Modern Icelandic — 54
3.4 Dorsal spirants in Standard German — 59
3.5 Summary — 63
3.6 Suggested further reading — 64

4 The syllable — 66
4.1 Introduction — 66
4.2 Some simple English syllables — 67

vi   *Contents*

	4.3	Empty onsets: French *h-aspiré*	69
	4.4	English onsets and rhymes	72
	4.5	Nasal assimilation or nasal place sharing in English	78
	4.6	Nasal place sharing in Dutch and German	82
	4.7	Nasal place sharing in Polish	86
	4.8	Summary	89
	4.9	Suggested further reading	90

5 More on codas 91
	5.1	Introduction	91
	5.2	Word-final consonants in Irish	92
	5.3	English word-final consonants and internal codas	96
	5.4	Nasal–obstruent place sharing continued	101
	5.5	Consonant sequences starting with [s]	107
	5.6	Summary	116
	5.7	Suggested further reading	117

6 Some segmental regularities 118
	6.1	Introduction	118
	6.2	Turkish vowel harmony	119
	6.3	Vowel reduction in English	124
	6.4	Polish nasal vowels	130
	6.5	Obstruent sequences in Icelandic	134
	6.6	Russian vowel reduction	139
	6.7	German final devoicing	145
	6.8	Summary	154
	6.9	Suggested further reading	156

7 Syllable structure and phonological effects: quantity in Icelandic 157
	7.1	Introduction	157
	7.2	Preliminaries	157
	7.3	Open syllable lengthening	159
	7.4	Word-final consonants and vowel length	161
	7.5	Codas, onsets and vocalic quantity	163
	7.6	Quantity as evidence for syllabification	167
	7.7	Coda–onset contacts in Icelandic	178
	7.8	Length in compounds	181
	7.9	Summary	184
	7.10	Suggested further reading	185

8 Segmental double agents 186
	8.1	Introduction	186
	8.2	Icelandic vowel length: an extension	187

	8.3	Russian labial fricatives	193
	8.4	Polish dorsal obstruents	197
	8.5	Welsh vowels	200
	8.6	Summary	203
	8.7	Suggested further reading	204
9	**Words and feet: stress in Munster Irish**		**205**
	9.1	Introduction	205
	9.2	Stress and nuclei	206
	9.3	Stress and feet	214
	9.4	Summary	222
	9.5	Suggested further reading	223

Conclusion 224
Appendix The phonetic alphabet of the International Phonetic Association 226
References 227
Index 233

Preface

This book is intended as an introduction to phonology for students who have not previously been exposed to this area of linguistics. It contains material which can be covered within one academic year and provides guides for extensive further study. While it does not presuppose any knowledge of phonology, it does assume prior familiarity with the basic terminology of articulatory phonetics and some background in general linguistics. For this reason notions such as *morpheme* or *spirant* are not explained here – readers needing assistance with such terms should consult other sources, such as, for example, Trask (1996).

Because the objective of the book is to provide a manageable introduction to the field it has been necessary to exercise maximal restraint as far as the issues covered are concerned. As is well-known, phonology, just like any other branch of linguistics, is not a uniform discipline. Quite conversely, the field is theoretically vibrant, with several substantially different models currently vying for the dominant position, a situation which confuses not only the beginner student. It has been decided that introducing all or even a few of these models would amount to a fairly superficial survey of different techniques of description, or would require a book much broader in scope (and in length). It is quite unlikely that a textbook of that sort could be used by the introductory student with much profit, and a course based on it would last much longer than one year. Assuming that students do not live by phonology alone, there is only so much that can be covered within a single course. For these reasons a different perspective has been adopted.

Leaving aside the significant theoretical variation among different phonological models, it is possible to identify a body of data that most or perhaps all models would regard as calling for a phonological description. These are the issues that would need to be described in any model, even if there is a measure of disagreement concerning some specific sets of data. In this book we have adopted the view that the student should try and see what qualifies as a phonological issue and how it may be interpreted. Thus we do not set off by assuming that we know what the problem is, and define our task as basically capturing the problem in terms of some theory. Obviously, phonology means making theoretical assumptions and proposing hypotheses – we have not tried to avoid these. Phonology also means looking for and finding the relevant data, a task which is anything but easy. In this book we make an effort to avoid creating the impression that phonology amounts to merely providing a neat formula for a handful of examples taken from a workbook. For this reason, although we obviously start with quite simple cases, our data become progressively more complex, and the regularities involved are seen to be intricately interwoven with others. In general, the emphasis is not on formalising or providing definitive answers but on identifying issues and pointing out the consequences of adopting specific theoretical positions. This approach has been motivated by the desire to convince the reader from the start that neither the author nor the classroom instructor know all the answers to the questions raised in this book. They do not. But they definitely know more questions than the student, and are aware of various attempts which have been made to grapple with these questions.

It is this attempt to identify phonological problems and provide a possible theoretical framework for them that is the focus of interest in the following nine chapters. No specific theoretical doctrine/approach/theory is explicitly adopted or adhered to, and hence practitioners of any particular model may be disappointed or may want to take issue with the particulars of what follows. This does not mean that the author has no theoretical preferences or that these preferences are not reflected in the book: the notion of a theory-free theoretical approach is an absurdity. No instructor or practising phonologist will have any difficulties in identifying the theoretical proclivities of the present author. As far as possible, however, we have tried to avoid model-specific machinery and theory-internal issues. For the same reason we have refrained from adopting any specific phonological alphabet (distinctive features, particles, elements) and used instead the traditional labels of phonetic description such as velarity, voicedness, rounding etc. It is hoped that the gist of our proposals will be acceptable to different frameworks and that most of the interpretations we offer can be translated into the distinctive theoretical language of individual models. Students should constantly be invited to venture their own reanalyses of the textbook cases and, where possible, search for new or additional sources of data. Partly for this reason some of the analyses we provide are deliberately provocative and can – or should – be challenged.

The constraints adopted here mean also that this textbook should not be viewed as a survey of the various types of phonological regularities in existence. Both the scope of the book and its author's competence (or lack of it) preclude any such attempt. Economies had to be effected and the results will hardly please everybody. The author remains solely responsible for the individual selections and for all other failures and misdemeanours.

A short comment is in order with respect to the vexed problem of transcription. Although the number of languages used for discussion and illustration is very small, the phonetic tradition behind the various sources varies considerably. To make the task easier for the student we have ruthlessly unified the different systems by bringing them maximally close to the current IPA notation as presented in the *Handbook of the International Phonetic Association* (1999). The IPA chart is included in the Appendix and should be regularly consulted in case of doubt.

Every chapter is supplied with a list of suggested further reading. These lists comprise sources used in the body of the chapter and indications as to where the problems or the theoretical issues following from them have been discussed previously. Some references to different theoretical frameworks will be found there. The listings are deliberately restrictive since they relate directly to some issues discussed in the body of a given chapter; we believe that an introductory text is not the place for extensively documenting the development of the discipline in general or of the history of specific problems and their solutions. By consulting the works mentioned the student will be able to find his/her way to more advanced phonological work. This strategy is in line with a leitmotif of this book: models come and go, problems remain. It is hoped that the reader will discover some of the reasons why both of these statements are true, and in doing so come to realise why phonology is such a fascinating study.

The writing of this book has taken an inordinately long period of time. Two people were involved in its inception: Heinz Giegerich first suggested to me the idea of writing an introduction to non-derivational phonology, and Judith Ayling of Cambridge University Press helped me thrash out a general framework within which the discussion could be cast. During the writing of the book I have received support from two institutions and a number of individuals. My work on Irish was aided by the Cultural Relations Committee of the Irish Ministry for Foreign Affairs through grants supporting research into Irish in Poland. I also received a grant from the Stofnun Sigurðar Nordals in Reykjavík which allowed me to pursue my work in Icelandic. I am deeply obliged to both institutions for their support.

A number of people have read and commented on parts of the book at the different stages of its gestation, and also responded to questions about language data. I would like to single out in particular Aidan W. Doyle who read individual parts of the manuscript and also its prefinal version, raising doubts and helpful questions which forced me to clarify numerous points. Colin Ewen read the typescript for Cambridge University Press and provided a massive amount of feedback which has affected the shape of the book. Special thanks go to the copyeditor,

Citi Potts for the energy and commitment that went into tracing errors and inconsistencies, for divining my meanings and prompting clearer alternatives. For comments and advice I am also grateful to Eugeniusz Cyran, Bogdan Szymanek, Bożena Cetnarowska, Anita Buczek-Zawiła, Olga Molchanova, Kristján Árnason, Silja Aðalsteinsdóttir and Jeroen van de Weijer. Finally I wish to acknowledge the great help I have received from Andrew Winnard of Cambridge University Press whose quiet competence and unfailing responsiveness have been invaluable.

Abbreviations

acc.	accusative
adj.	adjective
augmen.	augmentative
dat.	dative
def.	definite
def. art.	definite article
dim.	diminutive
express.	expressive
fem.	feminine
gen.	genitive
imper.	imperative
indef.	indefinite
instr.	instrumental
loc.	locative
masc.	masculine
n.	noun
neut.	neuter
nom.	nominative
part.	participle
pl.	plural
sg.	singular
vb.	verb
vb. n.	verbal noun
voc.	vocative

1

Sounds and segments

1.1 Introduction

It is a commonly held view that speech consists of sounds: morphemes, words, phrases and sentences are thought of as made up of a series of sounds, one following the other. Speakers of English will readily agree that a word such as *plot* starts with the sound [p], which is followed by [l], then the vowel [ɒ], and ends with a [t] sound. Likewise, speakers of French are not likely to object to the word *garder* 'look after' being recorded as [gaʁˈde], and speakers of Icelandic will find nothing strange about *bráðum* 'soon' being transcribed as [ˈprauːðʏm]. Phonetic transcription, just like the alphabetic writing systems on which it is modelled, encourages the view that speech consists of individual, separate or discrete sounds strung together in much the same way as beads on a string. Although there exist non-alphabetic orthographies which do not necessarily impose this view, phonetic transcription, which is believed to be an objective record of pronunciation, leaves no doubt as to the divisibility of speech into small chunks called sounds; within this system of recording speech, separate symbols are available for what are regarded as sufficiently different sound units. The procedure whereby words are divided into smaller units is called **segmentation**.

Phonetic transcription was originally devised to remove ambiguities that conventional spelling systems could not cope with: in English what is spelt *wind* can be pronounced [wɪnd] or [waɪnd], depending upon the meaning, while *lower* can be either [ləʊə] or [laʊə], again with different meanings; conversely, the same phonetic chunk [æŋ] is spelt as differently as *ang* and *ingue* in *bang* and *meringue* respectively, while what is phonetically [ʃuː] can be spelt – depending on the word that is intended – either *shoe* or *choux*. Although English offers probably an extreme example of the discrepancy between sounds and spelling, arguably all languages which have an orthography display some orthographic departures from a consistent one-letter–one-sound and one-sound–one-letter model. The system of phonetic transcription, which is intended to overcome the various ambiguities, adopts the basic mechanism of any orthographic convention, as it embraces the assumption that speech is segmentable, with vowels and consonants following each other in different arrangements. The intuitive recognition of the segmentable nature of speech is thus reinforced by the linguistic tradition of phonetic transcription.

Speakers' intuitions and traditional orthography find support in the way the segmented chunks of sound function in languages. It is frequently the case that by replacing one sound with another we obtain different words; a substitution test of this kind shows that speech does indeed consist of **segments** or significant sounds which can be called independent sound units of the language. Consider the following set of English words:

[1] met [met]   net [net]   pet [pet]
     bet [bet]   let [let]   set [set]
     get [get]   vet [vet]   debt [det]
     het [het]   yet [jet]   wet [wet]
     jet [dʒet]

In all these words there is a chunk which is repeated, i.e. [et], and an initial consonant which differs in every case. Since we are dealing with separate words, the initial segment must be regarded as the first independent unit of the word. If we replace the vowel [e] by the diphthong [ai], in several cases the result is an existing English word:

[2] might [maɪt]   night [naɪt]   bite [baɪt]
     light [laɪt]   site/sight [saɪt]   white/Wight [waɪt]

to which others may be added:

[3] kite [kaɪt]   fight [faɪt]   rite/right [raɪt]
     tight [taɪt]   (in)dict [daɪt]

Finally, while maintaining the first two segments we can replace the last consonant in the words:

[4] Meg [meg]   men [men]
     mess [mes]   met [met]

It is also possible to omit the consonant preceding the vowel [5a] or the one following it [5b], e.g.

[5]
a.   ate [et]   egg [eg]   Ed [ed]
     isle [aɪl]   aim [eɪm]   oak [əʊk]
     earn [ɜːn]   eel [iːl]   ooze [uːz]
b.   sigh [saɪ]   pie [paɪ]   vie [vaɪ]
     guy [gaɪ]   tie [taɪ]   rye [raɪ]
     dye/die [daɪ]   by/buy [baɪ]   lie/lye [laɪ]
     nigh [naɪ]   why [waɪ]

The replacement tests show very clearly that the intuitive division of the words in [1] into three segments, confirmed by the transcription, is linguistically real since the language exploits the three separate chunks for making different words. Admittedly, it is not the case that every possible combination is actually attested as a real word – hence there are gaps – but these gaps must be regarded as an accident. The following could be regular words of English which just happen not to have found their way into dictionaries:

[6]   pite/pight [paɪt]   vite [vaɪt]
        weg [weg]   kie [kaɪ]

Sound combinations such as those in [6] are referred to as **potential words** while those in [1] – [5] are **attested words**. This distinction is generally recognised in phonology (linguistics) as it reveals an important property of language: it is not a closed system but has the potential to expand and develop.

Speakers' intuitions, phonetic transcription and the replacement test all tell the same story: speech is segmental, words consist of sequences of units following each other. As we will see below, this very simple statement will need to be seriously revised and modified. Caution must be exercised in the use of the very notion of **speech sound** or **segment**.

The popular conviction that speech is segmentable and each word can be broken up into a limited number of sounds leads to the conclusion that each language has at its disposal a definite number of such sounds which it uses in different combinations. Observation of the spoken language shows that this conclusion is very much oversimplified. Phonetic events by their very nature are unique; hence, strictly speaking, no two sounds are ever exactly identical even if they are perceived as such by users of the language: there are individual differences between speakers as far as their voice quality goes, and even the same speaker on different occasions will produce sounds that differ, for example, in loudness. These differences can be identified and described by means of the rigorous physical methods of acoustic phonetics but they contribute little to the way sounds are used for linguistic purposes. All linguistic practice tends to disregard such minute phonetic distinctions, but this means the sounds we speak of are in reality not physical but **abstract sounds**. For practical reasons we continue to use the term **sounds** but it is worth keeping in mind that this is nothing but a convenient shortcut.

There is a linguistically more relevant difficulty connected with the notion of sounds. It is easy to see that what speakers treat as the same sound displays marked differences depending on the context in which it appears. Such **contextual variability** of sounds is found in every language. Phonetically we can describe the different sounds, for example, by indicating the articulatory differences involved such as degree of length or voicing, presence or absence of aspiration and the like. Phonetics, however, will not tell us that we are dealing with contextual variability of what are in some sense the same sound units. This constitutes one of the areas of interest of phonology. To see what is involved in the variation of sounds and how this affects the very notion of a language sound, we shall now look at a few examples, starting with a simple case of consonant differences in English.

1.2 Aspiration of plosives in English

English voiceless plosive consonants – the initial sounds in words like *peace, tease, keen* – are pronounced with a puff of air called **aspiration** and transcribed by means of the diacritic [ʰ] following the plosive: [pʰiːs], [tʰiːz], [kʰiːn]. No aspiration is found when voiceless plosives appear after [s]; as a result we find pairs of very similar consonants: [pʰ – p], [tʰ – t], [kʰ – k]. In [7] we list some words differing in the presence or absence of the initial fricative which consequently differ slightly as regards the following plosive.

[7] pain/pane [pʰeɪn]   Spain [speɪn]
     teem/team [tʰiːm]   steam [stiːm]
     key/quay [kʰiː]   ski [skiː]

English dialects, it should be added, differ considerably with respect to the extent and details of this phenomenon. Below we describe the situation found in the variety of southern British English known as Received Pronunciation (RP). It should be kept in mind, however, that in this dialect, just like in any other, some variation is bound to occur. In general, a voiceless plosive before a stressed vowel is accompanied by strong aspiration. As mentioned above, no aspiration is found when a plosive appears after [s]. This is shown in [7] where the left-hand words begin with an aspirated stop, while the plosives following [s] in the right-hand column are all pronounced without aspiration. By and large, the same holds true for word-internal position as shown in [8a], although phonetic descriptions usually note that aspiration before an unstressed vowel is relatively weak. Word-finally the situation is slightly more complicated since single plosives may be either aspirated or unaspirated; furthermore, the aspiration may be reinforced or even replaced by the glottal stop [ʔ]. A word such as *kick* may be pronounced in any of the following ways: [kʰɪkʰ], [kʰɪk], [kʰɪʔk] or [kʰɪʔ]. Assuming the careful, perhaps somewhat studied pronunciation with the released plosive, we observe that an aspirated plosive after [s] is just as impossible in word-final position [8b] as it is word-internally [8b] and word-initially.

[8]
a. supper ['sʌpʰə]　　aspen ['æspən]
　　batter ['bætʰə]　　pester ['pʰestə]
　　acorn ['eɪkʰɔːn]　　husky [hʌski]
b. hope [həʊpʰ]　　gasp [gɑːsp]
　　hate [heɪtʰ]　　haste [heɪst]
　　break/brake [breɪkʰ]　　tusk [tʰʌsk]

Aspirated and non-aspirated plosives are phonetically different as sounds, but in English they are felt to be closely related. The question is how to express this relatedness in a phonological description.

One way of capturing the relatedness of aspirated and non-aspirated plosives in English words is to concentrate on the contexts in which they appear. Contexts where sounds occur are known technically as their **distribution**. RP requires aspirated plosives in some contexts whereas non-aspirated ones must occur in others. The plosives may be viewed as associated with specific positions within a word. Thus the position before a stressed vowel displays strongly aspirated voiceless plosives; after a stressed vowel, including the word-final position, there are weakly aspirated plosives; the postconsonantal position, regardless of stress, shows unaspirated voiceless plosives. By adopting this perspective we move away from individual sounds and concentrate on what is possible or impossible in specific points or positions in a word.

It must be added that the very existence and distribution of aspirated plosives is a fact about English phonology: there is no particular reason why voiceless plosives should be aspirated in the first place – French, Russian and numerous other languages do not have aspirated plosives – and, indeed, some dialects of English itself have no aspiration. Other languages aspirate some plosives but not others: in Modern Icelandic, where all plosives are uniformly voiceless, some words contain aspirated consonants, whereas others have non-aspirated ones, and thus aspiration is a property that distinguishes one group of words from the other. This gives rise to contrasting pairs such as those in [9]:

[9]　　panna ['pʰanːa] 'frying pan'　　banna ['panːa] 'forbid'
　　　　tæma ['tʰaiːma] 'empty, vb.'　　dæma ['taiːma] 'judge, vb.'
　　　　kola ['kʰɔːla] 'coal, gen. pl.'　　gola ['kɔːla] 'breeze'

The distribution of aspirated and non-aspirated plosives varies depending on the language. Note that before a following sonorant – liquid or semivowel – aspiration in English is not present while the sonorant is partly or completely voiceless.

In Icelandic, on the other hand, aspiration is realised on the plosives also in this context. Word-internally, however, when a weakly aspirated plosive follows a nasal or a lateral, these sonorants remain voiced in English and the plosive itself may in fact lose its aspiration. In Icelandic, instead of the expected aspirated plosives we find non-aspirated ones, while the preceding sonorants are partially or completely voiceless. Compare some examples from the two languages, noting that a circle under or over a consonantal symbol denotes voicelessness:

[10]

	English	Icelandic
a.	plate [pl̥eɪtʰ]	plata ['pʰlaːtʰa] 'disc'
	prone [pr̥əʊn]	prjóna ['pʰrjouːna] 'knit'
	tulip ['tjuːlɪpʰ]	tjörn [tʰjœrtn̥] 'lake'
	clear [kl̥ɪə]	klæða ['kʰlaiːða] 'dress, vb.'
b.	banker ['bæŋk⁽ʰ⁾ə]	bankar ['bauŋ̊kar] 'bank, nom. pl.'
	banter ['bænt⁽ʰ⁾ə]	panta ['pʰan̥ta] 'order, vb.'
	pamper ['pʰæmp⁽ʰ⁾ə]	lampi ['lam̥pɪ] 'lamp'
	silky ['sɪlk⁽ʰ⁾i]	túlkur ['tʰul̥kʏr] 'interpreter'
	filter ['fɪlt⁽ʰ⁾ə]	piltur ['pʰɪl̥tʏr] 'boy'

There is an aspect of the appearance of aspiration which we cannot discuss at any length here but which is worthy of note: as the English and Icelandic examples indicate, aspiration and sonorant devoicing seem to be connected or, in some sense, are really the same thing. Where the two languages differ is that in English a sonorant following a plosive is voiceless (e.g. *plate*), while in Icelandic it is a sonorant before a plosive that is voiceless (e.g. *piltur*). In general the existence of a particular property within a language and its distribution in the words of the language is subject to language-specific conditions. English plosives are aspirated most readily when they precede a vowel and do not follow a consonant, hence typically in word-initial and intervocalic position; word-finally, aspiration is subject to variation, while aspirated plosives do not occur before voiceless sonorants. Thus, the vocalic environment generally favours the appearance of aspiration, while consonantal contexts tend to disfavour it.

We started by noting that aspirated and non-aspirated plosives are phonetically similar but distinct speech sounds. In terms of the structure of English, however, their appearance is conditioned by the environment in such a way that where one appears, the other cannot. In this sense they are closely associated with specific positions. Below we will look at a few more examples of contextually conditioned segmental relatedness, concentrating on the factors in the context that determine the specific sound shape of segments.

1.3 The Muskerry Irish [ɑ – a] alternation

Consonants in Modern Irish are divided into **palatalised** and **velarised** groups. Palatalised consonants involve the secondary articulation of raising the front of the tongue towards the hard palate; in phonetic transcriptions such palatalised consonants are marked with the diacritic [ʲ], e.g. [pʲ, tʲ, gʲ], a practice we will adopt below. Velarised consonants display a secondary articulation whereby the back of the tongue is raised towards the soft palate; this property may be marked in transcription by the diacritic [ˠ], e.g. [pˠ, tˠ], but traditionally this diacritic is disregarded in order not to overspecify the consonants thereby making the transcription cumbersome and cluttered. We will adopt this practice but it should be kept in mind that consonants without diacritics are velarised, hence a word such as *madra* 'dog', which we transcribe ['mɑːdərə], would appear as ['mˠɑːdˠərˠə] in a detailed or narrow transcription. Finally, consonants whose primary articulation is palatal, as [ʃ], or velar, as [k, x], cannot have a secondary articulation of palatalisation or velarisation, e.g. *seo* [ʃo] 'this', *cá* [kɑː] 'where', *chun* [xun] 'towards'.

In what follows we shall be interested in the relation between consonants and the two low vowels – front [a] and back [ɑ] – in West Muskerry variety of southern Irish. The two vowels are restricted in their occurrence by the surrounding consonants in ways which are quite complex. We will consider only two possibilities, illustrated in the examples below.

[11]
a.   bagairt ['bɑgərtʲ] 'threat'
    capall ['kɑpəl] 'horse'
    bás [bɑːs] 'death'
    garda ['gɑːrdə] 'policeman'
    féileacán ['fʲeːlʲəkɑːn] 'butterfly'
b.   meaig [mʲagʲ] 'magpie'
    geaitire ['gʲatʲirʲi] 'splinter'
    oileáin [ə'lʲaːnʲ] 'island, gen. sg.'
    geáitse ['gʲaːtʲʃə] 'pose'
    milleáin [mʲi'lʲaːnʲ] 'blame, gen. sg.'

The first thing we note is that the appearance of a front or a back vowel is independent of its length – as the examples in [11] show, both long and short vowels can be back or front. Fundamentally, however, the nature of the vowel which can appear in words of the type illustrated in our examples seems to depend on the consonants flanking the vowel. In [11a] the back vowel [ɑ] is surrounded by velarised consonants, while in [11b] the front vowel [a] appears between palatalised consonants. Since velarised consonants involve the superimposition of the raising of the back part of the tongue on the primary articulation, they may be classified as back themselves; by the same reasoning palatalised consonants are front. Looking now at the two Irish vowels [a] and [ɑ] we can say that in a back environment, the intervening low vowel must itself be back and, conversely, a front vowel is required between two consecutive front consonants. This conclusion is strengthened by what might be called negative facts: there are no examples of words in this dialect with a back vowel between palatalised consonants or a front vowel between velarised consonants. This is to say, sequences such as, e.g. *[tʲɑtʲ] or *[tat] are not well formed and hence inadmissible as Muskerry Irish words – in the terminology we introduced above, these are not potential words in this dialect.

This very simple example is instructive since it casts some initial doubt on the view of speech which the notion of the segment entails. Recall that the ordinary assumption which we adopted at the outset is that linguistic units, such as words, consist of a series of segments. Thus the English word *apt* consists of three segments transcribed as [æptʰ]; since segments are separate units we can expect that they should be moveable, and this is indeed something which is partly attested in English, where we find the words *pat* [pʰætʰ] and *tap* [tʰæpʰ], although, of course, not *[tpæ] or *[ptæ]. Later on we will find reasons for excluding these ways of combining the three segments but even as things are *apt*, *tap*, *pat* show that the three segments are independent of each other. If the English situation were the norm, facts such as the Irish ones should not arise. However, the facts for the dialect of Irish in question are quite unambiguous: no front [a] vowel between back or velarised consonants and no front or palatalised consonants flanking the back [ɑ] vowel. If the segments were fully independent, there should be nothing unusual or unexpected about front consonants flanking both front and back vowels, for instance. This is simply not the case, which shows that segmental independence is anything but absolute. As we will see on many occasions below, segments are only partially independent of each other in a string and a degree of mutual interaction – or interdependence – is to be expected. The nature and degree of the interdependence are language-specific properties which contribute to the phonology of that language.

The full facts of Muskerry Irish determining the distribution of low vowels are much more complex than what we have presented above, since we have only singled out a uniformly palatalised or uniformly velarised environment. There are cases of consonant disagreement, i.e. cases when the consonants preceding and following a vowel do not belong to the same class. We shall not go into further detail here apart from noting that in the case of consonant disagreement, the frontness and backness of the vowel is partially unpredictable. Thus between a palatalised and a velarised consonant we find both the back vowel, e.g. *coileán* [kiˈlʲɑːn] 'pup' and the front one, e.g. *coimeád* [kiˈmʲaːd] 'keep'. If, however,

1.3 The Muskerry Irish [ɑ – a] alternation

in other forms of the words the two consonants are uniform, the quality of the vowel cannot differ from them in terms of frontness or backness. A case in point where the two consonants can be made uniform involves one of the morphological means found in the language for marking the genitive case of nouns, which consists in palatalising the final consonant. As an example we can offer two nouns from [11a]: *capall* ['kɑpəl] 'horse' and *bás* [bɑːs] 'death', which form their genitives as *capaill* ['kɑpəlʲ] and *báis* [bɑːʃ] respectively. Against this background consider the following nominative–genitive pairs:

[12]   coileán [kiˈlʲɑːn] 'pup'   coileáin [kiˈlʲaːnʲ]
         Seán [ʃɑːn] 'proper name'   Seáin [ʃaːnʲ]
         cineál [kʲiˈnʲɑːl] 'species'   cineáil [kʲiˈnʲaːlʰ]

The left-hand column nominatives show the back [ɑ] between consonants differing in their palatality–velarity value; the right-hand column genitives have uniformly palatalised consonants separated by a front vowel. Thus the genitives conform to the Muskerry Irish distributional requirement which disallows uniformly front or back consonants from being split by a low vowel of an opposite value. The examples in [12] illustrate what is traditionally known as an alternation: the presence of partially different phonetic chunks of what are otherwise the same words. We could say that the word for 'pup' has two **alternants** – [kiˈlʲɑːn] and [kiˈlʲaːnʲ] – or that the vowels [ɑː] and [aː] **alternate** in this word. The presence of partially different shapes of the same morpheme is quite common in languages and often offers evidence of a prevailing phonological regularity.

As another example of alternation revealing the Muskerry Irish vowel–consonant uniformity requirement we have been discussing, consider a suffix used to form verbal nouns. The suffix *-áil* forms verbal nouns, in some cases attaching to English stems; it appears in two shapes and provides an illustration of alternation. In the examples below we mark the boundaries between the stem and the suffix by placing a space before the suffix

[13]
a.   fadáil [fəˈd ɑːlʲ] 'delay'
        diúgáil [dʲuːˈg ɑːlʲ] 'drain'
        lódáil [loːˈd ɑːlʲ] 'load'
        cadragáil [kɑdrəˈg ɑːlʲ] 'chatter'
b.   tindeáil [tʲinˈdʲ aːlʲ] 'look after'
        graibeáil [grɑˈbʲ aːlʲ] 'grab'
        ciceáil [kʲiˈkʲ aːlʲ] 'kick'
        déileáil [dʲaiˈlʲ aːlʲ] 'deal'

In [13a] the verbal noun suffix contains the back vowel, and the surrounding consonants differ in their palatality–velarity specification; in [13b], however,

10   Sounds and segments

where the verbal stem ends in a palatalised consonant, the vowel of the suffix is sandwiched between two palatalised or front consonants and is itself front. The morpheme marking the verbal nouns appears in two alternating shapes – [aːlʲ] and [aːlʲ], where the nature of the vowel depends on the surrounding consonants. It is to be expected that if the final consonant in examples such as [13b] were to be made velarised, the preceding vowel should be back as it would no longer find itself between two palatalised consonants. This is exactly what is found in a group of agentive nouns based on verbal nouns.

In the examples below the verbal noun is morphologically turned into an agentive noun by means of the suffix [iː] which is attached to a depalatalised (or velarised) form of the verbal noun. Consider a few examples, where the verbal noun suffix is separated from both the preceding stem and the following suffix in the transcription:

[14]   bóiceáil [boːˈkʲ aːlʲ] 'brag'   bóiceálaí [boːˈkʲ ɑːl iː] 'braggart'
       beiteáil [bʲeˈtʲ aːlʲ] 'bet'   beiteálaí [bʲeˈtʲ ɑːl iː] 'one who
                                              makes bets, a better'
       cáibleáil [ˈkaːbʲəlʲ aːlʲ] 'prevaricate'   cáibleálaí [ˈkaːbʲəlʲ ɑːl iː]
                                              'prevaricator'
       póitireáil [ˈpoːtʲər aːlʲ] 'prepare delicacies'   póitireálaí [ˈpoːtʲər ɑːl iː] 'one
                                              who prepares delicacies'

The alternation [aːlʲ – ɑːl] in [14] is somewhat different from the alternation [aːlʲ – ɑːlʲ] that we saw in [13]. In the latter case we found that the verbal noun suffix had different forms when attached to different stems, depending on whether the stem ended in palatalised or velarised consonants; in [14] on the other hand, the same verbal stem can be followed either by [aːlʲ] or [ɑːl], the latter alternant appearing in the derived agentive noun. It is still true that between two palatalised consonants we cannot have a back vowel; this is possible only when the consonants have a different palatalisation–velarisation value, exactly as in [13a]. Thus the vocalic alternations are determined by the context in both sets of examples. In [14] we note additionally that the lateral consonants of the verbal noun suffix alternate: [lʲ – l]. What is significant about the alternation of the laterals is that it does not depend upon the neighbouring segments, i.e. in *bóiceálaí* [l] is followed by a front vowel [iː], but it is velarised. This independence of the laterals of the context is further demonstrated below.

[15]   áil [ɑːlʲ] 'wish, n.'   ál [ɑːl] 'litter, brood'
       síl [ʃiːlʲ] 'seed, gen. sg.' síol [ʃiːl], 'nom. sg.'
       míle [ˈmʲiːlʲə] 'thousand'   míola [ˈmʲiːlə] 'insect, nom. pl.'

The examples show clearly that the palatalised and the velarised lateral consonant can appear in the same context, irrespective of what follows or precedes, if anything. The two consonants are thus independent segments. The alternations of the laterals in [14] cannot be connected with the environment and thus will not be regarded as belonging to phonology proper. The phenomenon of alternations, viewed in a general way as the appearance of different shapes of the same morpheme, is only partially controlled by the phonology of the language. Numerous cases have to be subsumed by morphology or the lexicon. In English, for example, we find alternants such as *sing – sang – sung – song* [sɪŋ – sæŋ – sʌŋ – sɒŋ] or *clear – clar(ity)* [klɪə – ˈklær(əti)]; the appearance of a given alternant is not determined by the phonological context, hence such alternations are not the domain of phonology. Whether a given alternation is phonological or non-phonological cannot be determined in advance but must form part of the study of a specific language. We will now look at what is phonetically an almost identical alternation between laterals as that found in Irish, but whose function is very different. The language in question is English.

1.4 *Dark* and *clear l* in RP English

Most dialects of British English contain a velarised lateral, not unlike the Irish consonant discussed above. It is known by the traditional tag of *dark l* and transcribed narrowly as [ɫ]; just like the sound in Irish it is pronounced with a raising of the back part of the tongue towards the velum imposed on the primary alveolar lateral articulation. The so-called *clear l*, transcribed [l], is pronounced without such secondary articulation; it differs little from the Muskerry Irish palatalised lateral. The distinction between *clear* and *dark l* is characteristic of RP in particular; it is totally absent from American English, which predominantly displays only the velarised lateral in all positions, or from Hiberno-English which, in turn, admits only the non-velarised lateral. RP not only has the dark and clear laterals, but it also displays alternations involving these sounds.

The distribution of the two lateral sounds is illustrated in [16] for *clear l* and in [17] for *dark l*.

[16]	light [laɪtʰ]	loom [luːm]	London [ˈlʌndən]
	Dublin [ˈdʌblɪn]	allow [əˈlaʊ]	hilarious [hɪˈleərɪəs]
	belly [ˈbeli]	fillip [ˈfɪlɪpʰ]	pillow [ˈpʰɪləʊ]
	brilliant [ˈbrɪljənt]	failure [ˈfeɪljə]	tell us [ˈtʰelʌs]
	all over [ɔːˈləʊvə]	cool and calm [ˈkʰuːlənˈkʰɑːm]	
[17]	file [faɪɫ]	rule [ruːɫ]	dull [dʌɫ]
	dullness [ˈdʌɫnəs]	help [heɫp]	filter [ˈfɪɫtʰə]
	dangle [dæŋgɫ]	always [ɔːɫwɪz]	Salisbury [ˈsɔːɫzbri]
	Hilton [ˈhɪɫtn̩]	gamble [gæmbɫ]	belfry [ˈbeɫfri].

An inspection of the examples reveals a few striking regularities. First of all, the dark lateral never appears at the beginning of the word but is found word-internally before a consonant or at the end of a word. This is not to say that the *clear l* cannot find itself at the end of a word but this only happens when the next word begins with a vowel, e.g. *all over*. Additionally, the next word must be closely linked with the preceding one – if a major syntactic boundary separates the words, the first has the *dark l*, e.g. in *Bill, a student* the name is normally pronounced [bɪɫ]. The clear sound also appears word-internally before a vowel – whether the preceding segment is a vowel, e.g. *pillow*, or a consonant, e.g. *Dublin*, is irrelevant. In fact, the clear lateral appears almost exclusively before a vowel, the only consonantal exception being [j], e.g. *brilliant*; the remaining contexts, which embrace the word-final and the preconsonantal positions, display [ɫ].

As might be expected, alternations of the two laterals are frequently encountered.

[18] gamble [gæmbɫ]   gambling ['gæmblɪŋ]   gambler ['gæmblə]
      fail [feɪɫ]   fail it ['feɪlɪt]   failure ['feɪljə]
      oil [ɔɪɫ]   oily ['ɔɪli]   oil on troubled waters [ɔɪlɒn]
      dull [dʌɫ]   dullest ['dʌlɪst]   dull as ditch-water [dʌləz]

These alternations emerge as a result of the different lexical and syntactic modifications which change the environment following the lateral. In every case, however, the factors controlling the distribution are easy to define: the clear [l] appears before a vowel (and [j]), the dark [ɫ] occupies all remaining positions. It can be said that the distribution of the laterals is **complementary**: each of the two sounds occupies a position which complements the positions occupied by the other sound. Alternatively, we can say that the prevocalic position is reserved for the clear [l], while the preconsonantal and word-final position can be filled by the dark [ɫ]. On this interpretation the two sounds are related in that they are phonetically similar but attached to different positions.

1.5 Voicedness of fricatives in Old and Modern English

We will now look at anterior spirants in two periods of English separated by over a thousand years: Old and Present-Day English. These are the sounds transcribed [f, v, θ, ð, s, z], and although they appear in both periods of the history of the language, their position in the structure of the language is markedly different. Consider first some examples of the fricatives, also called spirants, in Old English words.

[19]
[f]   findan ['findan] 'find'   fōt [foːt] 'foot'
      sceaft [ʃaft] 'creation'   wīf [wiːf] 'wife'
      wulf [wulf] 'wolf'   lyffettan ['lyfːetːan] 'flatter'

1.5 Voicedness of fricatives in Old and Modern English

[v]	wulfes ['wulves] 'wolf, gen. sg.'	giefan ['jevan] 'give'
	earfoð ['æarvoθ] 'work'	nifol ['nivol] 'dark'
	æfen ['æːven] 'evening'	
[θ]	þegn [θejn] 'nobleman, thane'	þēod [θeːod] 'nation'
	bæð [bæθ] 'bath'	fȳlþ [fyːlθ] 'filth'
	sceððan ['ʃeθːan] 'harm'	
[ð]	bæðe ['bæðe] 'bath, dat. sg.'	cȳðan ['kyːðan] 'make known'
	weorðan ['weorðan] 'become'	hoðma ['hoðma] 'darkness'
[s]	sellan ['selːan] 'give'	spor [spor] 'trail, spoor'
	bletsian ['bletsian] 'bless'	prēost [preːost] 'priest'
	lǣssa ['læːsːa] 'less'	
[z]	wesan ['wezan] 'be'	cēosan ['tʃeːozan] 'choose'
	hāses ['haːzes] 'hoarse, gen. sg.'	horsum ['horzum] 'horse, dat. pl.'
	wīse ['wiːze] 'wisely'	

An inspection of the data shows some striking restrictions on the occurrence of voiced and voiceless spirants. Thus at the beginning and the end of words only voiceless consonants are possible – no Old English word can start with [v] or [z] for instance. When long (the term **geminate** is generally used), the fricatives are invariably voiceless, hence [ðː] is not found. (This is completely independent of how the sounds are spelt – in Old English manuscripts there are interchangeable spellings for the spirants: þeod or ðeod, sceððan or sceþþan.) It is clear that spirants are voiced when single – non-geminate – and surrounded by voiced segments, most frequently by vowels. The intervocalic position is the primary site where voiced spirants appear and from which the voiceless ones are banned; furthermore, voiced fricatives are not admitted in other environments. One may say, then, that the voiced and voiceless spirants are associated with specific positions in the word. Thus, from the point of view of the structure of the language they are not unlike the dark and clear lateral in the dialects of Modern English which have this distinction; in the same way that the *clear l* requires a following vocalic element, the voiced Old English spirants need to be surrounded by vowels. Also, just like in Modern English where alternations between clear and dark laterals are found (e.g. *sail – sailor*), a by-product of the Old English spirant distribution is the presence of partially different forms of what is the same morpheme, e.g.:

[20] sōð [soːθ] 'truth'   sōðe ['soːðe] 'truly'
      wulf [wulf] 'wolf'   wulfas ['wulvas] 'wolves'
      wīs [wiːs] 'wise'   wīse ['wiːze] 'wisely'

The appearance of the spirants is completely predictable: in the intervocalic position we only find the voiced ones, while word-initially and word-finally it is exclusively the voiceless ones that can appear. Although we have simplified the facts somewhat by restricting ourselves to anterior consonants only, it is legitimate to say that the voicedness of spirants is conditioned by the phonological environment in Old English.

In Present-Day English the distribution of the same spirants differs in some interesting ways. First of all, members of the [s – z] and [f – v] pairs can independently appear word-initially, word-internally and word-finally, as shown in [21].

[21]
a.   sing [sɪŋ]   zing [zɪŋ]
       fine [faɪn]   vine [vaɪn]
b.   messy ['mesi]   busy ['bɪzi]
       beefy ['biːfi]   beaver ['biːvə]
c.   bus [bʌs]   buzz [bʌz]
       leaf/lief [liːf]   leave [liːv]

In Old English, initially and finally we can only have voiceless spirants, while in Present-Day English both types of consonants are possible; similarly, while intervocalically voiceless spirants were not admitted in Old English, they are found in that position today. It thus seems that the restrictions imposed on the Old English spirants have been relaxed or that the voiced and voiceless consonants have grown independent of each other. However, the independence is not mechanical or absolute; leaving aside for the moment the interdental spirants [θ – ð], let us note that the voiced spirants [v – z], although enjoying more leeway as compared to their Old English predecessors, are still restricted. The voiceless spirants, both in Old and Present-Day English, can be followed by other consonants, e.g.:

[22]   flōd [floːd] 'tide'   flood [flʌd]
        fretan ['fretan] 'devour'   frog [frɒg]
        swefan [swevan] 'sleep'   sweet [swiːt]
        strengu ['strengu] 'strength'   strength [strenθ]

Although unlike Old English the voiced spirants can appear initially today, they still cannot be followed by other consonants, i.e. nothing like *[zrɒŋ] is possible in Modern English. Admittedly, there is a handful of words like *vroom*, *Vladimir*, *Zbig* but they are either extremely rare and unusual or strongly felt to be borrowings, hence ultimately exceptional. The freedom to combine with other consonants that the voiceless spirants show has not been extended to their voiced counterparts.

On the other hand the voice contrast has been extended in Modern English to include also the palatal spirant. While in Old English the palatal spirant [ʃ] was quite common in all three positions, i.e. initially *scūr* [ʃuːr] 'downpour, shower', medially *fiscere* ['fiʃere] 'fisherman', and finally *disc* [diʃ] 'dish', there was no voiced palatal spirant [ʒ] at all. In this sense the emergence in Present-Day English of [ʒ] in words like *treasure* ['treʒə], *vision* ['vɪʒən], *rouge* [ruːʒ] broadens the list of spirants existing in the language. Note that medially we can have either the voiced

1.5 Voicedness of fricatives in Old and Modern English

spirant as in *treasure* ['treʒə], *pleasure* ['pleʒə] or the voiceless one as in *fissure* ['fɪʃə], *mission* ['mɪʃən]. However, both the voiceless and the voiced spirants are extremely limited in their ability to combine with other consonants. [ʃ] can be readily followed only by [r] in native words, e.g. *shrewd* [ʃruːd], *shriek* [ʃriːk], while its voiced congener cannot be followed by any other consonant; additionally, initial [ʒ] is found only marginally, e.g. *genre* ['ʒɒnrə]. The case of the [ʃ – ʒ] distinction in Present-Day English is instructive as it shows that the phonological potential of a segment is not exhausted by its ability to appear in specific contexts: even if two segments can find themselves in the same environment, they can display marked differences in their combinability with other segments.

Another difference becomes apparent when we look at the length of consonants: in Old English it was possible for voiceless spirants to be long, i.e. to appear as geminates – recall *lyffettan, sceððan, læssa* in [19]. This option is no longer available in Modern English where long or geminate consonants only arise as a result of combining words, e.g. *bus stop*. Thus Present-Day English has certain possibilities which were not available in Old English (opposition of voiced and voiceless spirants of the *rise* [raɪz] – *rice* [raɪs] type), but it lacks others that used to be there (geminate spirants). The status of a segment as a phonological unit follows not only from its dependence on or independence of the environment, but also from its ability to combine with other segments. As a further example consider now the two interdental spirants [θ, ð] in Modern English; in contrast with the Old English situation where the voiced one only occurred in a voiced context, the current distribution of the two spirants is more complex.

In internal or intervocalic position both interdental spirants can be found [23a–b], which marks a departure from the Old English pattern, where only the voiced spirant was possible; word-finally, where Old English had only the voiceless consonants, there is no problem today in finding not only voiceless but also the voiced ones [23c–d]. Consider some examples.

[23]
a. other ['ʌðə]   southern ['sʌðən]
    father ['fɑːðə]   weather ['weðə]
    withy ['wɪði]   bother ['bɒðə]
b. apathy ['æpəθi]   author ['ɔːθə]
    pithy ['pɪθi]   ether ['iːθə]
    Dorothy ['dɒrəθi]   breathy ['breθi]
c. sleuth [sluːθ]   oath [əʊθ]
    labyrinth ['læbɪrɪnθ] hyacinth ['haɪəsɪnθ]
    beneath [bə'niːθ]
d. seethe [siːð]   scythe [saɪð]
    smooth [smuːð]   loathe [ləʊð]
    breathe [briːð]   bathe [beɪð]

The examples in [23b] and [23d] illustrate a situation which would be impossible in Old English but which parallels the intervocalic and word-final distribution of the other spirants we have discussed above: [s, z, f, v] (see [21b–c] above).

Consider now the initial situation. Unlike in Old English, it looks as if both spirants can also occur at the beginning of the word, as illustrated in [24].

[24]
a. think [θɪŋk]   therapy ['θerəpi]
    thimble [θimbl̩]   thrive [θraɪv]
    thorn [θɔːn]   thick [θɪk]
b. this [ðɪs]   those [ðəʊz]
    thither ['ðɪðə]   thus [ðʌs]
    they [ðeɪ]   them [ðem/ðəm]
    the [ðə/ðiː]

Although formally both fricatives are found initially, there can be no doubt that the words in [24a] are very different from those in [24b]. The voiceless spirant appears in major class words, such as nouns, verbs and adjectives, whereas the voiced one is to be found in a small number of pronouns, adverbs, and the definite article, which are jointly referred to as **function words**. The difference between the two classes is that the former group is open-ended, while the latter one is restricted to a dozen or so words. Note that there is not a single noun or verb which begins with [ð], e.g. *[ðeɪnt], *[ðræmp] are not potential words of English. Even if it is possible to find occasional pairs of words differing in the voicing of the initial interdental spirant (e.g. *thy* [ðaɪ] – *thigh* [θaɪ]), the general absence of the voiced spirant from the initial position can hardly be an accident. Note that with the other spirants we have no difficulty in supplying words belonging to the same grammatical class but differing in the initial consonant, be they nouns such as *fine* [faɪn] – *vine* [vaɪn], or verbs such as *sip* [sɪp] – *zip* [zɪp]. Also it is worth noting that while the voiceless spirant can be followed by another consonant, e.g. *throng* [θrɒŋ], *thwart* [θwɔːt], the voiced spirant can only be followed by a vowel. In sum, then, we conclude that the voiced interdental spirant is only marginally tolerated initially in Modern English. On a more general level, we see that the Modern English pairs of voiced and voiceless spirants show different phonological properties. These can be appreciated by considering not only pairs of words differing in some sound or other, but by inspecting the factors which condition the appearance of segments and their combinations with other segments. In subsequent chapters we will have occasion to extend and enrich these considerations.

1.6   Summary

The common sentiment that words consist of individual sounds in linear order, with one sound following the other, is reflected in the linguistic concept of segmentation. This entails the conviction, or assumption, that larger linguistic units can be chopped up into independent segments. We have seen that segments can be exchanged and the process of replacement may produce different words (*pet – pit – bit – bed – bad – bat*...). In this sense the mechanism of replacement supports the segmentability of speech and the everyday intuition that there are such objects as independent sounds which can be combined to make up words. Most of this introductory chapter has been devoted to showing that this view is in serious ways inadequate.

Cases can easily be found which undermine the notion of segmental independence. Very often the appearance of a specific sound is strictly connected with the neighbouring sounds or with the position within a word. Voiceless plosives in RP are aspirated or not depending on what precedes and follows, and thus the 'independence' of, say, [t^h] is curtailed by its having to be followed by a stressed vowel and not preceded by a consonant. The 'independence' of the vowels [a] and [ɑ] in Muskerry Irish is seriously restricted by the consonants which flank them. Similarly there are factors which control the distribution of laterals in RP or the voicing of fricatives in Old English. Sounds can thus be seen primarily as somewhat artificial results of the segmentation procedure rather than as independent units which can be strung together to make up words. The independence of the front [a] in the Muskerry Irish word *meaig* [m^{j}aɡ^j] 'magpie', or the velarised lateral in the English word *help* [heɫp] is illusory since in the particular environment the low vowel in Muskerry Irish *must* be front and the lateral in English *must* be velarised. These properties of the two sounds are totally dependent upon the context.

A certain conflict or contradiction emerges from our discussion so far: on the one hand we see that sounds appear to be independent because they can be replaced by other sounds. On the other hand they appear to be inseparably linked with the environment. This is one of the issues that we will need to resolve. At the very least, however, segmentability of speech must be viewed with caution (or suspicion). In the next chapter we will see that the notion *sound* which we have been using in its everyday sense must be regarded linguistically as a complex structure.

1.7 Suggested further reading

The principles of phonetic transcription are laid out in the *Handbook of the International Phonetic Association* (1999). This book also contains a brief phonetic description of over two dozen languages where the principles of transcription are put to use and tested.

On abstract and concrete sounds see also Jones (1939).

The literature on alternations is vast and almost invariably linked to a specific theoretical framework. Kilbury (1976) offers a survey of the area, while Lass (1984: chapter 4) is a much more succinct summary. The relevant parts of Fischer-Jørgensen (1975) and Anderson (1985) are very much worth consulting, but a beginner might find them difficult to follow.

Data on RP English phonetics can be found in most textbooks, e.g. Jones (1975) or Gimson and Cruttenden (1994), and in the standard pronouncing dictionaries of Wells (1990) and Jones (1997). For Icelandic aspiration and sonorant voicelessness see Einarsson (1945), Kress (1982) and Gíslason and Þráinsson (1993); for Muskerry Irish consult Ó Cuív (1944); for Old English see Campbell (1959), Mitchell and Robinson (1992) or Hogg (1992).

2
The melody and the skeleton

2.1 Introduction

As we have seen, segments can be pronounced in somewhat different ways depending on the context in which they appear; they also vary in their ability to combine with other segments. There are other properties of phonological units which deserve attention and which should be reflected in a description. Some of these properties are language-specific, while others characterise a great many or perhaps all languages; in the latter case such properties are not part of individual language systems and their phonology but rather belong to the theory of language and its phonology. The theory of phonology reflects our current understanding of the organisation and the working of the sound system of languages. A general problem in this theory is the question of whether the segments that we identify in languages are indivisible units or whether they have an internal structure.

In what follows we shall argue that segments are complex structures. Each segment comprises a slot, or a position, linked to a group of phonetic properties. The phonetic properties are called **the melody**, while the slots with which they are associated make up what is known as the **skeleton**. The slots which make up the skeleton can be thought of as a sequence of x's so that a word like *America* can be represented as a two-layered structure with melodic units attached to skeletal positions in the following way:

[1]   x x x x x x x
         | | | | | | |
         ə m e r ɪ k ə

This representation offers an extremely simple case since there is a one-to-one relationship between melodic units and skeletal positions. If this were always the case, the skeletal level – as an addition to the melodic one – would be superfluous; there is quite a lot of evidence, however, which shows the need for the skeleton apart from the melodic representation. In what follows we shall review some of the evidence and relate it to specific phonological phenomena.

2.2 Equivalence of long vowels and diphthongs in English

The vowels or **vocalic nuclei** of Modern English comprise at least three types of objects:

vowels which are short and lax, e.g. [ɪ, ʊ, ɒ] *bitter* ['bɪtə], *soot* [sʊt], *folly* ['fɒli]
vowels which are long and tense, e.g. [iː, uː, ɔː] *lead* [liːd], *stool* [stuːl], *lawn* [lɔːn]
diphthongs, e.g. [aɪ, ʊə, əʊ] *revile* [rə'vaɪl], *allure* [ə'ljʊə], *notice* ['nəʊtɪs]

The phonetic tradition recognises an additional category of triphthongs for some varieties of English, illustrated by [aɪə] in *Messiah* [mə'saɪə] or [eɪə] in *layer* [leɪə]. We need not be concerned with this complication here – suffice it to say that such complex phonetic units could be interpreted as sequences of a diphthong followed by a vowel, i.e. as [aɪ] or [eɪ] plus [ə].

Another issue which deserves mention is the question of vowel quantity. As is well known, vocalic length depends to some extent on the environment, so that the vowel in *bit* [bɪt] is longer than the first one in *bitter* ['bɪtə], but the nucleus in *bid* [bɪd] is longer than either of these. Such contextually determined length distinctions should be carefully distinguished from the more basic contrast where the vowel of *bit* or *bid* is distinct from that of *beet/beat* [biːt] or *bead* [biːd]. The somewhat varying quantitative differences accompany a basic difference in quality often referred to as a **tense–lax** vowel opposition. Tense vowels are said to require a greater articulatory effort and a more significant departure from the neutral position than lax vowels. Thus tense vowels are both higher and longer as compared to the lax ones. Thus the English short or long vowels are in reality quality–quantity complexes of lower or more open and relatively shorter nuclei as against closer and relatively longer ones. The difference between short and long nuclei, then, involves not only duration but also tenseness. Long vowels which might be said to be of the same duration as diphthongs differ from them in maintaining their articulatory configuration throughout. Diphthongs modify the configuration so that [aʊ], for example, starts as an open front vowel and ends as half close back. The identification of three vocalic categories – short vowels, long vowels and diphthongs – is thus phonetically motivated. There are, however, serious considerations which force us to look at the three classes in a different way.

Consider the vocalic nuclei which can appear before the velar nasal and a sequence of a labial nasal and another consonant within English morphemes. There are words like *wrong* [rɒŋ], *link* [lɪŋk], *lump* [lʌmp], *timber* ['tɪmbə] in which the vowel preceding the nasal is short; words with either a long vowel or a diphthong are impossible in this position, i.e. things like *[reɪŋ], *[laɪŋk], *[laʊmp] or *['təʊmbə] are not possible words of English. There is a phonological regularity which only allows a short vowel in such positions; in other words, long vowels **and** diphthongs are banned from this environment. We see that these two distinct nuclei groups – long vowels and diphthongs – are treated in a uniform way in English.

The non-appearance of long vowels and diphthongs before the velar nasal and certain nasal consonant sequences is part of a more general regularity. Specifically, before a sequence of two consonants a short vowel is the preferred option as shown in [2a]; long vowels and diphthongs, while not totally excluded, are seriously restricted [2b].

[2]
a.   nymph [nɪmf]   fact [fækt]
       sombre ['sɒmbə]   sceptre ['septə]
       bump [bʌmp]
b.   salt [sɔːlt]   hind [haɪnd]
       child [tʃaɪld]   paint [peɪnt]
       fiend [fiːnd]

Without going into details (we return to this question later on), short vowels are tolerated in a broader range of contexts than long vowels and diphthongs. The latter are most frequently found before a sequence of **coronal** consonants, i.e. those whose primary articulation is located in the dental and alveolar region. This means that although short nuclei are possible before a coronal context (as in [3]), long ones and diphthongs are normally not tolerated before non-coronal clusters, i.e. *[paʊmf], *[klaʊkt], *[seɪptə] etc.

[3]   melt [melt]   bond [bɒnd]
       Hilda ['hɪldə]   mint [mɪnt]
       hand [hænd]

These two groups of vocalic elements, which we shall call **complex nuclei**, are subject to the same restriction.

A very different case where complex nuclei pattern together concerns stressed word-final vowels. In English short stressed vowels are impossible in the final position, i.e. there are no words ending in any of the following stressed segments [ɪ, e, æ, ɒ, ʌ, ʊ]. Combinations of segments such as *[rə'bæ], *[ɪn'tɒ], *[æblə'me] are not potential English words. The vowels we find regularly in stressed word-final positions are complex nuclei, i.e. either long vowels or diphthongs.

[4]
a.   see [siː]   absentee [æbsən'tiː]
       accrue [ə'kruː]   hullabaloo [hʌləbə'luː]
       flaw [flɔː]   macaw [mə'kɔː]
       spa [spɑː]   bizarre [bɪ'zɑː]

b. sty [staɪ]   apply [ə'plaɪ]
    ploy [plɔɪ]   destroy [də'strɔɪ]
    glow [gləʊ]   below [bə'ləʊ]

Although we may not be able to find examples for every single diphthong, the general pattern is unmistakeable: short vowels are strictly excluded from the position in question while there is no problem about either long vowels or diphthongs appearing there. English phonology treats complex nuclei one way, and simplex ones differently.

As a final argument let us note that there is variation between long vowels and diphthongs in dialects of English. In some dialects the nucleus which we have represented as [eɪ], e.g. *tale* [teɪl] can be more adequately transcribed by means of a long vowel, i.e. [teːl]; conversely, the long vowels [iː, uː] in e.g. *beam* [biːm], *boom* [buːm], in certain other dialects or even varieties of the same dialect should be represented as diphthongs [i̯i, u̯u] (or [ij, uw]). Quite obviously, apart from the monophthongal or diphthongal pronunciations of certain vocalic nuclei, the phonological systems of the dialects treat them uniformly. This goes to show that English interprets long nuclei as equivalent to diphthongs.

We have seen a few instances of the split among English vocalic elements into two classes: simplex or short vowels and complex or long vowels and diphthongs. The phonetic distinction into three groups we noted at the outset reduces to a phonological division into just two classes. The complex nuclei form a single group and hence we need a mechanism for treating them as a unit: referring to a disjunction of long nuclei *and* diphthongs fails to achieve this aim, since a class of two objects could, in principle, comprise any two groups. Thus, theoretically, we could have a class comprising long vowels and short rounded vowels, or long vowels and diphthongs ending in [ɪ] etc. What we need is to separate what we have called simple nuclei from complex ones. This is where the skeletal representation proves useful. A short vowel corresponds to a single skeletal point while both a long one and a diphthong represent a two-point structure. The skeletal and melodic representation of the words *sit, seat* and *sight* take the shape in [5].

[5]   x   x   x   x   x   x   x   x   x   x   x
        | | | | \ / | | | | |
        s   ɪ   t   s   i   t   s   a   ɪ   t

Within a representation such as [5], a short or simplex vowel is defined as a melodic unit – in this case [ɪ] – associated with a single skeletal position, while a long vowel or a diphthong is a melodic unit associated with two such positions. Our phonological observations referring to short vowels or long vowels and diphthongs can be translated into statements about single or double skeletal slots with associated vocalic melodies:

> before a labial or velar nasal followed by a plosive only a single nuclear position is possible
> two vocalic positions are only possible before coronal clusters
> a stressed final nucleus must contain two positions

In no case do we need to refer to a disjunction of either a long vowel or a diphthong since from the phonological point of view they form a unity. This unity is reflected in their being attached to two skeletal slots. The phonological regularities invoked above refer not so much to any vocalic melodic properties but to the duration of the melodies, which can be either short or non-short; whether the latter type has a stable melody, yielding a traditional long vowel, or a changeable one, yielding a diphthong, is immaterial from the point of view of these regularities. Hence we only need to refer to the skeletal structure of words. The split of segments into a two-layered representation is thus justified: we need both the melodic level and the skeletal tier. An important condition on the elements of the two tiers is that they must be linked: the units of the melodic tier must be **associated** with skeletal positions, as it is only together that they form complete structures. Neither melodic elements on their own nor skeletal points without associated melodies can be pronounced, i.e. they do not constitute pronounceable phonological expressions. This we shall refer to as the **Association Condition**. Below we present other arguments attesting to the reality of the tier split and the need for association between the levels.

2.3 Germanic and Finnish nuclear simplifications

A different instance illustrating a similarity in phonological behaviour that is puzzling at first blush comes from developments in early Germanic dialects. It is generally recognised that in unaccented syllables long vowels tended to become short and short ones to disappear. Similar, more detailed claims can be made for the grammars of individual languages: in Old English short vowels were lost and long vowels were shortened. As an example, and leaving aside various details which would be required in an exhaustive description of the phenomena, consider the reconstructed form **þēodænæs* 'prince, gen. sg', pronounced presumably something like ['θeːodænæs], which yielded Old English *þēodnes* ['θeːodnes]: here the middle vowel is lost; on the other hand, the earlier **stānæ* ['staːnæː] 'stone, dat. sg.' and **blindūst* ['blinduːst] 'blindest' became first **stānæ* ['staːnæ] and **blindust* ['blindust], before emerging as *stāne* ['staːne] and *blindost* ['blindost] in classical Old English. Additionally, diphthongs become monophthongs, as in the second syllable of *arbaiþ- ['arβaiθ] 'trouble' which became the historical form earfeþ ['æarveθ].

We seem to be dealing with not two but three independent regularities: vowel loss, vowel shortening and finally monophthongisation of diphthongs; the only thing the regularities have in common is that the nuclei they affect all appear in unstressed positions. In principle, the three phonological mechanisms could be independent of each other, and the fact that they apply in the same context of an unstressed syllable could be an insignificant accident. However, the recurrence of such accidents in the languages of the world suggests that this interpretation should be ruled out and a more fundamental phonological reason should be sought. If we look at the Germanic phenomena from the point of view of the skeleton, we detect a very simple pattern: unstressed nuclei lose one skeletal position. The monophthongisation of diphthongs is the loss of one position, as is the shortening of long vowels. The loss of a position singly associated with a vowel melody means that the vocalic melody will be unassociated to the skeleton and hence, in accordance with the Association Condition, will not be pronounced. Thus the superficially three distinct operations are merely different manifestations of one and the same mechanism: the removal of one position dominating an unaccented vocalic melody. We will now look at some of the complex vocalic alternations in modern Finnish which seem to mirror closely the situation in early Germanic.

The superlative degree of adjectives in the nominative singular of Finnish is formed by adding the suffix -in to the adjectival base, which ends in a vowel. Note what happens to the final vowel of the base in the examples in [6]:

[6]
a.   vanha ['vanha] 'old'   vanhin ['vanhin]
     köyhä ['køyhæ] 'poor'   köyhin ['køyhin]
     suure- ['suːre] 'great'   suurin ['suːrin]
b.   tärkeä ['tærkeæ] 'important'   tärkein ['tærkein]
     lyhye- ['lyhye] 'short'   lyhyin ['lyhyin]
     pimeä ['pimeæ] 'dark'   pimein ['pimein]
c.   tervee- ['terveː] 'healthy'   tervein ['tervein]
     rakkaa- ['rakːaː] 'beloved'   rakkain ['rakːain]
     oppinee- ['opːineː] 'learned'   oppinein ['opːinein]

The stems in [6a] lose the final vowel before the superlative suffix. In [6b] the adjectival base contains a sequence of two vowels but, just as in [6a], the final vowel is lost and the remaining two vowels appear to yield a diphthong. The stems in [6c] shorten their final long vowel and the resulting combination of two vowels again looks like a diphthong. We are, then, dealing with vowel loss and vowel shortening, a configuration that is largely parallel to what we found in the

2.3 Germanic and Finnish nuclear simplifications

early Germanic examples above. The contexts of the changes are different but the virtual identity in the treatment of long and short nuclei is something that should be captured in phonological terms.

Let us approach the data with the skeleton–melody distinction in mind. Loss of a vowel, it will be recalled, means that a given vocalic melody has no skeletal position associated with it and as such is not pronounced. In other words, vowel loss is skeletal position loss. In Finnish this happens to the stem-final vowel, no matter whether this melody is itself preceded by a consonantal or a vocalic melody. The mechanical addition of the suffix to the stem would result in the representation in [7a] and [7c], while what we actually find is depicted in [7b] and [7d].

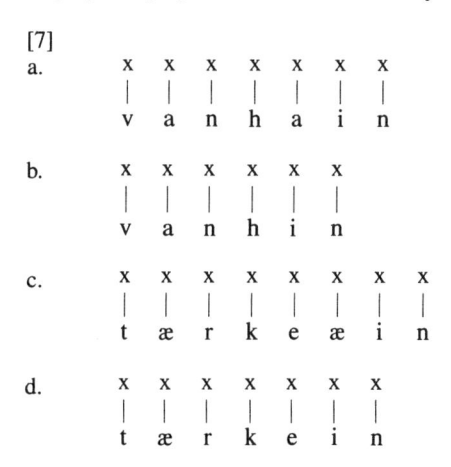

[7]
a. x x x x x x x
    | | | | | | |
    v a n h a i n

b. x x x x x x
    | | | | | |
    v a n h i n

c. x x x x x x x x
    | | | | | | | |
    t æ r k e æ i n

d. x x x x x x x
    | | | | | | |
    t æ r k e i n

Consider now the shortening of long vowels. Within the skeleton–melody model, a traditional long vowel is a single melody attached to two skeletal positions (see [5]). Given this we need to say nothing new about the Finnish data – vowel shortening is another instantiation of the same nuclear simplification mechanism following the removal of the skeletal position preceding the ending -*in*. Consider the pre-loss configuration in [8a] and the attested representation in [8b]:

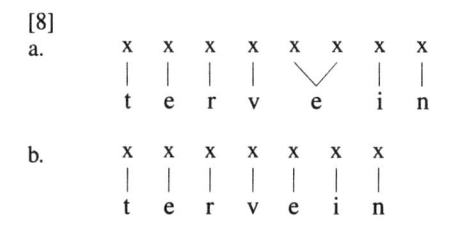

[8]
a. x x x x x x x x
    | | | | \ / | |
    t e r v e i n

b. x x x x x x x
    | | | | | | |
    t e r v e i n

Vowel loss and vowel shortening turn out to be mechanical consequences of the suppression of a single skeletal position. The same is obviously true about the early Germanic simplifications which we briefly illustrated above: short vowels are lost when the one and only skeletal point associated with them is removed. Long vowels and diphthongs, when one skeletal position is taken away, become short vowels. Thus the same mechanism is involved in what are phonetically different effects. The regularities can be formulated as a single operation only when the skeletal level is recognised as distinct from the sequence of melodic units.

We thus conclude that the representation of melodic elements which is linguistically relevant consists in the association of the melodic unit with one or two skeletal slots or positions. If one melodic unit corresponds to one skeletal point, we are dealing with what is traditionally called a short vowel or a short consonant [9a]. If a single unit is associated with two slots we end up with a long vowel or a long consonant, normally called a geminate [9b]. The Finish adjectives *rakkain* 'most beloved' and *oppinein* 'most learned' in [6b] contain geminate plosives which in traditional phonetic transcription one denotes by means of ː, i.e. [kː], [pː]; such a transcription should be seen as a shortcut or replacement for the phonologically more adequate representation as a two-tiered structure. Diphthongs within this system denote a situation where a complex melodic unit is attached to two consecutive skeletal positions [9c].

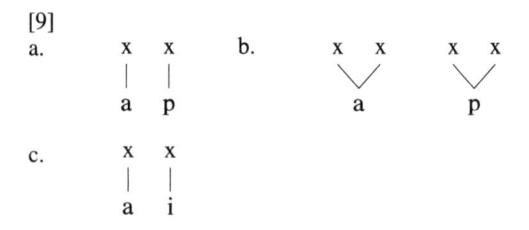

[9]
a. x x   b.   x x   x x
    | | \ /   \ /
    a p   a   p

c. x x
    | |
    a i

The fact that a single melodic unit can be associated with two skeletal positions making up a long vowel or a geminate consonant means that the segments in question are at the same time single entities (melodies) and complex structures (skeletal sequences). The fundamental function of the skeletal tier is to capture the purely quantitative or temporal properties of linguistic forms, while their qualitative properties are located on the melodic level. It should be stressed that the representation of long segments in [9b] makes the specific claim that melodically the segments are single and hence they are expected to function in a unitary fashion. On the other hand, it should be possible to have a sequence of two identical slot-melody associations, which would provide evidence against the conflation of the melody to a single unit. Consider in this context the English negative prefix *un-*, e.g. *unstable* [ʌnˈsteɪbl], *unkind* [ʌnˈkaɪnd] and the present participle suffix *-ing*, e.g. *building* [ˈbɪldɪŋ], *dashing* [ˈdæʃɪŋ]. In forms such as *unnecessary* [ʌnˈnesəsəri], *unnatural* [ʌnˈnætʃərəl] we have a sequence of two nasals which happen to be next to each other in much the same way as they are neighbours in *ten names* [tenneɪmz] or *tin knife* [tɪnnaɪf]. The very clear morphological boundary falling 'in the middle' of the long nasal in forms like *unnatural* argues for two melodic nasal segments not unlike the two melodic segments which are recognised at the boundary in *unstable* for example. Similarly in *studying* [ˈstʌdiɪŋ] or *carrying* [ˈkæriɪŋ], we do not want to talk about a long vowel [iː] but rather of a sequence of two melodic units and their associated skeletal positions which happen to occur together. Such sequences of ostensibly long consonants are often called spurious or **fake geminates**. Fake geminate consonants, like the nasal of *unnecessary* or pseudo-long vowels such as the vowel of *carrying*, will be represented as sequences of simplex structures:

[10] x   x   x   x
      | | | |
      n   n   ɪ   ɪ

The system separating temporal from qualitative properties predicts the possibility that a complex vocalic or consonantal melody could be attached to a single slot. This is borne out by language data: in the former case we encounter the so-called short diphthongs found, for example, in Modern Icelandic; their consonantal equivalent are affricates, combinations of plosives and spirants within a single segment found in numerous languages. The Icelandic word *hætta* [ˈhaihta] 'stop' with the short diphthong [ai] and the German word *zehn* [tseːn] 'ten' with the affricate [ts] can be represented in the following ways:

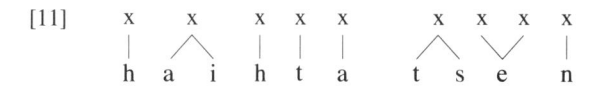

[11] x   x   x x x   x x x x
      | ∧ | | | ∧ ∨ |
      h   a i h t a   t s e n

Further implications of the two-level representation will become evident in subsequent discussion. For the moment we recognise four possibilities for the melody-to-skeleton association:

one-melody–one-skeletal position (traditional short vowels and consonants)
one-melody–two-skeletal positions (long vowels, geminate consonants)
two-melodies–one-skeletal position (short diphthongs, affricates)
two-melodies–two-skeletal positions (diphthongs, vowel and consonant sequences)

2.4 Compensatory lengthening in Germanic and Turkish

The view of the phonological structure of words presented so far entails the claim that the two levels of representation – the skeletal tier and the melodic one – are independent of but associated with each other. To be pronounced a melodic unit must be connected with one or two skeletal positions and, likewise, a skeletal point without an attached melody is silent. A further confirmation of the existence of the skeletal level of representation comes from a phenomenon called **compensatory lengthening**. This notion, functioning both in synchronic and diachronic studies, refers to a situation where a skeletal position exists independently of the melody to which it was originally attached. In other words, a skeletal slot may be shown to persist independently of its melody, thereby strengthening the argument for the skeletal level of representation. We will first look at a historical example involving old Germanic, and then consider a case taken from Modern Turkish.

When certain Old English (OE) forms are compared with those of a related Germanic language such as Old High German (OHG) or Gothic (G), it can be seen that a long vowel in English corresponds to a sequence of a short vowel and a consonant in the other language(s). Consider the pairs of words in [12], concentrating on the quantitative differences:

[12]   [oː] – [an]   OE gōs 'goose'   OHG gans
              OE ōþer 'other'   G anþer, OHG ander
       [oː] – [am]   OE sōfte 'softly'   OHG samfto
       [iː] – [in]   OE līþe 'gentle'   OHG lindi
       [iː] – [im]   OE fīf 'five'   G fimf
       [uː] – [un]   OE ūs 'us'   OHG, G uns
              OE dūst 'dust'   OHG tunst

The examples show clearly that a long vowel in Old English must historically come from a sequence of a short vowel and a nasal consonant before a spirant. This is normally explained as being due to the loss of the nasal, which is compensated for by the lengthening of the preceding vowel. Note that in our terms a long vowel is a two-slot segment; a short vowel followed by a nasal consonant likewise embraces two slots in the skeletal representation. Thus the development of compensatory lengthening can be represented as a case of reassociation where a vowel and a nasal, each associated with single skeletal positions, is replaced by a representation where the vowel is attached to two positions while the nasal remains unattached. The unattached nasal might have remained in the phonology of the speakers who introduced the change, but it was bound to disappear from later representations since subsequent generations of speakers would have no base for assuming any

2.4 Compensatory lengthening in Germanic and Turkish

nasal in such words at all. Once the sound change was complete, a word such as *ūs* [uːs] would contain a two-skeletal vocalic melody followed by a fricative. A possible scenario for the change is suggested in [13].

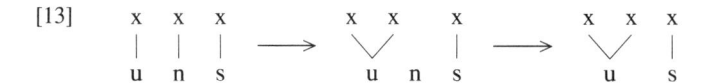

[13]
```
    x x x         x x x         x x x
    | | |    →    \ / |    →    \ /  |
    u n s         u n s          u   s
```

What is important here is that if phonological representations consisted solely of segmental melodies, the lengthening of a vowel attending the loss of a consonant before another consonant would have to be an accident. The Germanic case shows that the skeletal representation remains stable so that a short vowel followed by a consonant at some stage corresponds to a long vowel at a later stage. The lengthening of a vowel entails the loss of a consonant; this is possible since the skeletal point associated with the consonant, rather than being lost like its melody, is combined with the melody of the preceding single slot. What the operation yields is a phonetically long vowel.

In Modern Turkish we find a very similar case. Rather than being an instance of historically related forms, however, this case involves phonological **optionality**, i.e. the ability of some forms to appear in two or more phonetic shapes. This is rather like having the English words *prints* pronounced both [prɪnts] and [prɪns] or *French* as [frentʃ] and [frenʃ], depending perhaps upon the tempo and style of speaking. In Turkish we find numerous words where short vowels are followed by the consonants [h], [j], [v] and another consonant. The first consonant can be optionally deleted; if this happens the preceding vowel is lengthened in a way which is strikingly similar to the Germanic change. Both can be said to represent the process of compensatory lengthening. In Germanic the change is prehistoric and has to be reconstructed; Modern Turkish is caught in the act with speakers free to choose either the form with the short vowel and two following consonants the first of which is one of [h, j, v], or a form with a long vowel and the first consonant of the cluster lost. Consider these examples of alternations resulting from the existence of both options in the language.

[14]
a.   kahya [kah'ja] 'steward'   [kaː'ja]
        tahsil [tah'sil] 'education'   [taː'sil]
        Ahmed [ah'met] 'name'   [aː'met]
b.   eylül [ej'lyl] 'September'   [eː'lyl]
        düğme [dyj'me] 'button'   [dyː'me]
        seyret [sej'ret] 'watch'   [seː'ret]
c.   sevmek [sev'mek] 'love'   [seː'mek]
        övmek [œv'mek] 'praise'   [œː'mek]
        savmak [sav'mak] 'repel'   [saː'mak]

The alternations in [14] show that speakers of Turkish have at their disposal two different pronunciations of the same lexical items. The optionality is phonological and phonetic since it amounts to variant realisations of the same forms: long vowels accompany the suppression of the immediately following consonantal melody. This is a synchronically motivated case of compensatory lengthening and documents the perseverance of the skeletal representation, hence its independence of the melodic structure. Consider the alternative representations of the pronunciation of the word *sevmek* 'love':

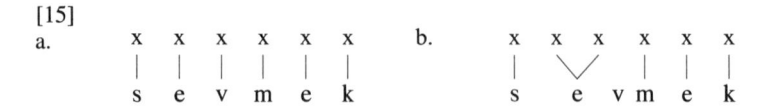

[15]
a. x x x x x x   b.   x x x x x x
    | | | | | | | \/ | | |
    s e v m e k   s e v m e k

As the representations show, the two different phonetic realisations are not due to different melodic or skeletal structures: the word consists of the same number of skeletal points and the same melodic units arranged sequentially, one after the other. The alternative pronunciations emerge as the result of different associations between the units on the two tiers; specifically, the spirant [v] is unassociated in [15b], hence it is not phonetically audible. The skeletal position to which it is attached in the careful or monitored pronunciation does not disappear but is linked to the preceding vowel. The vowel is rendered phonetically long. Turkish compensatory lengthening presents a situation where a unit present in the melody may be realised directly when associated with its slot, or may remain unrealised; alternatively we could say that the unit is realised indirectly through the association of its slot with a different – neighbouring – melody.

As noted above, compensatory lengthening in early Germanic is a historical mechanism. It is assumed in order to account for certain correspondences between related languages: one of the languages deriving from the same hypothetical proto-language, in this case the predecessor of Anglo-Saxon, compensatorily lengthens some vowels, whereas other languages preserve the original situation. The crucial point is that at the Old English stage, a word like *gōs* 'goose' containing the long vowel [oː] which is the result of a historical compensatory lengthening (cp. OHG *gans*), is not phonologically different from a word such as *dōn* 'do' having the same vowel [oː] which continues an earlier long vowel. There is nothing to make these two vowels different. In other words, one cannot talk about any compensatory lengthening in synchronic Old English phonology. It may be legitimate to involve compensatory lengthening as a historical mechanism, but synchronically Old English *gōs* contains no traces of a short vowel and a following nasal. The Turkish situation is drastically different since the long vowel alternates with a sequence of a short vowel and a consonant; thus compensatory lengthening in Turkish is a synchronically **productive** phonological regularity.

The discussion so far indicates that a segment must be seen as a skeletal-melodic complex whose interpretation depends on the nature of the association between its component parts. In the most straightforward case each unit of the melody is attached to one or two skeletal positions. The Turkish case shows that this simple relation can be disrupted by leaving melodic units stranded. A somewhat more complex case is provided by the phonological aspects of English inflectional morphology, to which we now turn. This new material will allow us to study a different factor conditioning the association between the melody and the skeleton.

2.5 The phonology of English inflectional morphology

The inflectional morphology of English is extremely simple. In the present-day language we have in the nominal system the regular ending of the plural, e.g. *bat – bats*, the regular ending of the genitive singular, e.g. *tailor – tailor's*, and the genitive plural of irregular nouns, e.g. *children – children's*. Apart from these regular endings we also encounter irregular nominative plural forms such as *sheep – sheep, ox – oxen, foot – feet* etc. which as genuine irregularities need to be listed in the grammar or lexicon. In the verbal system there is the regular past tense, e.g. *walk – walked* which happens to coincide with the past participle, e.g. (*I have*) *walked*, and the ending of the third person singular present tense of most verbs, e.g. (*s*)*he walks*. As far as the actual endings go, the English system is frugal in the extreme; the phonological properties of the endings and their representations are what we are interested in. We will start with the regular plural morpheme, denoted in spelling by *-(e)s*.

The regular *-(e)s* ending corresponds to three phonetic forms, namely [s], [z] and [ɪz]. The distribution of the phonetic variants is strictly determined by the character of the final segment of the noun. Thus we find [ɪz] when the noun ends in one of the hissing fricatives or affricates [s, z, ʃ, ʒ, tʃ, dʒ], e.g.:

[16] buses [ˈbʌsɪz]   roses [ˈrəʊzɪz]
     ashes [ˈæʃɪz]   corteges [kɔːˈteʒɪz]
     entourages [ˈɒntʊrɑːʒɪz]   garages [ˈɡærɑːʒɪz/ˈɡærɪdʒɪz]
     watches [ˈwɒtʃɪz]   sausages [ˈsɒsɪdʒɪz]

The voiced spirant is the most liberally distributed variant in terms of the number of environments as it occurs after vowels and diphthongs, sonorants, voiced plosives and the voiced fricatives [v, ð], e.g.:

[17] laws [lɔːz]   remedies ['remədɪz]
     flies [flaɪz]   toys [tɔɪz]
     games [geɪmz]   drills [drɪlz]
     songs [sɒŋz]   ribs [rɪbz]
     beds [bedz]   rogues [rəʊgz]
     loves [lʌvz]   scythes [saɪðz]

Finally, [s] appears after voiceless plosives and the voiceless fricatives [f, θ], e.g.:

[18] lamps [læmps]   tickets ['tɪkɪts]
      sticks [stɪks]   roofs [ruːfs]
      myths [mɪθs]

It is evident that the contexts where the variants occur are mutually exclusive in the sense that in a given environment one and only one variant can appear; alternatively, wherever one variant appears, none of the others is allowed. Thus, for example, after [g] we can only have [z], and if we have [z] in some word, this is the only possibility in that context, hence [pɪgz] rules out *[pɪgs] or *['pɪgɪz]. The presentation of the variants as illustrated in [16 – 18] gives an account of the facts by **listing** the contexts where each of them appears. Listing forms is basically a way of recording exceptional or **unpredictable** properties of words: we list the comparative of *bad* as *worse* or the past tense of *sing* as *sang* but the regular comparative of, say, *small* or the regular past tense of *wait* require no individual listing. Listing individual contexts where each of the plural variants appears makes the implicit claim that their distribution is to a larger or smaller extent unpredictable and, in fact, could be very different. Thus our account would not be significantly altered if the facts of English were altogether very different; if, say, we had the ending [s] after plosives and vowels, the ending [iz] after diphthongs and voiceless spirants and [z] in all remaining cases, we would find it just as easy to produce a list-like solution, along the lines of [16] – [18]. All that would differ would be the specific contexts where each variant occurs. In other words, the list-like solution implies that the context where a given variant occurs is an accident, historical or otherwise, just like the comparative of *bad*. This implication is false: the comparative of *bad* could be *badder* just as the comparative of *sad* is *sadder*, but we will argue below that the plural of *lamp* could not be *[læmpz] or *['læmpɪz]. The distribution of the plural variants strictly depends on the final segment of the base – we can, in fact, say that the shape of the plural marker is conditioned by what ends the singular noun. A phonological account is interested in capturing this dependence.

Turning to the three variants we observe that one of them is pronounced with a vowel, i.e. it is vocalic ([ɪz]), while the other two are non-vocalic as they consist of just the single consonants [s] and [z]. Note also that the voiceless variant

2.5 The phonology of English inflectional morphology

[s] can appear exclusively after another voiceless consonant, whereas the voiced one can appear only after a voiced segment, be it a consonant or a vowel. Thus the spirant of the plural marker has the same voicing as the final segment of the stem. In this sense one can make the tentative observation that the two shapes are merely a manifestation of the requirement of voice agreement between consecutive obstruents that English seems to possess.

The variant with the vowel (i.e. [ɪz]) appears only when the stem ends in a hissing fricative or affricate; the consonants which make up this group constitute the class of hissing obstruents. The consonant of the plural ending is also a hissing obstruent, hence the vocalic variant occurs between two hissing obstruents. In all other contexts the non-vocalic variant is present. We can generalise these observations as follows: the plural marker in English contains two skeletal positions, of which the first is vocalic and the second is the voiced coronal spirant. The vocalic element is pronounced [ɪ] only when attached to a stem ending in a hissing coronal obstruent; if added to a different segment, it is only the coronal obstruent of the ending that is pronounced and, furthermore, it is realised as voiceless after a voiceless obstruent. A representation for the words *dogs*, *cats* and *leashes* is suggested in [19]; note that the melody of the ending should be specified in terms of properties such as [voicing], [hissing], [coronality] but the simplified representation is adequate for our immediate concerns.

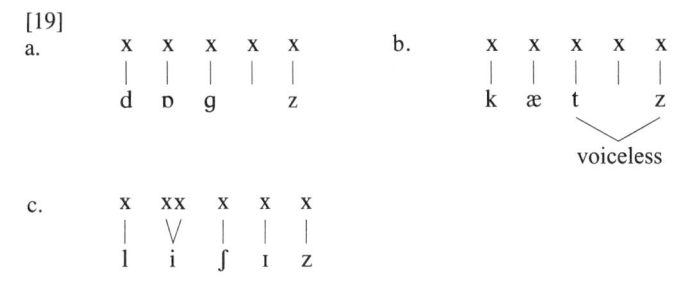

[19]
a.
```
    x   x   x   x   x         b.   x   x   x   x   x
    |   |   |   |   |              |   |   |   |   |
    d   ɒ   g       z              k   æ   t       z
                                                ⌣
                                              voiceless
```

c.
```
    x   xx  x   x   x
    |   \/  |   |   |
    l   i   ʃ   ɪ   z
```

In [19a] and [19b] the skeletal position preceding the final consonant has no melody attached to it – it is **an empty position**; the melody [ɪ] is attached only when the flanking consonants both belong to the same class of hissing obstruents, as in [19c]. Additionally, in [19b] the final consonant of the ending is specified as *voiceless* in agreement with the voicelessness of the stem-final plosive; a [z] which is specified as *voiceless* is, of course, nothing else than, phonetically speaking, [s]. We will say that voicelessness is **shared** by the two final consonants.

Since the final consonant of the ending varies between voiced [z] and voiceless [s] we might legitimately ask why it is the voiced consonant which appears in the representations in [19]. Our list-like interpretation in [16] – [18] makes it clear that after a voiced segment, be it vowel or consonant, the hissing obstruent of the ending must be voiced, while after a voiceless consonant, it must be [s]. Consequently we could adopt a different interpretation and claim that the final consonant is voiceless and acquires its voicedness from the preceding vowel or consonant. The words of [19] would then be represented in a slightly different way, namely as in [20]:

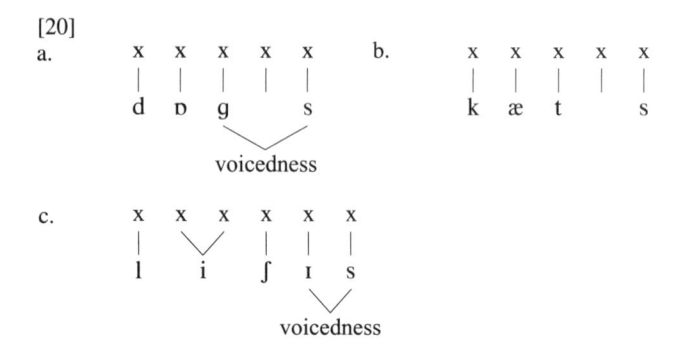

[20]
a.
```
        x x x x x        b.    x x x x x
        | | | | |              | | | | |
        d ɒ g   s              k æ t   s
             \_/
          voicedness
```

c.
```
        x x x x x x
        |  \/  | | |
        l  i   ʃ ɪ s
                \_/
             voicedness
```

As we can see, the facts of the English plural ending can be described in two ways. Which is correct?

The two interpretations make different claims or predictions. The analysis embodied in [19] says in effect that a sequence of a voiceless and a voiced obstruent is not acceptable in English; nor is a sequence of two hissing coronals. The analysis in [20] says that a sequence of a vowel and a voiceless hissing coronal is not tolerated in English and that is why the obstruent shares its voicing with the preceding vowel. This latter claim is factually incorrect since there is no shortage of words which end in a vowel and [s], words which are either morphologically simplex as in [21a], or morphologically complex as in [21b].

[21]
a. miss [mɪs]   bogus [bəʊɡəs]
    loss [lɒs]   mice [maɪs]
b. happiness ['hæpinəs] manageress ['mænɪdʒəres]
    hostess [həʊs'tes]   hopeless ['həʊpləs]

Furthermore, pairs of words such as those in [22] indicate that the voicing of the coronal spirant after a vowel is not phonologically determined, hence cannot be predicted.

[22] rice [raɪs]   rise [raɪz]
      bus [bʌs]   buzz [bʌz]
      miss [mɪs]   Ms [mɪz]

Thus the claim embodied in [20] is seen to be false: the voiceless spirant [s] is perfectly acceptable after a vowel in English. In fact, this analysis encounters other obstacles, since it would need to voice the final spirant not only after vowels but also after sonorants in words like *bills* [bɪlz], *lambs* [læmz], *rains* [reɪnz]. As there are words where the voiceless spirant [s] freely follows voiced sonorants, both within [23a] and across morphemes [23b], we conclude that just as in the case of vowels, there is no requirement that sonorants must be followed by a voiced hissing coronal.

[23]
a. pulse [pʌls]   false [fɔːls]
    ransom ['rænsəm]   dance [dɑːns]
    Samson ['sæmsən]
b. troublesome ['trʌblsəm] minstrelsy ['mɪnstrəlsi]
    insoluble [ɪn'sɒljʊbl]   youngster ['jʌŋstə]
    circumstance ['sɜːkəmstɑːns]

For these reasons the representations in [19] can be said to be phonologically motivated, while the alternative ones would be either at odds with the facts of the language or would require additional complications, e.g. we would need in some way to explain the voicing in *bills* as against its absence in *pulse*.

The analysis of the English regular plural ending reveals the existence of two phonological conditions of the language: (i) sequences of hissing coronals are not acceptable, and (ii) sequences of obstruents must agree in voicing. By a sequence we understand consecutive or directly adjacent skeletal positions with their melodic associations. Conditions of this sort will be referred to as phonological **constraints** of the language. We have seen independent evidence showing that it is the voiced coronal spirant in English that adjusts itself in voicing to the preceding voiceless consonant; also, the analysis calls for a skeletal position which is filled by a vocalic melody when a certain phonological constraint needs to be observed, while otherwise the slot remains empty.

The material discussed so far covers the regular plural ending in English. As we noted at the outset, the -(*e*)*s* ending also marks the third person present tense of most verbs, hence side by side with the examples of nouns in [16] – [18] we find verbs with a homophonous ending. In [24] there are verbs whose stem ends in a hissing coronal.

[24]   (s)he misses ['mɪsɪz]   rises ['raɪzɪz]
        bashes ['bæʃɪz]   garages ['gærɑːʒɪz] (or ['gærɪdʒɪz])
        watches ['wɒtʃɪz]   savages ['sævɪdʒɪz]

The voiced spirant occurs after vowels and diphthongs, after sonorants, after voiced plosives and the voiced fricatives [v, ð].

[25]   (s)he soars [sɔːz]   remedies [ˈremədiz]
       flies [flaɪz]   toys [tɔɪz]
       names [neɪmz]   drills [drɪlz]
       sings [sɪŋz]   robs [rɒbz]
       beds [bedz]   begs [begz]
       loves [lʌvz]   clothes [kləʊðz]

We are left with [s], which appears after voiceless plosives and the voiceless fricatives [f, θ].

[26]   dumps [dʌmps]   bites [ˈbaɪts]
       sticks [stɪks]   spoofs [spuːfs]
       sleuths [sluːθs]

On the face of it it is not surprising that what looks the same is pronounced the same way. However, the 'look' of sameness is highly misleading: a moment's reflection will convince us that although the -(e)s endings look identical, i.e. they are spelt in the same way, they are completely different entities. They represent different morphemes – plurality vs. third person singular present tense – and are attached to nominal or verbal bases. It is entirely possible that their phonetic realisations could be different – the verbal ending could have just two variants: [ɪz] in the contexts of [24] and [s] elsewhere, or transitive verbs could have one and intransitive verbs the other variant, to take just one possibility. If the variation were morphological or morphologically conditioned, any arrangement other than the one actually attested would be equally plausible. In actual fact, the two endings are morphologically distinct but the phonology treats them in the same way. In other words, they do not differ as phonological objects, they are subject to the same constraints and consequently display the same phonetic variation. At best we can talk about **morphological homophony** where different morphological categories are expressed by the same phonological means; another instance of such homophony in the area of derivational morphology is the suffix -er [ə]: it can denote agentive nouns *singer* [ˈsɪŋə], *player* [ˈpleɪə] or the comparative degree of adjectives, e.g. *broader* [ˈbrɔːdə], *darker* [ˈdɑːkə].

The morphological homophony in English involving the -(e)s ending is even broader. Apart from the two categories just discussed, a same-sounding ending also denotes the genitive singular, e.g. *George's* [ˈdʒɔːdʒɪz], *child's* [tʃaɪldz], *cat's* [kæts] and the genitive plural. The latter case is restricted to plurals formed in an irregular fashion, hence the examples are not very numerous, but they are completely unambiguous: *oxen's* [ˈɒksənz], *sheep's* [ʃiːps], *geese's* [ˈgiːsɪz]. In all these cases the phonological distribution is governed by the same constraints and the effects they induce are identical: voice agreement in obstruent clusters and the filling of the empty position by the vowel [ɪ] when the obstruents happen to be coronal hissing consonants. The identity of the phonological consequences means that the representation of all these different endings is the same: an empty position followed by the voiced coronal spirant.

Let us now turn to the other ending which practically completes the English inflectional inventory, namely -(e)d marking the regular past tense and the past participle. That these two categories are distinct can be seen in the irregular or semi-regular verb groups: thus the past of (*I*) *went*, (*I*) *showed* is distinct from the past participle of (*I have*) *gone* and (*I have*) *shown*. In the regular group of verbs no formal distinction is observed, hence in what follows, while keeping in mind the dual function of the ending, we will speak about the past only.

The past tense ending appears in three shapes whose distribution, illustrated in [27], can be formulated as follows: (i) [ɪd] with verbs ending in [t, d]; (ii) [d] with verbs ending in vowels, sonorants and voiced obstruents except for [d]; (iii) [t] with verbs ending in voiceless obstruents except for [t].

[27]
a.   wait [weɪt]   waited ['weɪtɪd]
       remind [rɪ'maɪnd]   reminded [rɪ'maɪndɪd]
b.   score [skɔː]   scored [skɔːd]
       supply [sə'plaɪ]   supplied [sə'plaɪd]
       repel [rɪ'pel]   repelled [rɪ'peld]
       wrong [rɒŋ]   wronged [rɒŋd]
       grab [græb]   grabbed [græbd]
       behave [bɪ'heɪv]   behaved [bɪ'heɪvd]
       clothe [kləʊð]   clothed [kləʊðd]
       advise [əd'vaɪz]   advised [əd'vaɪzd]
       charge [tʃɑːdʒ]   charged [tʃɑːdʒd]
       beg [beg]   begged [begd]
c.   sip [sɪp]   sipped [sɪpt]
       laugh [lɑːf]   laughed [lɑːft]
       bath [bɑːθ]   bathed [bɑːθt]
       pass [pɑːs]   passed [pɑːst]
       vanish ['vænɪʃ]   vanished ['vænɪʃt]
       coach [kəʊtʃ]   coached [kəʊtʃt]
       stroke [strəʊk]   stroked [strəʊkt]

As with the -(e)s ending, the distribution of the -(e)d variants is complementary; but the contexts for variation are partially different. It is true that the voiced/voiceless variants can appear after a voiced/voiceless segment only. This can be regarded as due to the regularity established above which requires that obstruent sequences should be uniform in voicing. However, the vocalic variant appears after hissing sonorants in the plural and third singular present, e.g. *hisses* ['hɪsɪz], and after a coronal plosive in the past tense, e.g. *waited* ['weɪtɪd]. As a result, a verb ending in a hissing sibilant takes the vocalic variant in the third person singular present tense but the non-vocalic one in the past: *miss* [mɪs] – *misses* ['mɪsɪz] – *missed* [mɪst]. Likewise a verb ending in a coronal plosive takes the non-vocalic present tense but the vocalic past tense variant: *fade* [feɪd] – *fades* [feɪdz] – *faded* ['feɪdɪd]. A closer look at the data reveals a certain similarity between the two groups: the variant containing a vowel appears when the consonant of the ending is similar to the final consonant of the base to which the ending is attached. Thus the hissing coronal spirant of the -(*e*)*s* ending is separated by a vowel from a hissing coronal obstruent terminating a base, and likewise the coronal plosive of the -(*e*)*d* ending is separated from a coronal plosive in the base – in some sense, then, English disallows sequences of too similar consonants and requires that the slot separating such consonants should be filled by a vocalic melody.

Viewed in this way, the three variants which we find in our endings are all governed by the same two constraints: (i) very similar consonants may not form a sequence but must have a vocalic melody between them and (ii) obstruent sequences must be uniformly voiced or voiceless. There is no need to list the individual variants or specify contexts for the distribution. Note specifically that the different contexts for the vocalic variants of the two endings (*misses – faded*) follow from the same, more general constraint disallowing sequences of similar obstruents and need not be specified separately for each of them. The representation of the endings is simply as follows:

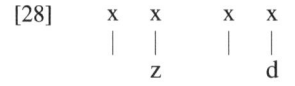

[28]   x   x   x   x
       | | | |
           z   d

Given these representations, we can provide an account of their variants by means of the two constraints. The variant phonetic forms constitute **an interpretation** of the representations in [28]. In other words, the phonetically attested variants are interpreted representations of linguistic forms.

We have been assuming so far – and this is reflected in the representations in [28] – that the empty vocalic position is filled under specified conditions, i.e. between similar obstruents. It is perfectly possible to imagine an alternative analysis, namely one where the vocalic melody is present in the representation and gets deassociated from the skeletal position when not surrounded by similar obstruents; with the association severed, the melody cannot be pronounced. Our main concern in this chapter is the separation of the melody from the skeleton; we also entertain the possibility that there may exist skeletal positions without any melody attached to them. From this point of view we do not have to make up our minds which of the two potential interpretations is to be selected – this is something that would

2.5 The phonology of English inflectional morphology

belong to a comprehensive account of English phonology. For our immediate purposes we note that slots without attached melodies will figure in both of the accounts: in the interpreted representations there are going to be slots with unassociated melodies, i.e. empty slots in one analysis, or slots with severed, hence also unassociated, melodies in the alternative one. It is worth pointing out, however, that there is some evidence which argues in support of the analysis which severs the association between the melody and the skeleton as against the empty position analysis presented above.

There are adjectives in English ending in *-ed* such as e.g. *witted* ['wɪtɪd] in *quick-witted*, which are related to the participle forms of verbs. In this case the *-ed* ending is pronounced in the same way as in the verb (*I have been out*)*witted* [aʊt'wɪtɪd], with the slot preceding the final consonant filled by a melody. In other cases, however, the ending has distinct pronunciations in the past tense and in the adjectival form:

[29] learned [lɜːnd]   learned ['lɜːnɪd] 'a learned person'
      aged [eɪdʒd]   aged ['eɪdʒɪd] 'an aged eagle'
      loved [lʌvd]   beloved [bɪ'lʌvɪd] 'the beloved country'

Similarly, when participles are turned into adverbs, there is a difference in the way the *-ed* ending is pronounced:

[30] advised [əd'vaɪzd]   advisedly [əd'vaɪzɪdli]
      deserved [dɪ'zɜːvd]   deservedly [dɪ'zɜːvɪdli]
      assured [ə'ʃʊəd]   assuredly [ə'ʃʊərɪdli]
      fixed [fɪkst]   fixedly ['fɪksɪdli]
      supposed [sə'pəʊzd]   supposedly [sə'pəʊzɪdli]
      pronounced [prə'naʊnst]   pronouncedly [prə'naʊnsɪdli]

The empty slot solution would need to fill the slot with the melody in the participles when used as adjectives or adverbs. Thus, in addition to the phonologically motivated slot filling when in the environment of similar consonants in nouns and verbs, this solution would also need to fill all slots irrespective of the context in adjectives and adverbs. The melody severing analysis does not need to say anything about adjectives and adverbs, as it merely severs the association in nouns and verbs when the vowel slot is not surrounded by similar consonants. This second solution is simpler and more direct and as such is perhaps preferable.

A more general argument in support of the second solution may derive from the fact that severing association lines between slots and melodies is well attested in other areas of English phonology. An illustration comes from the so-called **strong** and **weak forms**. We will consider just one instance of this phenomenon here, namely the verb *has*, pronounced [hæz] in its strong form, and [həz, əz, z, s] in the weak version.

Consider the forms [əz, z, s] which are highly reminiscent of the -(e)s variants found in the inflectional endings we have just discussed. That the distribution of the variants is identical in both groups can be illustrated by the following examples:

[31]
a. Tom's [tɒmz] car   Tom's [tɒmz] been here
b. Jack's [dʒæks] car   Jack's [dʒæks] been here
c. George's ['dʒɔːdʒɪz] car   George's ['dʒɔːdʒəz] been here

If we assume that the weak form of *has* is [əz], then the realisations found in [31] are due to the severing of the association between the slot and the vocalic melody and the observation of the two constraints formulated above. Voice agreement accounts for [31b], while the ban on consecutive similar obstruents accounts for [31c]. As [31c] shows, the form *George's* has two possible pronunciations in RP. The vocalic melody [ə] is the melody which has not been severed; by the same reasoning we may say that [ɪz] in *George's car* is the melody which has not been delinked in observance of the ban of adjacent similar consonants. This brings us again to the conclusion that the representations of the inflectional endings contain vocalic melodies. Thus, rather than [28] we may postulate [32] as the representation of the inflectional morphemes.

[32]   x   x   x   x
        | | | |
        ɪ   z   ɪ   d

We have considered two different analyses of the English data. They embrace a situation where a melody is de-associated from its skeletal position, or where a skeletal position has no melody. In other words, we envisage the possibility of a phonologically interpreted representation containing slots and melodies which remain phonetically inaudible. Another such case is discussed directly below.

2.6 English *linking r* and the unassociated melody

One of the differences among English dialects concerns the distribution of the sonorant [r]. There are dialects, called **rhotic**, where [r] occurs not only before vowels but also before consonants and word-finally. These dialects are to be found in large areas of the British Isles, in particular in Scotland and Ireland, and also in most of the USA. The **non-rhotic** dialects, which disallow preconsonantal and word-final [r], are, among others, those of southern Britain and the eastern United States. This means, in effect, that the distribution of the sonorant [r] within non-rhotic dialects is restricted to the position before a vowel and marginally also the semi-vowel [j] in unstressed positions, e.g. *bright* [braɪt], *berry* ['beri], *caress* [kə'res], *garrulous* ['gærjʊləs]. The distribution of [r], just like that of [ɫ], can be described as requiring the presence of a following vocalic element. Rhotic dialects are not restricted in this way since the sonorant can appear in non-vocalic contexts as well, e.g. *bark* [bɑrk], *bar* [bɑr]. If the differences were restricted to the presence as against the absence of a segment in a specified position, we would be dealing with a partially different distribution of a segment in some dialects of the language. However, the non-rhotic dialects which disallow word-final [r] admit it there in certain cases. Specifically, a final [r] is not possible when the next word begins with a consonant or when there is a pause; if the next word starts with a vowel, however, the final [r] must be pronounced. This final pronounced [r] is called *linking r* in the phonetic tradition. We shall consider the phonological significance of this phenomenon now, starting with a list of relevant examples.

[33] fear [fɪə]   fear of flying ['fɪərəv 'flaɪɪŋ]
      sure [ʃʊə]   sure of himself ['ʃʊərəv hɪm'self]
      share [ʃeə]   share of it ['ʃeərəvɪt]
      far [fɑː]   far above ['fɑːrə'bʌv]
      bore [bɔː]   bore us ['bɔːrʌs]
      for [fə]   for example [fər ɪg'zɑːmpl]

The left-hand column words all end in a vowel, while the same words end in [r] if followed by another word beginning with a vowel. The same regularity can be observed when a vowel-initial suffix is attached to a word that ends in a vowel. Consider the examples in [34].

[34] answer ['ɑːnsə]   answerable ['ɑːnsərəbl]
      cover ['kʌvə]   coverage ['kʌvərɪdʒ]
      appear [ə'pɪə]   appearance [ə'pɪərəns]
      declare [dɪ'kleə]   declarative [dɪ'klærətɪv]
      consider [kən'sɪdə]   consideration [kənsɪdə'reɪʃn]
      secure [sə'kjʊə]   security [sə'kjʊərəti]
      murder ['mɜːdə]   murderer ['mɜːdərə]

The vowel-initial suffixes of [34] behave in exactly the same way as words beginning with a vowel: [r] appears as the final consonant of the preceding word or morpheme. As noted above, within non-rhotic dialects the sonorant [r] must be followed by a vocalic element. In other words, it is only the presence of a following vowel that allows a preceding [r] to be pronounced – we shall use the term **licensing** to refer to this sort of situation, and say that [r] must be licensed by a following vowel in non-rhotic dialects. In rhotic dialects no licensing relation of this type is required.

The question might be asked as to how the alternations in [33] – [34] should be represented. If in absolute word-final position [r] cannot be licensed since no vowel follows it, the melody must remain unattached. If, however, a vowel follows – either as part of the following suffix in the same lexical item or in the following word – then the sonorant is licensed and retains the association between its melody and skeletal point. Consider the verb *answer* in *answer it* and *answerable*.

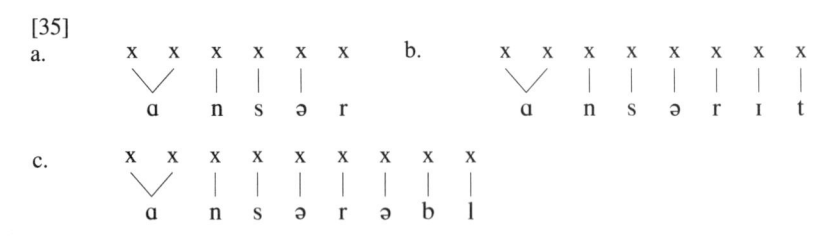

[35]
a.
```
x  x  x  x  x  x
 \/  |  |  |
 a   n  s  ə  r
```
b.
```
x  x  x  x  x  x  x  x
 \/  |  |  |  |  |  |
 a   n  s  ə  r  ɪ  t
```

c.
```
x  x  x  x  x  x  x  x  x
 \/  |  |  |  |  |  |  |
 a   n  s  ə  r  ə  b  l
```

In [35a] the final [r] is not licensed by a vowel, hence the association between the two constituent parts of the segment – the skeletal position and the melody – is not present (or has been severed) with the result that the segment is not pronounced. In both [35b] and [35c] the vowel following the sonorant in question licenses it, thereby maintaining the segment's internal association – consequently the sonorant is pronounced in this position. The representation [35a] is the one we are concerned with, as it offers another illustration of the absence of association between the skeleton and the melody resulting in the segment not being pronounced. In other words, the association is part of interpreted representations, and thus without it, the melody is only latently present. The alternations between [r] and zero in [33] – [34], just as the earlier alternations between [ɪ] and zero in inflectional endings, show that different factors determine the presence of association between the two tiers of representation: the nature of the surrounding consonants in one case, and the presence of a following vocalic melody in the other. As we will see in a number of cases below, phonological regularities result from the relations between neighbouring segments just as much as from the internal organisation of segments.

Before concluding this brief account of [r]-zero alternations in non-rhotic dialects of English, we would like to mention a phenomenon which often appears in the context of *linking r*, namely the so-called *intrusive r*. This is found in non-rhotic dialects and consists in the appearance of [r] at the end of a word before the vowel of the next word or a following suffix in forms which have no [r] in rhotic dialects (or in the spelling). The word *withdraw* [wɪð'drɔː] in non-rhotic dialects can be pronounced with [r] in *withdraw it* [wɪð'drɔːrɪt] or *withdrawal* [wɪð'drɔːrəl], while rhotic dialects tend to maintain the usual pronunciation of the infinitive in the other forms as well: [wɪð'drɔːɪt, wɪð'drɔːəl]. It seems that the non-rhotic dialects treat words like *withdraw* in the same way that they treat words like *answer*, i.e. with a final [r]-melody unassociated to a skeletal position. If a vowel follows, it licenses the association and the segment is pronounced. In rhotic dialects, the *intrusive r* phenomenon does not exist and we are dealing with representations without unassociated segments: words like *withdraw* simply end in a vowel.

2.7 Summary

This chapter has introduced the need for a layered view of phonological representations. Contrary to everyday intuitions, the linear sequence of segments provides only a small portion of the phonologically relevant information. Segments do follow each other in a linear sequence, but they also enter into such close-knit relationships with one another that it often becomes impossible to separate them, since certain properties belong to more than one segment at the same time. To reconcile the segmentability with the inseparability, phonological segments are viewed as consisting of skeletal positions and associated melodies.

Positions are basically temporal slots appearing in a sequence and thus they reflect the segmentability intuition. Melodies, while attached to skeletal positions, need not be singly attached but may at the same time span two or more such positions. The phonetic effect of such double – or multiple – attachment is the simultaneous presence of a given property in consecutive timing slots, in other words the inseparability of sounds.

A fundamental insight emerging from the skeleton–melody distinction is the independence of units at each level. Pronounceability requires that every melodic unit should be attached to some skeletal position and, conversely, that skeletal positions without any melody attached should remain silent. Thus, for example, a unit of vocalic melody attached to two skeletal positions corresponds to what is usually called a long vowel. Since, however, the two levels are independent, operations at one level do not influence the other. The removal of one skeletal position from a doubly attached melody will result in the shortening of that melody without affecting it in any other way. Similarly, the establishment of a melodic connection between consecutive skeletal positions will in no way influence the number or order of the positions. Phonological operations may affect either of the two levels and also the associations connecting them.

An important implication of such a model of organisation is the recognition of two types of phonological objects. On the one hand we can have skeletal positions without any attached melody (or with a severed melody) – these are the so-called empty positions. In this chapter we have come across one case of such a possibility, in the discussion of English inflectional morphology. Another object predicted by the model is unassociated melodies; obviously, if they are unassociated, they will remain inaudible but their existence must be justified by phonological evidence. In other words, the phonological evidence must call for the recognition of such unassociated melodies. This is the case of *linking r* in non-rhotic dialects of English.

In this chapter we have seen several instances, most of them quite simple, of what might be termed phonological generalisations. Such generalisations, also called constraints, may affect the melodic tier, the skeletal tier or the association between the two. Phonological regularities will occupy us for the rest of this book. To see how they can be established and justified we will look at a number of individual cases in some detail.

2.8 Suggested further reading

The relation between quantity and quality in English is covered by phonetic descriptions such as Gimson and Cruttenden (1994) or Jones (1975).

The Germanic lengthenings are described in grammars of older Germanic languages, in particular Meillet (1970) and Hogg (1992).

For the Finnish data consult Whitney (1959) and Morozova (1972); a more comprehensive account is to be found in Keyser and Kiparsky (1984).

Geminates have been subjected to numerous phonological analyses, e.g. Schein and Steriade (1986), Hayes (1986), the relevant parts in Kenstowicz (1994).

For the skeleton and compensatory lengthening see Prince (1984), Goldsmith (1990, chapter 2), Kenstowicz (1994, chapter 8), Harris (1994, section 2.2), Bickmore (1995), Perlmutter (1995).

The presentation of Turkish is based on the data in Sezer (1986).

For partially different accounts of the phonological regularities displayed by English inflectional morphology see Bloomfield (1933, chapter 13), Anderson (1974, chapter 4). Linking and *intrusive r*'s are reviewed and interpreted in Wells (1982), Giegerich (1992, 1999) and Harris (1994, chapter 5).

3
Domains and phonological regularities

3.1 Introduction

In the preceding two chapters we have seen that phonological representations of words consist of two separate tiers of which one – the skeleton – captures the linear and temporal order of units, while the other – the melody – provides the phonetic substance associated with skeletal positions. Crucially, we have seen that there does not have to be a one-to-one correspondence between the units of the melodic and the units of the skeletal subrepresentation: a certain melodic property may be associated with more than one position and, conversely, skeletal positions may have no melody attached to them and thus remain empty. Phonological regularities can hold between units of either of the two tiers or may invoke more complex structures at both levels. In subsequent chapters we will explore in greater detail the nature of phonological regularities by analysing individual phonological problems. The complexity of the problems will increase since it seldom happens that phonological phenomena can be formulated as single regularities: normally they are intertwined with other phenomena, and this often means that in order to interpret what looks like a simple regularity we need to study a number of other factors. Before we plunge into such complex patterns and the concomitant theoretical machinery we need to clear the stage a bit more.

In the present chapter we shall consider, among other things, the scope of phonological regularities. So far we have been assuming without justification that words constitute the domain of phonological phenomena. Quite apart from the fact that the notion **word** is very difficult to define, we will see that for phonological purposes we need a more subtle notion than words as found in a conventional dictionary. The relevant notion, called the **phonological domain** or just **domain** for short, will be introduced below in a discussion of several phonological regularities in English. This will give us a chance to broaden our view of the mechanisms which languages use in their sound structures. We will subsequently show how other linguistic regularities also need to refer to domain structure if they are to be formulated in a satisfactory manner. We start our investigation with an extended discussion of English nasal consonants.

3.2 The velar nasal consonant in English

Phonetically speaking there are a number of nasal consonantal sounds in English: the nasal in *smile* [smaɪl] differs from the one in *mile* [maɪl] since the former is partly devoiced and should be, strictly speaking, transcribed in a way reflecting this difference, say as [sm̥aɪl]; similarly the [n] of *tenth* [tenθ] is not identical to that found in *ten* [ten] as the place of the contact between the tip of the tongue and the teeth-ridge is different. Although the actual number of such distinct nasal consonants is quite large, it is normally recognised that only three such sounds are 'significantly different', namely those broadly described as the bilabial [m], the alveolar [n] and the velar [ŋ]. Pairs and sequences of words differing in just these sounds can easily be found:

[1]   fan [fæn]   fang [fæŋ]
       lame [leɪm]   lane [leɪn]
       brim [brɪm]   bring [brɪŋ]
       sun [sʌn]   some [sʌm]   sung [sʌŋ]
       win [wɪn]   whim [wɪm]   wing [wɪŋ]

Thus the phonetic contrasts seem to require that we treat the three nasals as peers which differ in the place of articulation in exactly the same way as the triplet [b – d – g]. This phonetic conclusion is at odds with native speakers' intuitive judgements, which seem reluctant to treat the velar nasal as yet another nasal consonant in the way they treat the velar plosive as another plosive consonant. Of course, speakers' intuitive judgements are not a very reliable criterion on which to base a phonological analysis. Fortunately, the structure of English reveals some deep-rooted evidence for the special status of the velar nasal in its sound pattern. The evidence has to do with distributional restrictions affecting the nasal consonants in the language.

Note first of all that both the bilabial and the alveolar nasal occur at the beginning of words: there is no shortage of words like *many* ['menɪ], *mist* [mɪst], *millionaire* [mɪlɪə'neə] or *noble* [nəʊ bl], *knowledge* ['nɒlɪdʒ], *need* [niːd]. The same is true about bilabial and alveolar plosives, e.g. *bite* [baɪt], *pail* [peɪl], *tale* [teɪl], *drum* [drʌm]. However, while velar plosives also occur initially, e.g. *kind* [kaɪnd], *glib* [glɪb], no word beginning with [ŋ] exists in English; furthermore, artificial words like *[ŋəʊt], *[ŋaɪlə], *[ŋepi] seem impossible – they are not potential words. We would appear to need a separate statement in the form of a distributional restriction barring the velar nasal from word-initial position. If the velar nasal were just another nasal consonant, the existence of such a restriction would be somewhat puzzling.

Another remarkable property of the velar nasal is the fact that unlike the other two nasals, it cannot occur after a long vowel or a diphthong; we again find numerous

3.2 The velar nasal consonant in English

words like *lime* [laɪm], *perfume* ['pɜːfjuːm] or *plain* [pleɪn], *balloon* [bə'luːn] but words like *[luːŋ] or *[blaʊŋ] are not even vaguely possible in English. If the three nasals differ only in their place of articulation, this restriction singles out – yet again – the velar nasal for special treatment.

Let us now consider nasals morpheme-internally, that is cases where these consonants appear in the middle of single morphemes. It is easy to point to words like *summer* ['sʌmə], *rumour* ['ruːmə] or *minor* ['maɪnə], *annoy* [ə'nɔɪ] where the bilabial or alveolar nasal appear intervocalically; nothing of that sort is possible for the velar nasal *['krɒɲi], *[ɪ'ɲaɪ]. The restriction of this regularity to the morpheme-internal position is important since in purely phonetic terms one does find the velar nasal intervocalically, e.g. *singer* ['sɪŋə], *singing* ['sɪŋɪŋ] etc. It goes without saying, though, that these are not simplex words since they contain the vowel-initial suffixes *-er* [ə] and *-ing* [ɪŋ]; hence the preceding velar nasal is morpheme-final in these complex words. The fact that in purely phonetic terms the velar nasal appears intervocalically must be regarded as due to chance, i.e. due to morpheme combinations. Thus the properties found at some morpheme boundaries are different from those found within morphemes, a point to which we will return presently. Here let us stress again that if the velar nasal were just 'an ordinary nasal' we should expect to find it within single morphemes between vowels just as we find the other nasals there, e.g. *simmer* ['sɪmə], *honour* ['ɒnə]. This does not happen.

In sum then, the velar nasal cannot start a morpheme while morpheme-internally it cannot be followed by a vowel; wherever it does occur, it can only be preceded by a short vowel. These properties set it apart from the two other nasals and justify its special position. It appears then that the velar nasal – from the point of view of its behaviour – does not belong together with the bilabial and the alveolar nasals. If that is the case, then we might well ask what exactly it is. To try and answer this question we need to look at combinations of nasals with other consonants.

As we have just seen, morpheme-internally the velar nasal cannot appear before a vowel; in fact it can only be followed by a velar plosive, be it voiced [2a] or voiceless [2b]. It is practically impossible to find this nasal in any other contexts:

[2]
a.   finger ['fɪŋgə]   angry ['æŋgri]   mango ['mæŋgəʊ]
     Bangor ['bæŋgə]   mongrel ['mʌŋgrəl]   bungalow ['bʌŋgələʊ]
     sanguine ['sæŋgwɪn]
b.   anchor ['æŋkə]   tinkle ['tɪŋkl]   donkey ['dɒŋki]
     monkey ['mʌŋki]   wrinkle ['rɪŋkl]   uncle ['ʌŋkl]
     tankard ['tæŋkəd]   plankton ['plæŋktən]

Before proceeding further it is necessary at this point to revert to the issue of single morphemes. As we have indicated above, phonological regularities are to be sought morpheme-internally; although this statement will be sharpened and revised later, it is important to stress here that the domain of phonology in most cases will not coincide with traditional words. It might be objected that by restricting ourselves to smaller domains we are simplifying the facts of the language. This is not the case. In an attempt to discover the phonological regularities we have to make a number of assumptions, not in order to disguise the facts, but in an attempt to discover the **relevant** phonological facts of the language. This is because the linguistic reality does not display obvious or crude signals of its structure; furthermore, since larger linguistic units (sentences, phrases, words) are made up of smaller ones, it frequently happens that accidental properties which are the result of the mechanical joining together – or **concatenation** – of units occur together with systematic properties. It is the task of the phonologist to separate the true regularities from accidental pseudo-regularities in the domain of sounds; in doing so it becomes necessary to make assumptions and consciously restrict the facts selected for inspection. Obviously a complete analysis should be compatible with what was originally omitted or simplified. To make this question slightly more concrete, let us take orthographic words as the domain of our observations and ask what the velar nasal can be followed by. Here are some examples:

[3] longs [lɒŋz]   longed [lɒŋd]   strongly ['strɒŋli]
     prolongment [prə'lɒŋmənt]   nothingness ['nʌθɪŋnɪs]   kingship ['kɪŋʃɪp]
     wrongful ['rɒŋful]   wellington ['welɪŋtən]   songster ['sɒŋstə]
     strength [streŋθ]   longwinded [lɒŋ'wɪndɪd]

As the examples show, word-internally [ŋ] can be followed by [z, d, l, m, n, ʃ, f, t, s, θ, w]; if we were to include proper names such as *Longbridge* ['lɒŋbrɪdʒ] or various compounds such as *stronghold* ['strɒŋhəʊld], *strongroom* ['strɒŋrʊm], we might well conclude that the velar nasal can be followed by any consonant whatsoever. To say that some sound can be followed by any other sound amounts to nothing more than saying that sounds follow each other. It is rather like saying that a word ending in [ŋ] can be followed by another word – in *long zebra crossing, long did they wait, strong local beer, prolong my subscription, nothing needs to be done* we find the sequences [ŋz, ŋd, ŋl, ŋm, ŋn] which correspond to the first five examples of the word-internal clusters in [3]. Examples can easily be constructed for all the remaining combinations of [3] since there is nothing unusual about some words ending with [ŋ] and others beginning with an arbitrary consonant; what we are saying in effect is that the two consonants are there by chance. Thus our observation that the velar nasal can be followed by any consonant is trivial. Is this a correct observation? The answer to this question depends on what we mean by *correct*. If it means not contradicted by the available data, then our statement

3.2 The velar nasal consonant in English 49

is correct. But true generalisations of any nature make predictions with respect to data which are not taken into account in their construction; if approached in this way, the correctness of our generalisation can be seriously questioned. If it is the case that the velar nasal can precede any consonant in English, then we would predict that this generalisation should hold for single morphemes just as well – we would expect to find words such as *to angmo* *['æŋməʊ], *a bangsy* *['bæŋzi], *rangny* *['ræŋɲi] and many others.

The absence of such words, and some speakers would claim that they are downright non-English and impossible, also counts as evidence: since all the examples in [3] are cases of words which can easily broken up into smaller component parts (*longs = long + s, wrongful = wrong + ful* etc.), the conclusion suggests itself that from the phonological point of view it is the component parts that are the proper domain of phonological generalisations rather than the words as orthographic wholes. The insignificance of consonantal combinations in complex words follows from the fact that the same combinations arise across word boundaries. In this way we arrive at an important theoretical concept, namely **the phonological domain**. This is the domain over which the phonological regularities of a language must be defined. It is important to note that phonological domains cannot be mechanically identified with the traditional word. Nor can they be identified with the morpheme: not every unit identified by a morphological analysis is necessarily a phonological domain – as we will see on a number of occasions below, there are morphemes which are invisible to phonological regularities. Both single morphemes and morpheme combinations need to be carefully inspected before correct generalisations of a phonological nature can be extracted from them. In our discussion of the English velar nasal we have settled upon monomorphemic words, which, as it happens, form a category that appears to constitute a morphological, lexical and phonological domain: *king* [kɪŋ] for example is a single morpheme, a lexical unit (a word) and also a string over which we may specify phonological regularities. For our purposes, it is the last feature which is essential; the others are incidental. If there are generalisations that hold over phonological domains, then they should also be detectable in more complex structures, perhaps in addition to regularities that arise as a result of morpheme concatenations.

Having clarified the theoretical reasons for selecting monomorphemic words as the basis for our phonological observations, we can now return to the discussion of the English nasal consonants.

Using the concept of the phonological domain we can claim that the examples in [2] show that the velar nasal must be followed by a velar plosive domain-internally. If we consider the domain-final situation we note that it differs from the domain-internal one and to some extent depends upon the particular dialect or variety of English. In RP the velar nasal can appear as the last segment of the domain [14a] or it can be followed by the voiceless velar plosive [k] as in [14b]. It can never be followed by the voiced velar plosive, i.e. a sequence such as [ŋg] is totally impossible domain-finally in RP (*long* *[lɒŋg]*).

[4]
a. wing [wɪŋ]   sing [sɪŋ]   bang [bæŋ]
   bring [brɪŋ] hung [hʌŋ]
b. wink [wɪŋk] sink [sɪŋk] bank [bæŋk]
   brink [brɪŋk] hunk [hʌŋk]

On the face of it pairs like *wink – wing* seem to differ in that their first members contain a segment, namely [k], which the second members do not; thus they might be seen to differ in the same way as the pairs in [5]:

[5]   mill [mɪl]   milk [mɪlk]   skull [skʌl] skulk [skʌlk]
      fat [fæt]   fact [fækt]   bar [bɑː]   bark [bɑːk]
      buy [baɪ]   bike [baɪk]   soap [səʊp]   scope [skəʊp]

Here, too, the left-hand member of each pair differs from its right-hand partner in not containing the consonant [k], but it is quite obvious that the presence or absence of this consonant is an accident in that certain words contain it while others do not. In the same way, some words begin with a vowel and others with a consonant, or some begin with a nasal stop and others with a voiceless fricative. The velar nasal on the other hand must be followed by a velar plosive domain-internally, and either by a voiceless velar plosive or nothing domain-finally. There can be no doubt that the velar nasal is inextricably linked with a following velar plosive, and the only situation where this is not manifested phonetically is in the final position of the domain. It is this final position then that requires special attention. Let us summarise the observations about the occurrence of the velar nasal in RP English.

[6]   domain-internally   domain-finally
        ŋg ŋk   ŋ ŋk
        *ŋV   *ŋg

We thus encounter two slightly different situations and we can assume that one of them is a modification of the other. If we take the domain-internal case as the more basic one, then the non-existence of the velar nasal intervocalically requires no special comment. The velar nasal and the following velar plosive are linked through their common place of articulation – they are **homorganic**. The homorganicity of the two consonants can be called an instance of sharing a certain phonetic property. Looked at in this way, the velar nasal can be seen to be a complex sound, consisting of its nasal properties and a place of articulation which is shared with the following plosive consonant. The velar nasal cannot stand before a vowel since it exists only when it shares its velarity with a following plosive. The place of articulation is thus associated with two skeletal positions – it is doubly associated. The situation can be represented graphically in the following manner:

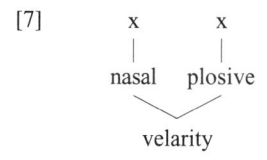

[7]
```
        x       x
        |       |
      nasal   plosive
         \＿＿＿/
          velarity
```

The representation in [7] shows two skeletal positions and the melodies associated with them. What is interesting about this structure is the absence of strict segmentation of the melody, since the place of articulation property straddles two skeletal positions. Unlike the pure long vowels or geminate consonants discussed in the previous chapter, where a single melodic complex is associated with two positions, here we have a case of partial identity of the two consonants; such segment combinations sharing a portion of the melody are referred to as **partial geminates**. The structure in [7] displays what is common to the [ŋk/ŋg] combinations in words like *anchor*, *finger*; obviously the two combinations differ as regards the voicedness of the final plosive.

The velar nasal is a good example of the complex nature of sounds. It constitutes a single sound unit in the sense that there is one skeletal position dominating parts of its melody, specifically nasality. Since, however, the element it shares with its neighbour, i.e. velarity, is doubly attached, the nasal itself must be seen as being interwoven with or partly contained in the following segment. In this way the velar nasal can be said to be both a single consonant and a special kind of consonantal or – more accurately – melodic cluster.

The domain-final situation, as we have seen, introduces a novel element since the voiced velar plosive cannot appear after the velar nasal. If we take the representation in [7] to be generally true of the English velar nasal, then we need an additional statement in order to account for it in the final position. One way of looking at the situation is to say that the plosive in the sharing relation is not itself licensed, or supported, domain-finally when it is voiced and hence is not pronounced. In other words the plosive's unshared properties are inaudible or suppressed. To say that a melody is not licensed or is suppressed and remains silent is to claim that the association between the skeletal position and the melody has been severed. In our case this might be represented as in [8]:

[8]   x   x
       |
       nasal plosive
           ╲__|
            velar
             |
            voiced

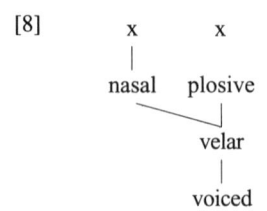

In [8] the final skeletal position has no properties associated with it since they are either severed or – as in the case of velarity – they are attached to a different slot. If a precondition for pronounceability of melodies is their association to skeletal positions, then the absence of such an association – or its severing – amounts to what traditionally is called **segment deletion**. This, however, is not a very felicitous term, since what we see is that the domain-final voiced velar plosive sharing its place of articulation with the preceding nasal is suppressed with respect to all its properties apart from the shared one. Although not audible phonetically, the final plosive is manifested indirectly through the cluster of features that make the velar nasal different from the other two nasal consonants. It is phonologically present even if phonetically we only have a trace of it in the form of the velarity of the nasal.

To sum up the discussion so far: the velar nasal in RP is fundamentally different from the two other nasals because it is bound to the following velar plosive with which it shares its place of articulation. Domain-internally the velar nasal appears exclusively as part of such consonant sequences. Domain-finally, the voiced velar plosive is not pronounced but remains in the representation of individual words. The velar nasal in every case, then, is the first member of a specific consonantal cluster and never a single consonant.

We can find some striking support for this interpretation in other dialects of English. We will restrict ourselves to two more varieties, one found commonly in parts of the British Midlands (M) and another one documented in Scotland (S). Let us bypass other differences between the two dialects and concentrate just on the velar nasal. The two dialects differ radically in the way they treat the voiced velar plosive in a sharing relation with the preceding nasal. In M both domain-internally [9a] and domain-finally [9b] the velar nasal is accompanied by a following [g]; in S, on the other hand, we find [ŋ] prevocalically in [9a] and word-finally in [9b].

[9]
a.   finger, angry, mango, Bangor, mongrel, bungalow,
b.   wing, sing, bang, bring, hung, longs, longed, strongly, nothingness, kingship, wrongful

The dialectal variation shows that the pronunciation of the voiced velar plosive after a nasal domain-internally is independent of the way the consonant is treated domain-finally. In RP, as we have seen, [g] is licensed domain-internally but not domain-finally while in M it is supported in all positions; in S on the other hand it is not accepted either internally or finally. This can be summarised in the following way:

[10]
	g-support domain-final	domain-internal
RP	NO	YES
M	YES	YES
S	NO	NO

Before concluding let us return to the main theoretical issue of this section, namely domain structure. We have seen clear cases where domain boundaries coincide with morphological divisions: the suffix *-ing* is separated from the base to which it is attached by such a domain boundary. This means that the sequence of a nasal and a velar plosive in the base (e.g. *sing*) is a domain-final sequence even if phonetically – and orthographically – it makes up a single unit with the suffix (*singing* etc.). In such cases phonological behaviour goes hand in hand with morphological complexity. We have stressed, however, that domain structure is a phonological rather than a morphological concept, which means that we cannot always expect a one-to-one correlation between the two. Specifically, there are numerous cases which are morphologically complex but which behave as single domains phonologically; and, conversely, there are phonologically complex domains which can constitute single morphological units. In subsequent chapters we will frequently encounter cases where phonological regularities hold in the same way for simplex words and for certain morphologically complex ones. In such cases we will say that the morphological boundary of the word is **invisible** to phonology or that the word makes up a single phonological domain. As an example, compare the word *velocity* [vəˈlɒsəti], which is morphologically indivisible in Present-Day English with *validity* [vəˈlɪdəti], which contains the suffix *-ity* attached to the base *valid*. However, both of them are stressed on the antepenultimate vowel, which suggests that from the point of view of stress placement the words have the same phonological structure. Thus the morphological complexity of *validity* is invisible to the phonology.

With regard to the second mismatch, i.e. the recognition of phonological domain structure without morphological evidence, we can offer some examples involving the velar nasal in English. There is a number of words for which it would be very difficult or downright impossible to justify a complex morphological structure. In such cases we would expect the velar nasal to be followed by a plosive on the pattern of *finger* words (in RP, of course), but this prediction is not always borne out. Some of these items are proper names such as *Birmingham* [ˈbɜːmɪŋəm],

Dingley ['dɪŋli] or *Wellington* ['welɪŋtən] where one might suggest pseudo-morphemes *-ham, -ley, -ton*. Others, such as *dinghy, hangar* admit two types of pronunciation, with and without a velar plosive following the nasal, i.e. ['dɪŋ(g)i, 'hæŋ(g)ə]; the variant with the velar plosive requires no comment, as this is precisely what we would expect. The variants ['dɪɲi, 'hæɲə] seem to call for a complex domain structure, a step which can be defended. The words *hangar, dingy* contain the vowels [ə] and [i] which frequently function as morphemes (e.g. *hanger, Johnny*), hence an enforced morphological division is not an unlikely possibility. The point is that enforced domain division is not morphologically justified: *dinghy* is not 'a small *ding' in the same way in which *Johnny* is 'small John'. By introducing domain structure into words like *dinghy* we consciously embrace the possibility of *false morphological segmentation* resulting in **pseudo-morphemes**. It should be kept in mind that such doctoring of representations is only to be recognised when a small number of words appears to contradict a reasonably convincing analysis. In every case it should be applied with caution and avoided if alternative solutions can be found. As such, even this limited need for artificial domain structure is a warning that the analysis we have arrived at may not be the definitive one.

3.3 Preaspiration in Modern Icelandic

A rather striking example of the role of domains in the functioning of phonological regularities can be found in the phenomenon of **preaspiration** in Modern Icelandic. This consists in the presence of the segment [h] before certain consonants and consonant combinations. Before we look at preaspiration in greater detail, we will review and extend some general facts about Icelandic consonants in addition to what was already said about the language in 1.2. Other information about the phonetics of the language will be supplied in chapter 7, which will be entirely devoted to selected Icelandic phonological phenomena; here let us note that stress is invariably initial, hence we do not include it in our transcriptions.

Plosives in Modern Icelandic are all invariably voiceless. They are divided into two classes distinguished by the presence and absence of aspiration, as in the examples below.

[11]   panna [pʰanːa] 'frying pan'   banna [panːa] 'forbid, ban'
        tala [tʰaːla] 'talk, vb.'   dala [taːla] 'valley, gen. pl.'
        kaldur [kʰaltʏr] 'cold'   galdur [kaltʏr] 'witchcraft'

The opposition between aspirated and non-aspirated plosives is most clearly visible in word-initial position; elsewhere in the word its presence is not always

3.3 Preaspiration in Modern Icelandic

directly observable. As an example: after a sonorant aspirated plosives are never aspirated. This does not mean, however, that a sequence of a sonorant and a plosive is always the same: although only unaspirated plosives are possible in such combinations, the sonorants can be either voiced or voiceless. Thus we find that *orka* [ɔr̥ka] 'energy' and *vanta* [van̥ta] 'want' are distinct from *orga* [ɔrka] 'scream' and *vanda* [vanta] 'do something carefully'. We have evidence showing that it is the aspirated plosives that render preceding sonorants voiceless; the evidence in question is the morpheme -*t*[tʰ] which marks the neuter gender of adjectives. When the suffix is attached to a stem ending in a sonorant, what emerges is a sequence of a voiceless sonorant and an unaspirated plosive as in [12].

[12] tóm [tʰouːm] 'empty, fem.'   tómt [tʰoum̥t] 'neut.'
      gul [kʏːl] 'yellow, fem.'   gult [kʏl̥t] 'neut.'
      dapur [taːpʏr] 'sad'   dapurt [taːpʏr̥t] 'neut.'
      brýn [priːn] 'urgent, fem.'   brýnt [prin̥t] 'neut.'

We can say that in such cases aspiration is realised as the devoicing of the preceding sonorant, but in strict terms it means that a sequence of a sonorant followed by an aspirated stop is pronounced as a voiceless sonorant followed by an unaspirated plosive (see also the examples [10b] in 1.2 above).

Another case where aspirated plosives appear without aspiration word-internally concerns geminate clusters; while geminate unaspirated plosives are pronounced as long consonants, e.g. *vagga* [vagːa] 'cradle', *labba* [lapːa] 'walk', *oddur* [ɔtːʏr] 'point', long aspirated plosives do not exist. If we take again the neuter adjective marker illustrated in [12] and attach it to stems ending in dental aspirated plosives, what emerges is a preaspirated plosive which itself is unaspirated, i.e. [ht]:

[13] heit [heiːtʰ] 'hot, fem.'   heitt [heiht] 'neut.'
      sæt [saiːtʰ] 'sweet, fem.'   sætt [saiht] 'neut.'
      fráleit [frauːleitʰ] 'absurd'   fráleitt [frauːleiht] 'neut.'
      hvít [kʰviːtʰ] 'white, fem.'   hvítt [kʰviht] 'neut.'

Thus we see that a potential geminate consisting of aspirated plosives is realised as a preaspirated plosive without postaspiration. Since this seems to be the general situation in the language, we conclude that preaspiration partly consists in replacing a sequence of aspirated plosives by the glottal spirant followed by a single unaspirated plosive.

Another context where preaspiration is found involves a sequence of a plosive and a stop sonorant, typically [l] and [n]. As above, the plosive must be unaspirated after preaspiration, hence we are talking about sequences [hpl, hpn, htl, htn, hkl, hkn], e.g.:

[14] epli [ɛhplɪ] 'apple' vopn [vɔhpn] 'weapon'
     ætla [aihtla] 'intend' batna [pahtna] 'improve'
     hekla [hɛhkla] 'crochet' læknir [laihknɪr] 'physician'

Although the plosives conditioning preaspiration are themselves not aspirated, they have to be distinguished from other unaspirated plosives. Phonetically the same consonantal sequences which in [14] are accompanied by preaspiration can be found without preaspiration:

[15] efla [ɛpla] 'strengthen' jafn [japn] 'even'
     kalla [kʰatla] 'call' barn [patn] 'child'
     sigla [sɪkla] 'sail' sagna [sakna] 'story, gen. pl.'

We encountered a similar situation above when sonorants were voiceless before some plosives but not others – recall the case of *vanta* [van̥ta] 'want' – *vanda* [vanta] 'do something carefully'. We argued that the voiceless sonorants manifested the aspiration of the following plosive; in support of this claim we supplied independent evidence. The same procedure will be followed here: we can find examples where the plosive of the preaspirated clusters appears (post)aspirated in other forms of the same morpheme. Consider the alternations below:

[16] deplar [tɛhplar] 'dot, nom. pl.' depill [tɛːpʰɪtl] 'nom. sg.'
     opna [ɔhpna] 'to open' opinn [ɔːpʰɪn] 'open, adj.'
     ketlar [cʰɛhtlar] 'kettle, nom. pl.' ketil [cʰɛːtʰɪl] 'acc. sg.'
     gatna [kahtna] 'street, gen. pl.' gata [kaːtʰa] 'street'
     jöklar [jœhklar] 'glacier, nom. pl.' jökul [jœːkʰʏl] 'acc. sg.'
     aukning [œihkniŋk] 'increase, n.' auka [œiːkʰa] 'increase, vb.'

The alternations in [16] show that the plosive is aspirated when followed by a vowel, as in the right-hand column, but loses the aspiration when followed by a stop sonorant; in the latter case the cluster is preceded by preaspiration. Speaking rather impressionistically, we could say that aspiration emerges as preaspiration if a plosive is directly followed by a stop sonorant. Consequently, in [15] – where no preaspiration is found – the right context is not met, i.e. the plosive does not contain aspiration which could be turned into preaspiration.

We can conclude this part of the description of preaspiration by repeating the two contexts where this phenomenon is found in Icelandic: (i) in place of the first part of an aspirated geminate; (ii) before an aspirated plosive followed by a stop sonorant. In both cases the plosive is phonetically unaspirated.

The description we have worked out so far covers a great number of forms of the language and appears general enough to qualify as a valid phonological generalisation. A question which must be answered at this stage is the scope of the

3.3 Preaspiration in Modern Icelandic

generalisation, i.e. what is the domain within which the preaspiration generalisation holds?

At first glance it might seem that it is the dictionary word that constitutes such domains, since no preaspiration effects are found when words follow each other in a sentence, e.g. in *kjöt nokkurt* 'some meat' there is no preaspiration before the final [t] of the first word, which is followed by [n] in the next word. However, a closer inspection of the Icelandic lexicon reveals that such a simple solution is not adequate. For one thing, Icelandic abounds in compounds, sometimes of considerable length and complexity; the notion of the word would have to take them into account in some way. Some such compounds, which function as single lexical items but consist of independent words, follow in [17].

[17]
a. hluttaka [l̥ʏːtʰːakʰa] 'participation' (hlut + taka)
b. bakljós [paːkʰljous] 'back light' (bak + ljós)
c. reknet [rɛːkʰnɛt] 'drift net' (rek + net)

The compound in [17a] has a long aspirated plosive, something which is not found word-internally; where such a combination arises at morpheme junctures, it is interpreted as a preaspirated plosive – see examples in [13]. Similarly, as shown by [14], the combination of an aspirated plosive and a sonorant should result in preaspiration – this does not happen in the compounds in [17b–c]. Phonologically, then, compounds display different properties from single morphemes or morphologically complex derivatives. It is necessary to restrict the operation of preaspiration in such a way as to exclude it at word junctures within compounds, while admitting it at morpheme junctures within words. A simple way of achieving this is to analyse the compounds in [17] as consisting of two phonological domains; in such a case the relevant consonant sequences are separated in the same way as words in a sentence and hence do not qualify for preaspiration effects. However, not all cases are so persuasive or so straightforward: the examples in [17] involve compounds with clearly visible constituent parts which delimit the area for the operation of phonological generalisations. Words with derivational suffixes are less clear in this respect.

Consider the stem *sjúk* [sjuːkʰ] 'sick, fem.'; when combined with the noun-forming suffix *-lingur* [liŋgʏr] it derives the noun *sjúklingur* [sjuhkliŋgʏr] 'patient' with preaspiration appearing in the required context. When the same stem combines with the adjective-forming suffix *-legur* [lɛɣʏr] or the noun-forming *-leiki* [leicʰɪ] we end up with derivatives without preaspiration: *sjúklegur* [sjuː kʰlɛɣʏr] 'sickly, peaky', *sjúkleiki* [sjuːkʰleicʰɪ] 'sickness'. Note that in the cases without preaspiration we find the same consonant sequence as in the cases with preaspiration. In other words, it is not the presence of specific consonants or the very fact of morphological complexity that determines the emergence of a phonological effect such as preaspiration. The suffixes which do not evince preaspiration, i.e. *-legur*, *-leiki* behave in the same way as the members of the compounds in [17] do. On the other hand, the suffix that does, i.e. *-lingur* behaves as if it formed a single domain with the preceding stem. In sum, then, preaspiration appears in the simplex form like *vættur* [vaihtʏr] 'supernatural being' or the loan-word *sígaretta* [siːkarɛhta] 'cigarette', and also in the morphologically complex *sjúklingur*. The latter word must be regarded as making up a single phonological domain.

It looks then as if certain suffixes are separated from the base by a domain boundary, while others form a single domain with the base. In [18] more examples are offered of the two types of derivatives: in [18a] the suffixes are invisible for the purposes of preaspiration, while in [18b] they form a barrier and no preaspiration is attested. The words in the right-hand column show the alternants with single aspirated plosives appearing before a vowel.

[18]
a. bæklingur [paihklɪŋɣʏr] 'pamphlet, booklet'   bækur [paiːkʰʏr] 'books'
   latneskur [lahtnɛskʏr] 'Latin, adj.'   latína [laːtʰina] 'Latin language'
   vitneskja [vɪhtnɛsca] 'knowledge'   vita [vɪːtʰa] 'know'
   undantekning [ʏntantʰɛhknɪŋk] 'exception'   undantaka [ʏntantʰakʰa] 'exclude'
b. hlutlaus [l̥ʏːtʰlœis] 'neutral, disinterested'   hluti [l̥ʏːtʰɪ] 'part, share'
   hlutleysi [l̥ʏːtʰleisɪ] 'neutrality'
   saknæmur [saːkʰnaimʏr] 'punishable'   saka [saːkʰa] 'accuse'
   saknæmi [saːkʰnaimɪ] 'punishability'
   sakleysi [saːkʰleisɪ] 'innocence'
   saklaus [saːkʰlœis] 'innocent'

It thus seems that the lexical entries for individual words include information about their phonological domain structure (cf. *dinghy* etc. in the preceding section). This information is **unpredictable** or **idiosyncratic**: there is no way of knowing in advance that *-ning* is not separated from the base by domain structure while *-laus* is. This must be part of what is specific about a given word, together with the rest of its phonological representation, its morphological properties, syntactic peculiarities and its meaning. An additional argument in favour of the idiosyncratic nature of the domain structure of words comes from words which are exceptional. Here we will just consider two examples which should help us reach a better understanding of the role of domains in phonology.

In [17] we illustrated a case where the consonantal clusters which arise at the boundaries between component parts of a compound do not constitute the right context for preaspiration. This is predominantly the rule in the language, although individual cases can be found which depart from this generalisation: the word *kaupmaður* 'merchant' is clearly a compound of *kaup* 'trade, business' and *maður* 'man' and as such should disallow preaspiration. While the preaspiration-less pronunciation [kʰœiːpʰmaðʏr] is a possibility, so is a variant with preaspiration: [kʰœihpmaðʏr]; it is the latter possibility which indicates that domain structure cannot be mechanically identified with morphological complexity and hence needs to be entered in the lexicon. In this particular case two alternative domain structures for the compound have to be recognised: one separating the two parts with a concomitant absence of preaspiration, and an alternative one with a single domain for the compound as a whole and preaspiration.

A somewhat different case can be observed in the word *vitlaus* [vɪhtlœis] 'crazy' with obligatory preaspiration. The suffix *-laus* is normally separated from its base by domain structure (cf. *hlutlaus* in [18b]) and thus its initial sonorant does not occur in a context inducing the emergence of preaspiration. The word *vitlaus*, however, having the morphologically transparent structure *vit + laus*, lit. 'witless', admits a pronunciation with preaspiration only. In our terms this means that the derivative does not contain an internal phonological domain. On a more general level the implication is that it is impossible to determine such domains for affixes once and for all. Rather, they belong to individual words and are subject to lexically unpredictable variation.

Domain structure is crucial for the statement of phonological regularities, most of which have a restricted scope. The point of the discussion above has been not so much the need for delimiting the areas where generalisations hold, but rather to demonstrate that domains must to some extent at least be regarded as arbitrary. While monomorphemic words usually automatically constitute domains, derivatives do not allow a simple solution. Some of them, although unquestionably complex morphologically, behave as if they were simplex forms, while in others morphological complexity goes hand in hand with domain structure. There is no single rule for deciding whether or not phonological domains can be identified with morphological ones. Phonology behaves in its own way, sometimes taking morphological structure as its own phonological domain, and at other times ignoring morphology altogether. We have seen cases where both options are taken (*kaupmaður* in Icelandic), or when phonological domain structure is introduced although it has no morphological support (English *hangar, dinghy*). Phonological analysis consists not only in identifying the right generalisations, but also in specifying the phonological domain structure of words, something which is only partly derivable from their morphological structure.

3.4 Dorsal spirants in Standard German

Modern Standard German contains two dorsal spirants, i.e. consonants whose articulation involves the back of the tongue: the velar [x] and the palatal [ç], both of them voiceless. The position of these two consonants in the phonology

60   *Domains and phonological regularities*

of German has been subject to much discussion in the phonological literature. Here we will consider the most important aspects of the problem and their implications.

The most direct piece of evidence showing that the two spirants are not just phonetically close but also phonologically related can be seen in morphological alternations. There are numerous morphemes in German which display the velar spirant in some forms and the palatal one in others. Some examples follow.

[19] Buch [buːx] 'book'   Bücher ['byːçɐ] 'pl.'
      Loch [lɔx] 'lake'   Löcher ['lœçɐ] 'pl.'
      Bach [bax] 'stream'   Bäche ['bɛçə] 'pl.'
      Strauch [ʃtʁaux] 'shrub'   Sträucher ['ʃtʁɔiçɐ] 'pl.'
      Sprache ['ʃpʁaːxə] 'language' sprechen ['ʃpʁɛçən] 'speak'
      schwach [ʃvax] 'weak'   schwächer ['ʃvɛçɐ] 'weaker'
      brach [bʁaːx] 'I broke'   brechen ['bʁɛçən] 'break'
      brauchte ['bʁauxtə] 'I used' bräuchte ['bʁɔiçtə] 'I would use'

An inspection of the contexts where the two spirants occur shows that the velar spirant invariably follows some back vowel or glide, whereas the palatal one appears after a front vowel or glide. We are not concerned here with the relatedness of the back and front nuclei, but merely note that the backness or frontness of the vowel goes hand in hand with the velarity or palatality of the dorsal spirant. This seems to be generally the case in German, quite irrespective of the existing alternations: as the examples in [20a] document, the velar spirant is invariably preceded by a back vowel, while a front vowel requires the following spirant to be palatal [20b]. The length of the preceding nucleus is seen to be irrelevant to the character of the following dorsal spirant.

[20]
a.   Nacht [naxt] 'night'   nach [naːx] 'after'
     Woche ['vɔxə] 'week'   hoch [hoːx] 'high'
     Flucht [fluxt] 'flight'   buchen ['buːxən] 'enter'
     rauchen ['ʁauxən] 'smoke, vb.'
b.   Sicht [zɪçt] 'sight'   siech [ziːç] 'infirm'
     Küche ['kyçə] 'kitchen'   psychisch ['psyːçɪʃ] 'psychological'
     Fächer ['fɛçɐ] 'fan'   Leiche ['laɪçə] 'corpse'
     meucheln ['mɔiçəln] 'assassinate' röcheln ['ʁœçəln] 'give the death rattle'

The combined evidence of [19] and [20] might suggest a very simple relation between a vowel and a following dorsal spirant: the vowel shares its frontness or its backness with the consonant, which is consequently pronounced in the two different ways. Thus the velar spirant [x] would be expected to appear exclusively after a back vowel, and the palatal spirant [ç] could only appear after a front vowel. Unfortunately, this simple generalisation is only partly true: while the velar

3.4 Dorsal spirants in Standard German

spirant does, indeed, only appear after back vowels, the palatal one is less restricted as it is also found after consonants [21a], and at the beginning of a word no matter what vowel follows or whether the next segment is a vowel or a consonant [21b].

[21]
a. Milch [mɪlç] 'milk' Strolch [ʃtʁɔlç] 'rascal'
Fenchel ['fɛnçəl] 'fennel' manche ['mançə] 'some'
Archiv [aʁ'çiːf] 'archives' horchen ['hɔʁçən] 'listen'
b. Chinin [çi'niːn] 'quinine' Chemie [çe'miː] 'chemistry'
Charisma ['çaːʁisma] 'charisma' Cholesterin [çolɛste'ʁiːn] 'cholesterol'
chthonisch ['çtoːnɪʃ] 'earthly' Chrisam ['çʁiːzam] 'chrism'

It thus seems that while the velar spirant is crucially dependent on the preceding back vowel for its existence, the palatal variant is subject to fewer restrictions. In actual fact, the only restriction that it must obey is that it cannot follow a back vowel, since this is reserved for the velar consonant. It is this latter regularity that needs to be stated as a phonological sharing generalisation: a back vowel shares its backness with the following dorsal spirant. We may recast this in the form of a general formula of the following sort:

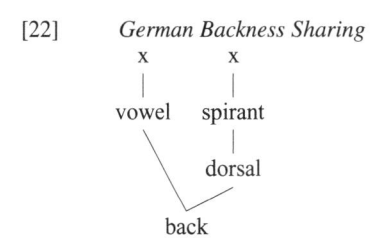

[22]   *German Backness Sharing*
```
        x       x
        |       |
      vowel  spirant
         \     |
          \  dorsal
           \__/
           back
```

This generalisation restricts the occurrence of the velar spirant to a well-defined context, connecting a feature of the context, i.e. vowel-backness, with the required nature of the spirant. In other words, the spirant is velar because the vowel is back. What about the other spirant? As we saw above, the palatal spirant has a distribution which is complementary to the velar one: it appears in all contexts apart from those involving a back vowel. We can reformulate this by saying that a dorsal spirant, unless it shares its backness with a preceding back vowel, is pronounced as [ç] in all contexts. In other words, the dorsal spirant in German is pronounced as palatal unless directed otherwise. The palatal pronunciation of the dorsal spirant is just a **phonetic effect** without a phonological motivation. More will be said about the concept of the phonetic effect in 3.5.

Let us now consider the other German spirants. These embrace:

[23] labio-dentals: [f], [v], e.g. *finden* [ˈfɪndən] 'find', *wieder* [ˈviːdɐ] 'again'
alveolars: [s], [z] , e.g. *beißen* [ˈbaɪsən] 'bite', *reisen* [ˈʁaɪzən] 'travel'
palato-alveolar [ʃ], e.g. *wünschen* [ˈvʏnʃən] 'wish'
glottal [h], e.g. *hundert* [ˈhʊndɐt] 'hundred'

Since the dorsal spirants vary between palatal and velar types, it might be suggested that the place of articulation is not an inherent property of theirs. As we have seen, the velar fricative [x] invariably shares its backness with the preceding vowel and for this reason it cannot appear at the beginning of a word or after a consonant. Thus the place of articulation of the spirant is what it has in common with the preceding vowel. If no sharing is involved, the fricative is pronounced as [ç]. On this interpretation we can slightly modify the formulation of backness sharing in German and remove the awkward combination of dorsality and backness. The revised formulation follows below:

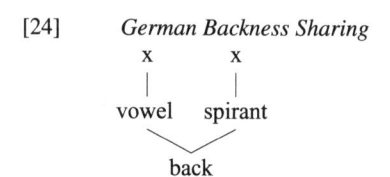

[24]   *German Backness Sharing*

```
     x      x
     |      |
   vowel  spirant
      \   /
       back
```

The condition states that a placeless spirant is back after a back vowel; otherwise it is palatal, with palatality being merely a phonetic effect with little phonological significance. The remaining fricatives in [23] contain place of articulation as part of their phonological specification.

The two dorsal spirants in German appear to show the predictability of distribution that is reminiscent of the RP *dark* and *clear l* as discussed in chapter 1. There is a difference, however. It has been generally observed that the pattern with the velar spirant after back vowels and the palatal one elsewhere is disrupted by a handful of forms such as those in [25].

[25]   Kuchen [ˈkuːxən] 'cake'   Kuhchen [ˈkuːçən] 'cow, dim.'
         tauchen [ˈtaʊxən] 'dive'   Tauchen [ˈtaʊçən] 'rope, dim.'

On the face of it, these pairs of words differ from the cases considered so far in that both spirants appear in exactly the same contexts. If the examples in [25] were to be taken at face value, we would have to conclude that our observations about the distribution of the spirants have to be revised, as the palatal spirant is also possible after a back vowel (*Kuhchen, Tauchen*) in contravention of the backness sharing constraint [24]. Before abandoning the generalisation we need to look a little more closely at the forms which appear to violate it, i.e. cases where the palatal consonant appears after a back vowel. What any morphological analysis of

German reveals is that the forms in the right-hand column in [25] are complex and consist of a stem *Kuh* [ku:] 'cow', *Tau* [tau] 'rope' and the diminutive-forming suffix *-chen* [çən]; the suffix is found in numerous other forms.

[26]   Hund [hʊnt] 'dog'   Hundchen ['hʊntçən] 'doggy'
        Vogel ['fo:gəl] 'bird'   Vögelchen ['fø:gəlçən] 'birdie'
        Fisch [fɪʃ] 'fish'   Fischchen ['fɪʃçən] 'little fish'
        Schwester ['ʃvɛstɐ] 'sister'   Schwesterchen ['ʃvɛstɐçən] 'little sister'

This very productive suffix always appears as [çən], with a palatal spirant. This is what we would expect of the word-initial position (see [21b]); we can adopt the view that the suffix is separated from the base to which it is attached by a domain boundary. In such a case the appearance of the palatal spirant after a back vowel has nothing to do with backness sharing in German; if anything, it is an accident that the domain-initial spirant follows a domain-final back vowel. It is not any different from [ç] coming after [a:] in *sah Chirurg* [za: çi'rurk] 'saw a surgeon' where – phonetically speaking – a back vowel is followed by the palatal spirant. The *-chen* counterexamples to the generalisations established so far can be dismissed as spurious: once domain structure is recognised, forms which initially appear to violate or contradict a generalisation turn out to support it.

3.5 Summary

Phonological regularities capture relations between consecutive skeleton–melody associations. What the evidence of this chapter shows is that these relations hold within chunks of the structure called phonological domains. The main point we have tried to make is that domains, just like regularities themselves, must be arrived at and established in the course of analysis. The difficulty facing an analysis is the necessity of disentangling both domain structures and phonological regularities: phonological regularities hold within domains, but domains can often be determined after achieving some preliminary understanding of the regularities. In the course of further analysis both domains and regularities should be made maximally precise. What must be kept in mind is that, in general, there are no mechanical methods of analysing the phonology of a language, whether we are dealing with regularities or domains.

What is relatively uncontroversial is that monomorphemic words, predominantly, constitute single phonological domains. This is true even if we have seen cases where morphologically simplex words may have to be assigned domain structure in order not to jeopardise a phonological generalisation. Words which are morphologically complex may, but do not have to, translate into phonologically complex domains. Whether they do or do not is an empirical question which can only be determined by an analysis of specific language data. In the case of complex units some mismatch between morphological structure and phonological domain organisation is the norm.

Although we have stressed the significance of domain structure for an adequate formulation of phonological generalisations, this is not to say that there are no phonological regularities holding between domains. In fact there is the ancient Sanskrit notion of **sandhi** phenomena, covering regularities emerging at word junctures. For the most part such phenomena lie outside the scope of this book.

Finally we introduced the notion of the phonetic effect, referring to sound properties which, in some sense, are not essential or are accidental. Phonetic effect covers that part of the phonetic substance which has little phonological significance and can vary a lot. The notion should be used with care as it can be abused in various ways. Its relevance cannot be doubted, however. A dramatic case in point is the variation in contemporary German among the various *r*-sounds; simplifying the matter considerably, two very different variants are normally identified in the language: the uvular fricative [ʁ] and the apical roll [r]. In phonetic terms these are very different sounds, one resulting from friction in the passage formed between the back part of the tongue and the uvula, and the other one from the tapping of the tip of the tongue against the gums. Not only articulatorily but also perceptually these sounds are markedly different. In the structure of German, however, they appear to exhibit very minor differences and the variation is regional: Bavaria in the south-east and Schleswig-Holstein in the north prefer the apical roll, while the uvular fricative predominates elsewhere. Thus, for example, [ʁ] appears in exactly the same positions in some dialects where [r] appears in others. The actual phonetic constitution of the sound and its physical nature are secondary to its phonological status, which can be determined by phonological analysis. What is crucial is the fact that the phonetic realisation of a segment says very little, sometimes next to nothing about its phonological properties and positioning in the system of the language, hence the designation of the phonetic (side-) effect.

In the following chapter we will need to broaden the notion of phonological organisation by considering units other than domains that determine the shape of regularities.

3.6 Suggested further reading

The velar nasal has figured prominently in the history of phonology, starting with Sapir (1925), whose paper involves both native speakers' judgements and language-internal arguments. For different analyses consult Vachek (1964,

1976), Chomsky and Halle (1968), Giegerich (1992), Gussmann (1998). See also Fromkin (1971) for a discussion of the status of the velar nasal as revealed through slips of the tongue.

Domain structure in phonology has been recognised in all frameworks, although sometimes under different names. The papers in Aronoff and Kean (1980) offer a selected survey of views; for an early statement and a relatively recent statement within the generative tradition, see Stanley (1973) and Kaye (1995) respectively.

Icelandic preaspiration has been described in traditional textbooks and grammars, such as Einarsson (1945), and interpreted phonologically in different ways in, e.g.: Thráinsson (1978), Árnason (1986), Gussmann (1999, 2000).

For an alternative analysis of the German dorsal spirants, see Hall (1992, chapter 5).

Sandhi phenomena in a variety of European languages are discussed at length in the papers in Andersen (1986).

4

The syllable

4.1 Introduction

The syllable, just like the sound, seems to be intuitively familiar but on closer inspection turns out to be a very vague notion. The familiarity is largely due to the fact that the term is part of colloquial speech and is often used in discussions where language and language-related issues appear. A case in point are the conventions of breaking words at the end of a line; these are orthographic devices of different sorts and involve the ban, for example in English or German, of breaking certain letter combinations which denote a single sound: *mother* cannot be divided as *mot-her or German *Bäche* 'stream, pl.' as *Bäc-he. The requirement imposed by such conventions in a variety of languages is that the constituent parts of a broken word should form individual syllables, hence in English *val-id* is acceptable, while *vali-d is not; in Polish *radość* 'joy' may be split up as *ra-dość* but not as *rado-ść. Examples of this sort of convention can be found in all languages using alphabetical writing, which of course means that children learning to write are exposed to the term **the syllable** quite early in life. Needless to say, a linguist cannot unquestioningly accept a notion used to define a spelling practice and apply it to the functioning of the sound system. What is needed are phonological rather than orthographic arguments demonstrating the relevance of the syllable; in the following pages we will attempt to provide these and to examine the nature of syllabic organisation a little more closely.

Thus far we have established the need for the skeletal level in addition to the melodic tier. The fundamental justification for the skeleton was connected with properties which could not be reduced to the melody. For one thing we saw the need for skeletal positions without any accompanying phonetic substance, so-called empty positions. On the other hand, some properties of the melody need to be split between two consecutive skeletal positions. It has been argued that there is no one-to-one relationship between the units of the skeletal level and those of the melodic one. Quite clearly, if every skeletal position corresponded to a melodic unit and vice versa, then there would be little or no need to separate the two levels. Putting the matter slightly more technically, the skeleton and the melody are independent levels, and though in many instances units at the two levels are coterminous, it is not the case that the skeletal level is just a projection of the melody. Each level is fundamentally independent of the other. If the division of linguistic forms into syllables, hence the recognition of yet another level of representation, is to be accepted, this means that the syllabic level must be independent of the segmental one. Syllables cannot be simple projections of sounds as there would be little obvious need for such projections. In constructing the syllabic level of representation, we have to keep in mind very clearly that it must offer something new, something which is not present in skeletal slots and melodies. This chapter and the following ones will try to show that phonological regularities in natural languages support this independent level of representation. These regularities can be formulated with greater insight only when related to syllabic constituents. The argument below starts with relatively unquestionable, hence uninteresting, cases where syllable structure coincides with melodic sequences, with more complex examples developed later.

4.2 Some simple English syllables

Let us consider a number of stressed words in English which are regarded as monosyllabic.

[1]
a.   oar, awe [ɔː]   eye, I [aɪ]   aye [eɪ]
       oh [əʊ]   err [ɜː]
b.   bay [beɪ]   lie [laɪ]   be, bee [biː]
       low [ləʊ]   sir [sɜː]   do [duː]
       row [raʊ]   pour, paw [pɔː]   bare, bear [beə]
       sear [sɪə]   dour [dʊə]

All these monosyllabic words end with a vowel, a situation for which the traditional term of an **open syllable** has been used. Additionally, words in [1a] contain nothing but a vowel; since there are no words without a vowel, this would suggest that the vocalic **nucleus** is an indispensable element of the syllable; as the forms in [1b] show, the nucleus may be preceded by a consonant. The consonantal sequence preceding the nucleus is termed the **onset**. Thus the open syllable in [1] contains a vocalic nucleus preceded by an optional consonantal onset. The onset is a constituent present in the syllabic structure of words even if it has no skeletal or melodic content. More will be said about such empty onsets as we proceed. Needless to say, the onset may contain two consonants rather than just one.

68   *The syllable*

[2]   play [pleɪ]   pry [praɪ]   tree [triː]
      glow [gləʊ]   blur [blɜː]   through [θruː]
      brow [braʊ]   draw [drɔː]   Clare [kleə]
      clear [klɪə]   pure [pjʊə]

As can be seen, onsets can comprise one or two skeletal positions in the same way as nuclei; an onset or a nucleus which straddles two slots is said to be **branching**. A constituent embracing just one position is said to be **non-branching**. The words *awe, bay, play* illustrate a branching nucleus preceded by an empty onset, a non-branching one and a branching one. Together with the melodic and skeletal representations, the onsets (O) and nuclei (N) of these words are presented in [3].

[3]   O   N   O   N   O   N
           /\ | /\   /\ /\
           x x   x x x   x x x x
           \/ | | | \/ | |
           ɔ   b e ɪ   pl e ɪ

The representations in [3] indicate that a syllable is made up of an onset followed by a nucleus even if the onset is empty, both skeletally and melodically. The nucleus is indispensable for syllables to exist.

An interesting property of such simple stressed English syllables is that while the onset need not have any melodic content, or may be non-branching or branching, the nucleus must be branching. Note that the following are not possible words of English: *[plæ], *[plʌ], *[bɒ], *[lɪ], *[tre], *[klʊ], i.e. a non-branching nucleus is ruled out in a stressed open syllable. Alternatively, we can say that a stressed open syllable must end in a branching nucleus. This is a phonological regularity of English which crucially involves the notion of the nucleus: there seems to be no natural way of expressing this without involving the nucleus, that is, as long as we restrict ourselves just to the skeletal and melodic levels. We could make a statement like the following: a word-final stressed vocalic melody must be attached to two skeletal positions (the *awe* case), or must be directly followed by another vocalic melody (the *bay/play* case). The disjunction contained in the statement betrays its artificial nature. Nothing in the skeleton or melody requires long vowels to pattern with diphthongs since they are independent units. By referring to nuclei, however, we dispense with the need for such unlikely rules as that above. All we need is a statement to the effect that in English stressed final nuclei must branch. Thus there is good reason for postulating the nuclear constituent.

The simple syllables we have discussed above comprise a sequence of an onset followed by a nucleus. The onset is an optional constituent in the sense that it may have no skeletal points attached to it, hence it may be phonetically inaudible. The nucleus is an obligatory part of the syllable in the sense that it always has a skeletal representation. In English the nuclear skeletal point is normally associated with a vowel melody; in a complete description of the language this statement would need to be modified since the nuclear position may be occupied by a sonorant, e.g. in *brittle* [brıtl̩] or *button* [bʌtn̩] there is only one phonetic vowel but the final lateral and nasal are said to be syllabic. A syllabic consonant denotes a consonantal melody associated with the nuclear position. This category of syllabic elements provides an additional argument in favour of the syllabic tier of representation as well as the skeletal and melodic ones. Note that skeletally and melodically there is very little difference between the initial and the final laterals in, say, *little* [lıtl̩], bypassing the distinction between the clear and the dark variants. The phonological distinctness of the two laterals is due to the fact that the first occupies the onset while the last one is attached to the nucleus, i.e. the difference is in syllabic affiliation, as shown below:

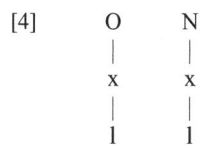

[4] O   N
     | |
     x   x
     | |
     l   l

Syllabic consonants, then, support the decision to introduce an additional level of representation apart from the skeleton and the melody, a level which comprises the sequence of an onset and a nucleus traditionally subsumed under the term of the syllable.

4.3 Empty onsets: French *h-aspiré*

Before proceeding further in our discussion of the structure and composition of syllabic constituents it will help to consider in detail an idea which was introduced above, i.e. the existence of empty onsets. These have been assumed above to be of two kinds: an onset is empty when it contains no skeletal position (and hence obviously no melody), or when it does contain a skeletal position but has no melody attached to it. In both cases the phonetic effect is the same, i.e. no consonant melody precedes the nuclear portion. However, if there exist two different structures producing the same effect, we might legitimately ask what justification there is for the diversification of structure. In other words, if we decide to postulate two different structures, we should expect different types of behaviour to follow from them. This is exactly what we find in the case of the French phenomenon referred to as *h-aspiré*.

The term is traditional and comes from orthography since in Modern French no [h] sound exists. It refers to the situation where some words spelt with *h* exert a different influence upon the neighbouring sounds than others; one type of *h* is called *h-aspiré* or 'aspirated h', and the other *h-muet* 'silent h', even though both of them are equally silent. Thus *hameau* [a'mɔ] 'settlement' and *hameçon* [amə'sɔ̃] 'hook' both begin with the vowel [a], and calling the former an *h-aspiré* word and the latter an *h-muet* one entails an intuition which needs to be made explicit in linguistic terms. In what follows we shall try to do so, using two phonological regularities of French, although it should be kept in mind that our discussion is intended to illustrate a general point rather than provide a definitive and detailed analysis of the French data. In fact readers familiar with Modern French may want to pursue the problems raised by taking into account additional data, and thus elaborate our somewhat simplified presentation here.

The two phonological regularities mentioned concern the preservation and loss of vowels and consonants in certain positions. In general, vowel sequences tend to be avoided in French, hence the pronoun *je* [ʒə] is pronounced as such before a consonant-initial verb, e.g. *je vais* [ʒə'vɛ] 'I go' but without its vowel before a vowel-initial verb, e.g. *j'entre* ['ʒɑ̃trə] 'I enter'. The phenomenon of suppressing a vowel before a vowel, called **vowel elision**, shows that when two nuclei come to stand one after the other without a realised intervening onset, the first of the vowels is not audible phonetically. Two nuclei in such direct contact represent a situation in which the intermediate onset has neither a melody nor a skeletal point, as illustrated in the representations in [5].

[5]
a.　　 O N O N 　　b.　　 O N O N O N
　　　 |　|　|　|　　　　　　 |　|　　 |　/\　|
　　　 x　x　x　x　　　　　　 x　x　　 x　x x　x
　　　 |　|　|　|　　　　　　 |　|　　 |　|| 　|
　　　 ʒ　ə　v　ɛ　　　　　　 ʒ　ə　　 ɑ̃　t r　ə

In [5a] the two nuclei are separated by an onset with an attached melody, whereas in [5b] the skeletal positions and melodic content of the two nuclei are directly adjacent; the latter situation results in the first nucleus not being pronounced. The necessary condition for elision is that the onset as a syllabic constituent separating two nuclei cannot itself have either a melodic or even a skeletal representation.

Let us now observe what happens when the definite masculine article *le* [lə] is attached to the two nouns starting with an orthographic *h*: *le hameau* [lə'mɔ] – *l'hameçon* [lamə'sɔ̃]. Vowel elision fails in one but not the other case. The two *h*-initial nouns behave in the same way as the verbs in [5], where the preceding vowel is elided in one case [5b] but not in the other [5a]; the difference is, of course, that phonetically both nouns begin with a vowel. A possible way of capturing the difference without distorting the facts is to claim that vowel elision occurs if and

4.3 Empty onsets: French h-aspiré

only if the two nuclei are directly adjacent melodically **and** skeletally. Elision is not expected to occur if the two nuclei are separated by an onset with a skeletal position but no attached melody. On this account the two nouns differ in that the one disallowing elision (the *h-aspiré* noun) starts with an onset which dominates a melodically empty position. The other noun starts with an onset which is empty both melodically and skeletally, and hence vowel elision follows. Consider the representations below.

[6]
a. O N O N O N
    | | | | | |
    x x x x x x
    | | | | |
    l ə   a m ɔ

b. O N O N O N O N
    | | | | | | |
    x x   x x x x x
    | | | | | | |
    l ə   a m ə s õ

The representations in [6] illustrate the consequences of having two different types of empty onsets: one with and one without an accompanying skeletal point. It is only the onset without any skeletal representation that is fully empty, while the presence of the skeletal position allows the onset to function differently. Evidently French elision is barred when the intervening onset dominates a skeletal position, irrespectively of whether the position itself dominates a melody or not. On this interpretation, the *h-aspiré* words are items whose initial onset contains a skeletal position, while *h-muet* words have fully empty onsets. In this way certain vowel-initial words are treated as if they were consonant-initial without actually having the consonants pronounced.

A phenomenon closely related to vowel elision is the pronunciation of word-final consonants before vowel-initial words and their loss before consonant-initial words, all subject to further conditions that we will not go into here. This phenomenon, known in French grammars as *liaison* 'linkage', is not unlike the *linking-r* found in some English dialects (see our discussion in 2.6) but it works on a far broader scale in French. For example, the pronoun *ils* 'they' appears as [il] in isolation and before a consonant and is thus homophonous with the pronoun *il* [il] 'he'. Before a vowel *ils* – but not *il* – appears as [ilz]. Consider the relevant examples in [7]:

[7]   il montre [il 'mɔ̃tʁ] 'he shows'   il arrive [il a'ʁiv] 'he arrives'
      ils montrent [il 'mɔ̃tʁ] 'they show' ils arrivent [ilz a'ʁiv] 'they arrive'

72 *The syllable*

The generalisation appears clear enough: a consonant is suppressed before a consonant, just as in the case of elision a vowel was suppressed before a vowel. Other examples of the loss of the final consonant when the word is pronounced in isolation or before a consonant, and the preservation of the consonant before vowels, can be seen in [8]:

[8]   trop [tʁo] 'very'   trop heureux [tʁop ør̥ø] 'very happy'
        grand [gʁɑ̃] 'great'   grand homme [gʁɑ̃t ɔm] 'great man'
        un [ɛ̃] 'a'   un enfant [ɛ̃nɑ̃'fɑ̃] 'child'
        porc [pɔʁ] 'pig'   porc-épic [pɔʁk e'pik] 'porcupine'
        les [le] 'def. art. pl.'   les enfants [lez ɑ̃'fɑ̃] 'children'

As might be expected, the appearance of a consonant before a vowel is not a watertight rule. There are numerous cases where the consonant which emerges before some vowels, e.g. *ils arrivent*, fails to do so before others, e.g. *ils haletent* [il a'let] 'they gasp', *ils haussent* [il ɔs] 'they raise' etc. Keeping in mind the alternations in [8], note that the same left-hand column words behave differently in [9], with no consonant appearing before the vowel of the next word.

[9]   trop [tʁo] 'very'   trop hideux [tʁo i'dø] 'very ugly'
        grand [gʁɑ̃] 'great'   grand Hollandaise [gʁɑ̃ ɔlɑ̃'dɛːz] 'great Dutchman'
        un [ɛ̃] 'a'   un hangar [ɛ̃ ɑ̃gaʁ] 'hangar'
        les [le] 'def. art. pl.'   les haches [le aʃ] 'axe, pl.'

Thus the right-hand column words beginning with vowels behave as if they had an onset. This is, of course, completely parallel to the failure of vowel elision before certain ostensibly vowel-initial words. As before, we can assume that the disparity in the behaviour is due to differences in structure: both the failure of vowel elision and the failure of the *liaison* consonant to appear result from the fact that the word-initial nuclei in fact are not initial but are preceded by onsets containing a skeletal point. Such onsets block vowel elision and constitute the required context for consonant elision; they are not associated with any melody, which produces the phonetic effect of vowel-initialness. The dual pattern that initial vowels display can be systematically correlated with the two possibilities that phonology recognises for empty onsets: they can be empty both on the skeletal and melodic level, or on the melodic one only.

4.4   English onsets and rhymes

4.4.1   Onsets

The onsets of the simple syllable types presented in the first section of this chapter may be non-branching, when they dominate a single skeletal slot, or branching when two such slots are attached to a single onset node. We have seen that stressed final nuclei must be branching in English, although this is by no means the case for other positions. Domain-internally non-branching nuclei can be found in any number of words, e.g. *lid* [lɪd], *letter* ['letə], *lumber* ['lʌmbə], *bother* ['bɒðə], *soot* [sʊt], *rapid* ['ræpɪd]. Thus both onsets and nuclei can be branching and non-branching. In what follows we shall refine this observation somewhat and claim that syllabic constituents can only be binary branching, i.e. they can dominate no more than two skeletal positions. If true, this statement rules out three-member syllabic constituents.

With reference to nuclei, the binary branching claim has seldom been challenged: in numerous languages we find a distinction between short and long vowels or diphthongs, while no convincing case has ever been made for a three-way length distinction – such as short, medium and long vowels – that would be phonologically significant. Triphthongs as phonetic sequences of three melodic units are attested but on closer scrutiny they turn out to be combinations of simpler elements. A case in point is English where we have [aɪə, ɔɪə, əʊə, aʊə] in words such as *higher* [haɪə], *employer* [ɪm'plɔɪə], *mower* [məʊə], *plougher* [plaʊə]. In all these words the triphthongs are clearly divisible into a diphthong [aɪ, ɔɪ, əʊ, aʊ] and the final vowel [ə], in particular since the final vowel is a separate morpheme, indicating the comparative degree in *high+er*, or marking an agentive in the remaining examples. We can extend this observation to cases which allow no morphological division – such as *fire* [faɪə], *paranoia* [pærə'nɔɪə], *flower* [flaʊə] – and conclude that the superficial triphthongs of English are just sequences of nuclei, the first of which is branching and the second non-branching. The words *plougher* and *paranoia* will have the following representations:

[10]   O   N   O   N   O N O N O   N   O N
          /\   /\ | | | | | | | /\ |
          x x x x x   x x x x x x x   x
          | | | | | | | | | | | | |
          p l a ʊ ə   p æ r ə n ɔ ɪ   ə

An additional remark about the representations in [10] needs to be made, or repeated: the syllabic level consists of sequences of onsets and nuclei even if a particular constituent happens to have no skeletal or melodic content. This follows from an initial assumption we made, to the effect that the syllabic level of representation is not derivative of the other levels but is an independent one. In many, perhaps most cases, the units of the skeletal, the syllabic and the melodic tiers will dovetail. This is, however, not always true, precisely because the onsets or nuclei are not projections of vocalic or consonantal melodies. We expect to find syllabic constituents to which nothing corresponds on the other levels. More cases of the same sort will be presented in subsequent sections and chapters.

74   *The syllable*

A minor conclusion following from our assumptions is that consecutive units of a melody may belong to different syllabic constituents. A clear case are sequences of more than two consonants: if onsets can be maximally binary, i.e. embracing two skeletal positions, then sequences of three or more consonants can never belong to the same onset. As an example consider English consonant sequences starting with [s] and followed by two consonants, e.g. *spring* [sprɪŋ], *sclerosis* [sklə'rəʊsɪs], *splash* [splæʃ], *stretch* [stretʃ] etc. Our reasoning leads us to conclude that the *s*+consonant sequences do not all belong to single onsets. We must also make the general observation that the word-initial position cannot be mechanically identified with the syllable onset: while in many cases the two will be the same, this is not always so. Thus, the very presence of a specific consonant sequence at the beginning of a word does not necessarily mean that this sequence is a possible syllable onset. A consonantal sequence beginning a word may be an onset but does not have to be. We will consider the position of [s] in such sequences later on the basis of English and other languages; for the moment we will concentrate on other types of branching onsets in English apart from *s*-initial clusters.

Typically, branching onsets comprise a sequence of a true consonant (an obstruent) followed by a sonorant. Thus in [11a] we have plosives and in [11b] fricatives as the first member of an initial cluster.

[11]
a. plot [plɒt]   blow [bləʊ]   prison [prɪzn]
    brought [brɔːt]   treat [triːt]   drain [dreɪn]
    twist [twɪst]   dwell [dwel]   crave [kreɪv]
    grim [grɪm]   clout [klaʊt]   glib [glɪb]
    quite [kwaɪt]   Guatemala [gwɑːtə'mɑːlə]
b. flop [flɒp]   fret [fret]   throng [θrɒŋ]
    thwart [θwɔːt]

An inspection of the examples shows that of the theoretical combinations of a plosive and a sonorant, some are strikingly absent. For one thing, the sonorant is never nasal. Also, while the velar plosives can precede the sonorants [l, r, w], neither of the remaining classes of plosives is so tolerant: after the coronals [t, d] the liquid [l] is impossible, while after the labials [p, b] the labio-velar semivowel [w] is not permitted. It is probably not an accident that the liquid which is disallowed after coronals is itself coronal or that the labial semivowel is not possible after a labial plosive. Both cases show that homorganic sequences are not possible in branching onsets. We can formulate a condition on English branching onsets stipulating that they must consist of an obstruent followed by a non-homorganic non-nasal sonorant.

4.4 English onsets and rhymes 75

The view that syllabic structure is independent of the melody means that once branching onsets are recognised, they should be attested both word-initially and word-internally. Examples of the latter situation are not hard to find:

[12] diplomat ['dɪpləmæt]   ablative ['æblətɪv]   apricot ['eɪprɪkɒt]
      abrupt [ə'brʌpt]   attract [ə'trækt]   address [ə'dres]
      abattoir ['æbətwɑː]   Edward ['edwəd]   decline [də'klaɪn]
      Anglican ['æŋglɪkən]   acrobat ['ækrəbæt]   aggravate ['ægrəveɪt]
      adequate ['ædɪkwət]   anguish ['æŋgwɪʃ]   Africa ['æfrɪkə]
      arthritis [ɑː'θraɪtɪs]

However, word-internally we also encounter combinations which are not possible word-initially, such as those which appear to violate the homorganic ban. Some of these examples can be easily dismissed by invoking domain structure: in words such as *quietly* [kwaɪətli], *deadly* [dedli] the adverb-forming suffix *-ly* is separated from its base which forms a domain of its own, and hence the combinations [tl, dl] do not form branching onsets. The same could be said about the suffix *-less* in *effortless* ['efətlɪs], *endless* [endlɪs], where the sequences [tl, dl] are not different from those we find when words are joined together, e.g. *let Liz*, *led Liz*. Once all such cases have been taken care of, including various real or pseudo-compounds like *outline* ['aʊtlaɪn], *headlong* ['hedlɒŋ] etc., we are still left with a handful of words for which no non-arbitrary morphological domain structure can be posited. A reasonably exhaustive list is offered in [13].

[13] Atlantic [ət'læntɪk]   antler ['æntlə]   butler ['bʌtlə]
      atlas ['ætləs]   athlete ['æθliːt]   motley ['mɒtli]
      medley ['medli]   maudlin ['mɔːdlɪn]   bedlam ['bedləm]

Our line of reasoning so far has been the following: sequences of a plosive and a homorganic sonorant seem inadmissible as branching onsets. They never appear in word-initial position, and word-internally they are due to the domain structure in most cases. The words in [13], while hardly susceptible to the domain interpretation, display internal sequences which are impossible branching onsets. If our reasoning is correct, then the only conclusion we can draw from forms like these is that the plosive–sonorant homorganic sequences are not what they cannot be, i.e. they are not branching onsets. In other words, rather than belonging to a single constituent, the onset, the offending consonants have to be split between two onsets. An onset is only possible where there is a nucleus, so we are led to conclude that the plosive in the clusters must be followed by a nucleus. Since the nucleus has no phonetic content, it must be empty; recall that we encountered the need for empty nuclei in our discussion of English inflectional morphology in 2.5. A possible representation of the word *medley* is suggested in [14].

76   *The syllable*

[14]
```
O   N   O   N   O   N
|   |   |   |   |   |
x   x   x   x   x   x
|   |   |       |   |
m   e   d       l   i
```

The words in [13] differ from words like *dill* [dɪl], *tell* [tel] in that they have a nucleus with no melody attached to it. A further piece of evidence supporting the existence of a nucleus between the obstruent and the sonorant is that there are words of the relevant structure with alternative pronunciations with and without a melody. A case in point is the noun *athlete* and the derived adjective *athletic*. These are usually pronounced ['æθliːt] and [æθ'letɪk] respectively. However, these words are pronounced by some speakers with the vowel [ə] appearing between the members of the homorganic cluster: ['æθəliːt] and [æθə'letɪk]. The existence of such pronunciation variants strengthens the conclusion that the counterexamples to the homorganicity ban are only apparent: they involve either domain structure or an empty nucleus separating the plosives from the following homorganic sonorant. In other words, their neighbourliness is only superficial and misleading. True branching onsets are different, in that they do not violate the homorganicity ban.

4.4.2   Rhymes

The open syllables that we have just briefly discussed presuppose the existence of closed syllables, i.e. cases where the nucleus is followed by a consonant which is not in the onset of the following syllable. In words such as *panda* ['pændə], *Rambo* ['ræmbəʊ] the nasal consonant belongs together with the first nucleus rather than the second onset; the consonant in such positions is called the **coda** and together with the preceding nucleus it forms the **rhyme** of the syllable. Properly speaking, then, the syllable breaks up into the onset and the rhyme; the latter dominates the vocalic nucleus but it can also contain a complement in the form of a consonantal coda, which is also called the **rhymal complement**. If a rhyme contains just a nucleus, the syllable is said to be open, while it is closed if a consonantal coda complements the nucleus. In our representations we will often take shortcuts and if reference to the coda is not explicitly required, we will continue to divide syllables into onsets and nuclei.

Given what has been said so far about the relation between the melodic and syllabic structure it comes as no surprise that the same consonants, when differently arranged in words, will be associated with different syllabic constituents. Consider

4.4 *English onsets and rhymes* 77

the consonants [b] and [l] in the words *publicity* [pʌbˈlɪsəti] and *alba* [ˈælbə]. In the first word they appear as [bl] with the obstruent preceding a lateral with which it is not homorganic – the cluster thus meets the criteria for onsethood. In *alba* the sequence is [lb], hence it cannot constitute an onset and must be broken up between the rhymal complement of the first and the onset of the second syllable. The representation of the two words is given below.

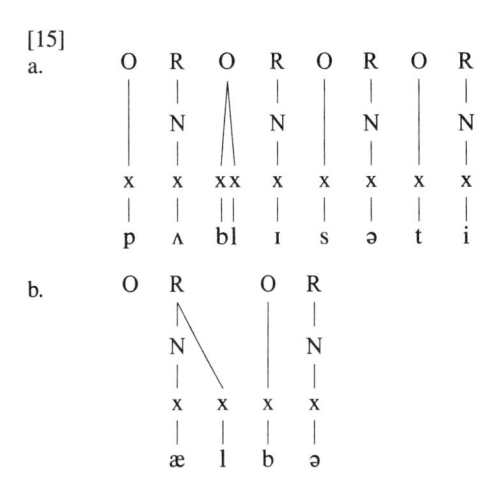

[15]
a.

```
O   R    O   R    O   R    O   R
|   |    |   |    |   |    |   |
|   N    |   N    |   N    |   N
|   |    |  /|    |   |    |   |
x   x   xx  x     x   x    x   x
|   |   ||  |     |   |    |   |
p   ʌ   bl  ɪ     s   ə    t   i
```

b.

```
O   R        O   R
|  /|        |   |
| N \        |   N
| |  \       |   |
x x   x      x   x
| |   |      |   |
æ l   b      ə
```

As can be seen from the representations, the consonants appearing as the coda–onset sequence in [15b] are the reverse or mirror-image of those found in the onset in [15a]. This combination constitutes only a subpart of all the coda–onset possibilities. Let us consider in somewhat greater detail the options open to the coda and compare them to the onset.

One combination which, as we have seen, is banned from the onset position is a cluster of homorganic consonants. Rhymal sonorants homorganic with onset obstruents are well attested, as is the combination of a nasal and a following plosive, something which is not allowed in the onset even in the order plosive – nasal, e.g. *[knɒt], *[pmæŋ]. The available coda–onset combinations are illustrated below.

[16]   [lf] alphabet [ˈælfəbət]   [lv] Elvis [ˈelvɪs]
       [lθ] healthy [ˈhelθi]   [lt] helter-skelter [ˈheltəˈskeltə]
       [ld] boulder [ˈbəʊldə]   [ls] calcium [ˈkælsɪəm]
       [lz] palsy [ˈpɔːlzi]   [lʃ] revulsion [rəˈvʌlʃən]
       [ltʃ] pilchard [ˈpɪltʃəd]   [ld] nostalgic [nəˈstældʒɪk]
       [lk] milky [ˈmɪlki]   [lg] vulgar [ˈvʌlgə]
       [mp] tempest [ˈtempɪst]   [mb] chamber [ˈtʃeɪmbə]
       [mf] symphony [ˈsɪmfəni]   [nf] infant [ˈɪnfənt]

78 *The syllable*

[nv] invalid [ɪnvəlɪd]   [ns] rancid ['rænsɪd]
[nz] frenzy ['frenzi]   [nt] mountain ['maʊntɪn]
[nd] bandit ['bændɪt]   [nʃ] tension ['tenʃən]
[nʒ] lingerie ['lænʒəri]   [ntʃ] concerto [kən'tʃɜːtəʊ]
[ndʒ] manger ['meɪndʒə]   [ŋk] anchor ['æŋkə]
[ŋg] finger ['fɪŋgə]

The examples show that the range of possible coda–onset combinations far exceeds the reverse sequences found in the onsets. Even if some of the clusters are not very frequent, they are undoubtedly possible, whereas the same sequences in onsets are totally ruled out in English, e.g. *[lvɪk]. In brief, we see that the coda sonorant can be followed by practically any obstruent, irrespective of any homorganicity holding between them. However, the range of consonants that can occupy the coda position is not restricted to sonorants only. As the examples in [17] demonstrate, the coda can also be a plosive or a spirant.

[17]   [dg] Edgar [edgə]   [kt] factory ['fæktəri]
    [pt] baptise ['bæptaɪz]   [pʃ] Egyptian [iː'dʒɪpʃən]
    [gd] Magdalen [mægdələn]   [gz] zigzag ['zɪgzæg]
    [ft] crafty ['krɑːfti]   [sp] aspen ['æspən]
    [st] custard ['kʌstəd]   [sk] rascal ['rɑːskəl]
    [zd] Mazda ['mæzdə]

Although plosives in the rhymal complement position are not as numerously attested as sonorants, their existence in that position is definitely possible. An exhaustive study of English phonology would need to provide a detailed account of the coda possibilities, something that is not our aim here. Suffice it to say that in English a coda can be a sonorant or a simple obstruent (plosive, spirant) and that these precede the obstruent of the following onset. Facts similar to those of English can be found in other languages, a situation which suggests that they all reflect certain general properties of the phonological organisation of language.

4.5 Nasal assimilation or nasal place sharing in English

As noted above, the rhymal complement position is frequently occupied by a sonorant while a following onset dominates an obstruent. We would like now to consider a specific instance of this configuration, one where the rhymal position is filled by a nasal consonant. This combination is frequently found in a variety of languages and in some sense appears to be natural, being favoured especially when the nasal is homorganic with the following onset obstruent. We will look at this form of nasal–obstruent homorganicity in a few languages, starting with English.

4.5 Nasal assimilation or nasal place sharing in English

A typical structure for the homorganic nasal–obstruent sequence can be illustrated by the English word *dingo* ['dɪŋgəʊ]:

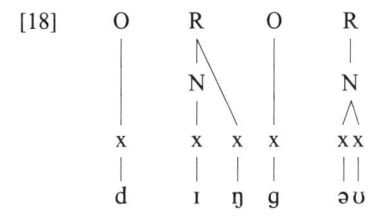

[18]
```
     O   R      O    R
     |   |\     |    |
     |   N \    |    N
     |   |  \   |    /\
     x   x   x  x   x x
     |   |   |  |   | |
     d   ɪ   ŋ  g   ə ʊ
```

This is the syllabic structure of the velar nasal in English which we discussed in 3.2. Recall that we argued there that the velar nasal always appears before a following velar plosive, in other words, the two consonants are homorganic. This is true even if the voiced velar plosive itself remains inaudible in the domain-final position, e.g. *king* [kɪŋ]. In effect, then, the distribution of the velar nasal is seriously restricted in English.

An inspection of other combinations of a nasal and a plosive reveals that domain-internally they are almost exclusively restricted to homorganic clusters, either bilabial or alveolar.

[19]
a. bimbo ['bɪmbəʊ]   Cumbria ['kʌmbrɪə]   bamboozle [bæm'buːzl]
    lumber ['lʌmbə]   samba ['sæmbə]   rhombus ['rɒmbəs]
b. rampant ['ræmpənt]   limpid ['lɪmpɪd]   dimple ['dɪmpl]
    crumpet ['krʌmpɪt]

Here we have the bilabial nasal preceding either a voiced or voiceless bilabial plosive – the homorganicity requirement seems fully observed. One admittedly does find words like *gimcrack* ['dʒɪmkræk], *lambkin* [læmkɪn] with a bilabial nasal before a velar plosive, or *sometimes* ['sʌmtaɪmz], *amtrack* ['æmtræk] where the bilabial is followed by a coronal plosive. However, all such forms are morphologically complex and hence it is perfectly legitimate to claim that the bilabial nasal is not directly adjacent to the following plosive since the two consonants belong to different domains; thus the [mk] of *lambkin* is not different from what we find in *tomcat* ['tɒmkæt]. As we argued in chapter 3, domain structure can be utilised in cases where morphological motivation may not be obvious, such as place names and personal names. Given a name such as *Fromkin* ['frɒmkɪn], rather than abandon the homorganicity generalisation we can propose that it comprises two domains and as such the bilabial nasal does not form a coda which is directly followed by an onset plosive.

Although such a procedure might appear somewhat ad hoc and intended to patch up holes in the analysis, it should be kept in proper perspective: the absolute majority of English words does conform to the homorganicity generalisation, while some of those which do not are clearly morphologically complex and in this sense remind us of the ordinary concatenation of words within larger speech chunks, e.g. the [mk] of *Tom can* [tɒm kæn]. Note that an alternative analysis of the offending forms would probably be far less acceptable as a general statement about English. Imagine that on the basis of forms such as *gimcrack* etc. we abandon the homorganicity generalisation. That would mean that in effect nasals can be followed by any plosives whatsoever. In such a case the offending forms and the non-offending majority would have an equal status in English phonology, so that we would expect to find single morphemes like *['bæŋti], *[frɪŋkə] etc. The question we would find difficult to answer would be why there are so few words of the latter type, just a handful in fact. Their very paucity speaks for their exceptionality, which is dealt with by the postulation of a (morphologically) unmotivated domain structure.

Just as the bilabial rhymal nasal is homorganic with the onset plosive, so is the alveolar one homorganic with the following onset, regardless of whether it is voiced or voiceless, e.g.:

[20]
a.   thunder ['θʌndə]   kindle [kɪndl̩]   random ['rændəm]
          window ['wɪndəʊ]   abandon [ə'bændən]   abundant [ə'bʌndənt]
b.   mentor ['mentə]   until [ʌn'tɪl]   lentil ['lentɪl]
          entry ['entri]   gentile ['dʒentaɪl]   Benton ['bentən]

Keeping in mind our discussion of the velar nasal and its implications we can say that a rhymal nasal and a following onset plosive share their place of articulation. Whatever forms appear to contradict this generalisation are not exceptions, but rather arise as a result of the nasal and the plosive not occupying contiguous syllabic positions. They are either separated by an empty nuclear position or they belong to distinct phonological domains.

Although we have explicitly restricted ourselves above to sequences of nasals and plosives, it is easy to observe that the homorganicity requirement generally holds for any combination of a nasal and a following obstruent. Thus before the coronal fricatives and affricates [s, z, ʃ, ʒ, tʃ, dʒ] the nasal is coronal although it may be either alveolar or postalveolar, just like the following obstruent, e.g.:

[21]   fancy ['fænsi]   answer ['ɑːnsə]   density ['densəti]
          ancestor ['ænsestə]   bonanza [bə'nænzə]   Kensington ['kenzɪŋtən]
          benzine ['benziːn]   ancient ['eɪnʃənt]   detention [dɪ'tenʃən]
          banshee ['bænʃiː]   differential [dɪfə'renʃəl]   lingerie ['lænʒəri]
          rancho ['rɑːntʃəʊ]   concerto [kən'tʃɜːtəʊ]   Winchester ['wɪntʃəstə]
          enfranchise [ɪn'frentʃaɪz] angel ['eɪndʒəl]   angina [æn'dʒaɪnə]
          danger ['deɪndʒə]   Benjamin ['bendʒəmɪn]

4.5 Nasal assimilation or nasal place sharing in English

Although sequences violating homorganicity are in certain cases immediately assignable to domain structure, e.g. *himself* [hɪm'self], we should, for the sake of completeness, note the few words which do not in any obvious way lend themselves to such treatment. Examples are very few: *damsel* ['dæmzəl], *crimson* ['krɪmzən], *flimsy* ['flɪmzi], *clumsy* ['klʌmzi]. They can be handled in either of the two ways – arbitrary domain structure or separating the consonants by a nucleus with no melody. The extreme rarity of such forms follows from their unsystematic nature.

Before the labio-dental spirants [f, v] we normally find either the labio-dental nasal [ɱ] or, in careful speech, the coronal nasal [n], e.g. *invalid* ['ɪɱvəlɪd] or ['ɪnvəlɪd], *infant* ['ɪɱfənt] or ['ɪnfənt]; before the voiceless interdental spirant [θ] – there seem to be no examples for the voiced [ð] – the nasal is normally dental, e.g. *epenthesis* [i'pen̪θəsɪs], *anthem* ['æn̪θəm], *anthropology* [æn̪θrə'pɒlədʒi], etc. Once again, it is significant that there are no words containing sequences such as [mθ, ɲf], which would require some extra adjustment of the general rules.

The discussion of the English nasal plus obstruent sequences reveals that a rhymal nasal **always** shares its place of articulation (POA) with the following onset, i.e. the relevant representation is

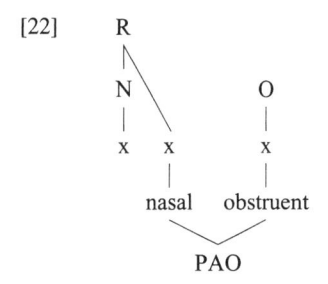

[22]

```
        R
       /\
      N  \    O
      |   \   |
      x   x   x
          |   |
        nasal obstruent
           \_____/
             PAO
```

We may call the above constraint *POA Sharing*. A crucial property of forms meeting this condition is that the nasal and the obstruent are directly adjacent within a phonological domain with the obstruent following the nasal. Whenever an apparent violation emerges, it really indicates that the two consonants do not form a coda–onset sequence and thus fail to meet the syllabic requirements for *POA Sharing*.

The POA agreement captured in [22] is traditionally referred to as nasal assimilation. There is a certain difference between the two formulations: an assimilation formula implies that something gets more similar to something else. In other words, at first the two consonants are different but they become more similar as a result of the assimilation process. This prompts a temporal sequence involving a stage before and after a change, and also suggests a dominating and a dominated partner in the relationship. *POA Sharing*, on the other hand, has no such implications: it states simply that in English a coda nasal and a following onset obstruent may not differ in their place of articulation, without entailing any temporal – or before-and-after – considerations, and without taking a stand on whether it is one or the other consonant that exerts the assimilatory influence. Put simply, a formulation like [22] says that English words do not violate the specified configuration. There are no stages or derivations but a static description of the way things are. The derivational statement may be more adequate for historical purposes, where time and different representations of what is the same unit play a role. For example, historically the homorganic [mp] in *empower* [im'pauə] may derive from the [n] of *en-* assimilating to the following bilabial plosive. Synchronically, however, the claim that the nasal gets assimilated to the plosive is no more justified than the reverse view: given a sequence of a rhymal nasal [m] followed by an obstruent, the obstruent assimilates to the place of the nasal. What we have is necessary identity of the place of articulation in two consonants meeting specified conditions. Any reference to derivations is nothing but a historical metaphor or a terminological shortcut. If we occasionally use it, it should be understood as just such a shortcut.

4.6 Nasal place sharing in Dutch and German

The constraint imposing place of articulation sharing between a rhymal nasal and an onset obstruent (*POA Sharing*) is also found in two closely related languages, namely Dutch and German, although some differences will also need to be noted. In principle, however, we find sequences of homorganic nasals and obstruents. In Dutch these comprise the labial, labio-dental, dental, palatal and velar consonant areas. Consider some examples:

[23]
a. gember ['gɛmbər] 'ginger' inpakken ['ɪmpɑkən] 'wrap up'
    aanbod ['ambɔt] 'offer' riempje ['rimpjə] 'belt, dim.'
    sympathiseer [sɪmpati'zeːr] 'sympathise' stiekempjes ['stikəmpjəs] 'stealthily'
b. onfatsoenlijk [ɔɱfɑt'sunlək] 'indecent' onvast ['ɔɱvɑst] 'unstable'
    inwijden ['ɪɱʋɛidən] 'initiate'
c. ponton ['pɔntɔn] 'pontoon' alliantie [ali'ɑntsi] 'alliance'
    financieel [finɑn'ʃeːl] 'financial' presidentieel [prɛzidɛn'ʃeːl] 'presidential'
    wandelen ['wɑndələn] 'walk, vb.' antiek [ɑn'tik] 'antique'
    gewoontjes [ɣə'ʋontjəs] 'ordinarily'

4.6 Nasal place sharing in Dutch and German

d. Spanje ['spaɲjə] 'Spain' bonje ['bɔɲjə] 'fight'
   oranje ['oːraɲjə] 'orange, adj.'
e. tango ['taŋgoː] 'tango' onkies [ɔŋ'kis] 'indecent'
   ongeluk ['ɔŋɣəlʏk] 'mishap' koninkje ['koːnɪŋkjə] 'king, dim.'
   fungeren [fʏŋ'ɣɛrən] 'function, vb.'

It does not matter in our interpretation that some of these words are morphologically complex: what is significant is that nasals and obstruents are neighbours, which translates into homorganicity. What requires attention are the cases where homorganicity is not observed. As in English this is found primarily with productive inflectional morphology, e.g. *roemde* ['rumdə] 'praise, past', *mengde* ['mɛŋdə] 'mix, past' (compare the infinitives *roem* [rum], *meng* [mɛŋ]) and thus invites an interpretation involving either domain boundaries or empty nuclei between the nasal and the dental of the past tense suffix. In this sense it parallels the English forms like *seemed* [siːmd], *hanged* [hæŋd] where the nasals are also followed by a non-homorganic alveolar plosive. In both the Dutch and the English cases the phonological identity of the verbal base in both the infinitive and past suggests that the consonant of the suffix is not directly adjacent to the final consonant of the stem, hence place of articulation sharing is not possible.

As in English there are further examples of morphological compounds. These, just like words joined in a sentence, tolerate phonetic sequences of non-homorganic consonants: they are possible because in phonological terms they do not form a coda–onset combination which constitutes the required context for homorganicity. Thus in *damkampioen* ['damkampijun] 'draughts champion' or the careful pronunciation of the name *Uhlenbeck* ['ylənbɛk] (side by side with ['yləmbɛk]) the [mk] and [nb] phonetic sequences do not undermine the general conditions on place of articulation sharing; rather they indicate that the nasal and the following stop do not conform to the conditions for *POA Sharing*. Similarly in words like *imker* ['ɪmkər] 'bee keeper' or *hemdje* ['hɛmtjə] 'shirt, dim.' the non-homorganic sequences mean, quite simply, that the consonants are not adjacent: in all probability they should be separated by an empty nucleus which is phonetically inaudible and produces the impression of a phonetic sequence of non-homorganic consonants. It is also possible that different domains are involved.

A complete description of nasal sharing in Dutch would need to include related phenomena which depend not only on the phonological composition of adjacent segments and the phonological domain structure of words, but also on factors such as the position of a given word in a syntactic configuration and the tempo of speech. One phenomenon should be noted here: in compounds and in connected speech the alveolar nasal before a continuant can be suppressed while the preceding vowel is nasalised (and somewhat lengthened). In other words, rather than producing nasal sharing, this context admits merger of the nasal with the preceding vowel, e.g.

on-zeker 'uncertain' and *on-gewoon* 'abnormal' can be pronounced [ɔ̃'zekər] and [ɔ̃ɣə'ʋon] side by side with the more studied variants [ɔn'zekər] and [ɔŋɣə'ʋon]. The fact that contact between two consonants may result in either place sharing or partial elimination of one of the parties involved suggests that there exist options which an individual language may select. While the general tendency for a nasal and an adjacent consonant to be homorganic is well attested, other ways of interpreting this configuration are available. We have seen that Dutch place sharing in certain ways is different from English; below we will consider from this point of view the facts of another closely related language, German, and a somewhat more distant one, Polish. We will see that within the basic tendency towards place sharing certain minor and major differences can be detected.

The basic facts of the phenomenon in Modern German are very similar to those of Dutch, namely bilabial, labio-dental (optionally), alveolar and velar nasals share their place of articulation with directly following obstruents.

[24]
a. Tempo ['tɛmpo] 'tempo' Amboß ['ambɔs] 'anvil'
   kompetent [kɔmpe'tɛnt] 'competent'
b. Unfall ['ʊɱfal] 'accident' Konflikt [kɔɱ'flɪkt] 'conflict'
c. Stunde ['ʃtʊndə] 'hour' bändigen ['bɛndɪgən] 'tame, vb.'
   hänseln ['hɛnzəln] 'tease, vb.'
d. danken ['daŋkən] 'thank' Tango ['taŋgo] 'tango'
   fingieren [fɪŋ'giːrən] 'fake, vb.'

In some cases, most typically at morphological boundaries, forms with and without the shared place of articulation can be found. In our terms this means that the two consonants either are directly adjacent and consequently homorganic or are separated and hence no sharing is possible. Taking the word *Unglück* 'mishap' as an example we record two possible pronunciations: ['ʊnglʏk] without and ['ʊŋglʏk] with place sharing. If the condition for the sharing is direct consonant adjacency, then the two variants must have somewhat different representations. The form where the nasal is in the rhymal complement position and the plosive is in the onset will constitute the required context for the shared place of articulation; if the consonants belong to separate domains, or if they are separated by an empty nucleus, the nasal is alveolar while the plosive is velar. No interaction between the two consonants takes place any more than it does between two such consonants in separate words.

As in Dutch and English, forms can be found for which no domain structure can be justified in a natural way. The German place name *Lemgo* ['lɛmgo] or the word *Imker* ['ɪmkɐ] 'bee-keeper' are a case in point. Non-homorganic sequences emerge where the relevant consonants are not adjacent: in cases such as these the simplest solution is to suggest that an empty nucleus intervenes between the two consonants. This solution may apply not only to indivisible words but also to combinations arising as a result of morphological operations: in *träumt* [trɔɪmt] '(s)he dreams' a bilabial nasal is followed by an alveolar plosive, while in *singt* [zɪŋt] '(s)he sings' the velar nasal appears in the same context, which at first blush violates the homorganicity requirement. However, since the plosive clearly represents the ending of the third person singular present tense, it is natural to suppose that the consonants are separated by a nucleus (recall the English lack of homorganicity in *dreams* [driːmz] and *sings* [sɪŋz]). The words *Lemgo* and *träumt* could be represented as follows:

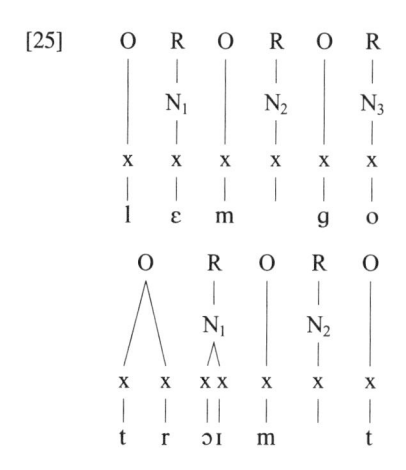

[25]   O   R   O   R   O   R
            | | |
            N₁   N₂   N₃
            | | |
        x   x   x   x   x   x
        | | | | | |
        l   ɛ   m   g   o

        O   R   O   R   O
       /\ | | |
      / \   N₁   N₂
     /   \   /\
    x   x   x x   x   x   x
    | | | | | | |
    t   r   ɔ ɪ   m   t

The presence of the inaudible nucleus (N₂) amounts to a claim that nasal sharing is general in German and the cases where it seems to be flaunted are only apparent. (The onset status of the final [t] in *träumt* will be discussed in the following chapter.)

A final point that should be made in connection with this brief overview of German nasal homorganicity concerns a certain difference vis-à-vis Dutch: as shown in [23d] Dutch has a palatal nasal before a following palatal. In German this does not seem to happen: taking the words *wünschen* ['vynʃən] 'wish' and *manche* ['mançə] 'some' as typical we observe the presence of an alveolar nasal both before the palato-alveolar [ʃ] and the palatal [ç]. While the palato-alveolar spirant could perhaps be interpreted as an alveolar consonant, this position cannot be adopted for the palatal spirant without gross violation of the phonetic facts. We must recall at this stage, however, that in 3.4 we discussed at length why the phonetically palatal spirant should be seen phonologically as just a spirant with

86   The syllable

no place of articulation specified in its melodic representation. In some dialects, including the standard variety, the spirant is palatal, but this is merely what we have called a phonetic effect without phonological consequences. The absence of place sharing in words like *manche* bears out the correctness of this interpretation: there is no sharing because the spirant has nothing to share as it is without place specification. In this way the facts of German place sharing support an observation based on completely independent evidence.

4.7   Nasal place sharing in Polish

In Modern Polish place sharing between a nasal and a following obstruent is amply attested and in certain ways it duplicates the Germanic situation. Thus before labial, dental, palatal and velar plosives and affricates we find nasals with the same place of articulation. Some examples follow in [26]. Stress is not marked in the transcriptions since it is invariably penultimate (at least in the words which appear below).

[26] labial
lampa [lampa] 'lamp' sępy [sempɨ] 'vulture, nom. pl.'
dębu [dɛmbu] 'oak tree, gen. sg.' rąbać [rɔmbatɕ] 'hew'

dental
ręce [rɛn̪tsɛ] 'hand, dat. sg.' wstędze [fstɛn̪dzɛ] 'ribbon, dat. sg.'
pętać [pɛn̪tatɕ] 'to fetter' nadęty [nadɛn̪tɨ] 'pompous'

palatal
pędzi [pɛɲdʑi] '(s)he rushes' rządzi [ʐɔɲdʑi] '(s)he governs'
sądzi [sɔɲdʑi] '(s)he thinks' chęci ['ɛɲtɕi] 'willingness, nom. pl.'

velar
księga [kɕɛŋga] 'book' uraga [urɔŋga] '(s)he abuses'
stęka [stɛŋka] '(s)he grumbles' obłąkany [ɔbwɔŋkanɨ] 'crazy'

More subtle divisions could be introduced, such as alveolar or prevelar but we need not be concerned with these here. The examples above show that Polish, too, enforces the requirement that a nasal and a following stop should share their place of articulation.

The examples above are restricted to the context of a nasal and a stop obstruent (plosive or affricate) for a very good reason: before a following spirant a new situation is attested. (Recall in this context the option available for Dutch nasals before spirants when a domain boundary follows.) In native vocabulary the nasal that appears before an adjacent fricative has the form of a short back nasal glide [$^{\tilde{w}}$] which forms a diphthong with a preceding vowel. Consider the examples in [27].

[27] wąwóz [vɔ̃ʷvus] 'ravine'   kąsa [kɔ̃ʷsa] '(s)he bites'
      męstwo [mɛ̃ʷstfɔ] 'valour'   mięsie [mʲɛ̃ʷɕɛ] 'meat, loc. sg.'
      więzi [vʲɛ̃ʷʑi] 'bond, gen. sg.'   więzy [vʲɛ̃ʷzɨ] 'fetter, nom. pl.'
      węszy [vɛ̃ʷʃɨ] '(s)he sniffs'   dąży [dɔ̃ʷʒɨ] '(s)he aspires'
      węchu [vɛ̃ʷxu] 'smell, gen. sg.'

One thing which transpires from examples such as these is that Polish nasal sharing before spirants differs from the straightforward homorganicity observed before other obstruents. As we will see in 6.4 there are additional factors which require that we treat the nasal diphthongs in a separate way from sequences of nasal consonants and plosive obstruents. It is the latter that we concentrate on here.

A by-product of Polish nasal sharing is the existence of alternations showing different nasal plus plosive sequences. The alternations arise when a given morpheme combines with inflectional and derivational affixes which require a somewhat different shape for the base. Consider the nouns in [28] with some of their closely related forms.

[28] ręce [rɛn̪tsɛ] 'hand, loc. sg.'   ręka [rɛŋka] 'nom. sg.'
      łąka [wɔŋka] 'meadow'   łączka [wɔntʃka] 'dim.'
      księga [kɕɛŋga] '(big) book'   księdze [kɕɛn̪dzɛ] 'dat. sg.'
      wstędze [fstɛn̪dzɛ] 'ribbon, loc. sg.'   wstęga [fstɛŋga] 'nom. sg.'

The different phonetic shapes of the same base morpheme, such as [kɕɛŋg-, kɕɛndz-] denoting 'book' all conform to the place sharing requirement in its Polish shape. In other words, a nasal is homorganic with a following plosive. In this sense the existing alternations merely conform to the pattern we have observed in non-alternating words such as those in [26]. Morphophonemic alternations play a significant role in phonological analysis since they may be used to identify existing phonological regularities. These, however, may also be established independently of such alternations, even when such alternations are absent in the language.

A far more significant observation is connected with the presence of words where nasal sharing seems to be disregarded. We have seen such instances in the Germanic cases – recall English words like *flimsy, banged* – but they were quite infrequent or formed large but regular morphological subclasses such as the past tense ending, for example. We accounted for these forms by suggesting that the relevant consonants are not adjacent, being separated either by an empty nucleus or a domain boundary. In Polish the number of forms that appear to violate the sharing property is quite considerable, but if our reasoning so far is correct we have to assume that the consonants in question rather than being adjacent are separated from each other. The following cases illustrate the problem.

88 The syllable

[29]
a. słomka [swɔmka] 'straw, dim.' ósemka [usɛmka] 'number eight'
ramka [ramka] 'frame, dim.' kłamcie [kwamtɕɛ] 'lie, imper. pl.'
zamknąć [zamknɔɲtɕ] 'close, vb.' mgła [mgwa] 'mist'
mgnienie [mɡɲɛɲɛ] 'twinkling'
b. państwo [paɲstfɔ] 'state' koński [kɔɲsci] 'equestrian'
maleńka [malɛɲka] 'little, fem.' wińsko [vʲiɲskɔ] 'wine, express.'
c. sanki [sanci] 'sled' rankiem [rancem] 'in the morning'
d. Irenka [irɛnka] 'name, dim.' piosenka [pʲɔsɛnka] 'song'
słonka [swɔnka] 'woodcock' cienka [tɕɛnka] 'thin, fem.'

In [29a] we find the bilabial nasal before a velar plosive, without the consonants showing any sign of sharing their place of articulation; in [29b] the palatal nasal appears before a non-palatal consonant, either the dental [s] or the velar [k], also in obvious violation of homorganicity sharing. In [29c] we find the dental (non-palatalised) nasal before the voiceless palatal plosive [c]. Finally in [29d] the dental rather than the velar nasal appears before the voiceless velar plosive. Following the reasoning established so far, we can say that if a nasal is not homorganic with an obstruent that follows it, the consonants are only superficially adjacent. A vowel must separate them and thus they must belong to consecutive onsets rather than forming a coda–onset sequence. The vowel itself has no melodic content and hence remains inaudible.

It might be objected that inaudible nuclei are just a device which allows us to maintain a uniform analysis of place sharing. Is there any evidence independent of the regularity of place sharing which would support our supposition that the nasals and the following non-homorganic obstruents in [29] are separated by a nucleus? The answer is that in some cases we can provide morphophonemic alternations where the nuclear slot between the nasal and the following obstruent is filled by a melody. Examples follow:

[30] słomka [swɔmka] 'straw, dim.' słomek [swɔmɛk] 'gen. pl.'
ósemka [usɛmka] 'number eight' ósemek [usɛmɛk] 'gen. pl.'
ramka [ramka] 'frame' ramek [ramɛk] 'gen. pl.'
zamknąć [zamknɔɲtɕ] 'shut' zamykać [zamɨkatɕ] 'imperfective'
sanki [sanci] 'sled' sanek [sanɛk] 'gen. pl.'
Irenka [irɛnka] 'name' Irenek [irɛnɛk] 'gen. pl.'
piosenka [pʲɔsɛnka] 'song' piosenek [pʲɔsɛnɛk] 'gen. pl.'
słonka [swɔnka] 'woodcock' słonek [swɔnɛk] 'gen. pl.'

It can be seen that the offending non-homorganic sequences in the left-hand column are all invariably separated by the vowel [ɛ] or [ɨ] in a different form of the word in the right-hand column. Thus our prediction, made on the basis of the general expectation that it is only directly adjacent sequences that are homorganic, is confirmed by independent morphophonemic alternations. Their existence strengthens the case for inaudible vowels, but it must be admitted that morphophonemic alternations are not available in every case. Nor is there any reason to expect that they should be: alternations are the result of specific morpheme combinations which depend on the shape and the category of the participating members. Recall that in English the nucleus of the plural and the past tense preserves its phonetic content only when the surrounding consonants are sufficiently similar, e.g. *watches, waited* vs. *watched, waits*. There are no alternations for words such as *flimsy, clumsy,* and the presence of nuclei between the consonants of the superficial clusters can only be deduced from the pattern established for the language as a whole. Similarly in Polish, some of the examples in [29] do not admit of alternants with a phonetic vowel in the required position, and this is nothing particularly surprising. We have enough cases of alternations together with massive evidence in favour of the place sharing generalisation to conclude that the non-alternating forms, if they contain non-homorganic clusters, are separated by inaudible or empty nuclei.

In our discussion of place sharing between a nasal and a following obstruent we have seen that the general tendency towards uniformity may be interpreted in partially different ways by individual languages. It is the task of the phonology of each language to specify the conditions under which full conformity to the required pattern is observed, and to describe the ways in which the sharing is implemented. The analysis forces us to look closely not only at consonant sequences within words, but also at morphophonemic alternations which help us to decide the phonological representation of specific words or which confirm the representations we suspect to be valid on other grounds.

4.8 Summary

The study of linguistics often involves fundamental reassessments and redefinitions of what appear to be familiar or 'obvious' notions. In phonology these include the word, the sound, the sound sequence and the syllable. In this chapter we started looking more closely at the concept of the syllable and its role in formulating generalisations.

The syllable and the syllabic level of representation need solid phonological backing if they are to be regarded as real components in the organisation of language. Intuitive judgements, often based on and deriving from orthographic conventions, are simply not good enough. In this respect phonology cannot be different from syntax where, say, constituent structure or case-marking must be established on syntactic rather than purely intuitive criteria.

English supplied evidence for the existence of nuclei and onsets. French went one step further and revealed that onsets can be either melodically empty or melodically and skeletally empty, with different consequences for vowel and consonant alternations.

Perhaps the main protagonist of this chapter has been silence or the motivated non-manifestation of a structural unit. This unit needs to be recognised for phonological reasons but has no phonetic realisation. A typical example of the use of silence is the presence of skeletal positions without associated melodies, the so-called empty positions. We have also seen that an onset may be unattached to a skeletal position, and in 2.6 we recognised unassociated melodies, sometimes called **floating melodies**.

Empty nuclei figured prominently in the analysis of onsets where we showed that a mere linear sequence of consonants does not necessarily amount to their being adjacent skeletally. If they are not adjacent skeletally, they cannot form a constituent such as an onset. The phenomenon of nasal sharing as illustrated in a number of languages served to demonstrate the same point on the basis of the coda–onset proximity. The existence of empty nuclei forces us to abandon what is probably an act of faith for most ordinary language users, i.e. the conviction that if sound *a* directly precedes sound *b*, then nothing separates *a* from *b*. We have seen evidence coming from phonological constraints, coupled with morphophonemic alternations, which shows that the common-sense view is a grand illusion. Progress in phonology is achieved by exposing illusions and formulating analyses without them, no matter how familiar or intuitively correct they may appear.

4.9 Suggested further reading

Different approaches to the syllable can be found in most surveys of phonological theory and the history of phonology. Some of the most relevant readings include Hooper (1972, 1976, chapters 11–12), Vennemann (1972), Anderson (1974, chapter 14), Selkirk (1982), Clements and Keyser (1983), Goldsmith (1990, chapter 3), Giegerich (1992, chapter 6), Harris (1994, sections 2.2 – 2.3), Kenstowicz (1994, chapter 6), Blevins (1995), van der Hulst and Ritter (1999). For the role of the concept in earlier phonological approaches see Fischer-Jørgensen (1975).

French facts are presented and analysed in a variety of ways in Clements and Keyser (1983, chapter 3.8), Durand (1986), Charette (1991) and Brockhaus (1995b).

Nasal assimilation in Dutch is presented in Booij (1995, sections 4.2.2 and 7.2.2); for German see Hall (1992, chapter 4) and Wiese (1996, section 7.3.4), for Polish see Gussmann (1980, section 3.1) and Bethin (1992, section 2.2.2).

5
More on codas

5.1 Introduction

In the previous chapter we concentrated on some basic properties of the syllabic organisation of language, that is on a level of organisation above and beyond the skeletal and melodic structure. This additional level of representation is necessary in order to formulate observations and generalisations which it would be very difficult or impossible to state otherwise. One point has been stressed repeatedly: syllabic organisation is not restricted to a mere division of segmental strings into chunks called onsets, rhymes, nuclei and codas. We have seen cases where syllabic units do not correspond to any segmental material, such as empty onsets or empty nuclei, which shows that syllabic organisation, while connected with the skeletal and melodic levels, comprises a fundamentally self-contained structure. The traditional notion of **syllabification**, i.e. the exhaustive division or compartmentalisation of a word into segments needs to be revised. In the past this was a relatively simple mechanical procedure whereby each segment was assigned to some syllabic unit with nothing left unsyllabified. While the need to incorporate melodic units into syllabic constituents is not controversial, we maintain that there may be syllabic units which are not directly manifested through segmental material. In other words, syllabification is an operation which involves the phonological structure of the language rather than just sequences of segments of phonetically transcribed words.

In what follows we shall continue to explore the syllabic structure of words. We will concentrate on cases where the phonological facts require that syllabification should depart from melodic sequences which are directly accessible for inspection. In particular, we will focus our attention on rhymal complements, i.e. codas. As we have seen, these are sounds like the sonorants [l] and [n] in words like *pilfer* [ˈpɪlfə] and *pundit* [ˈpʌndɪt] respectively, where they are followed by obstruents in the onsets of the following syllable. Additionally, nasals are homorganic with onset obstruents in a variety of languages, while the absence of homorganicity indicates that the nasal is not in the coda but rather in the onset and is followed by an empty nucleus, as in the English words *wronged* [rɒŋd] or *damsel* [ˈdæmzəl]. Rhymal complements followed by an onset obstruent can be called true codas since there is little, if any, disagreement among phonologists as to the syllabic status of such consonants. This stands in sharp contrast to the interpretations suggested for consonants appearing in word-final position. It is to such consonants that we now turn.

Traditional syllabification has no problems with the final consonants in *lad* [læd] and in *land* [lænd]: they are assigned to the coda, if only because there is nothing else they could be assigned to. This view identifies word-final consonants with the syllabic constitutent *coda*. If we accept this we are forced to recognise three-consonant codas, e.g. *lands* [lændz], *next* [nekst], four-consonant codas as in *sixths* [sɪksθs], and even an occasional five-consonant coda as in the Shakespearean (*thou*) *triumphst* [ˈtraɪəmpfst]. Other languages will likewise oblige in supplying long sequences: in Polish, words ending in three, four or even five consonants are not unusual, e.g. *łapsk* [ˈwapsk] 'paw, gen. pl.', *ostrz* [ɔstʃ] 'sharpen, imper.', *łgarstw* [ˈwgarstf] 'falsehood, gen. pl.', *następstw* [ˈnastɛmpstf] 'consequence, gen. pl.' etc. We will see presently that a theory which identifies word-chunks with syllabic constituents is seriously flawed. We begin by comparing the consonants that can appear in what is unquestionably a true coda position, i.e. before a following onset obstruent, with those that occur word-finally. Modern Irish furnishes the data for this.

5.2 Word-final consonants in Irish

In Irish the true coda position can be occupied by a sonorant as in [1a] or by a voiceless spirant [1b]. Consider the examples:

[1]
a. timpeall [ˈtʲiːmpəl] 'round'   iompair [ˈumpərʲ] 'carry'
    sláinte [ˈslaːnʲtʲə] 'health'   pionta [ˈpʲuntə] 'pint'
    ancaire [ˈaŋkərʲə] 'anchor'   ionga [ˈuŋgə] 'nail'
    ordóg [orˈdoːg] 'thumb'   garda [ˈgaːrdə] 'policeman'
    tarcaisne [ˈtarkəʃnʲə] 'contempt'   díoltas [ˈdʲiːltəs] 'revenge'
b. aspal [ˈaspəl] 'apostle'   báisteach [ˈbaːʃtʲəx] 'rain'
    treascair [ˈtraskərʲ] 'overthrow'   seachtain [ˈʃaxtənʲ] 'week'
    sneachta [ˈʃnʲaxtə] 'snow'

Single intervocalic consonants are assigned to the onset of the following syllable, e.g. in *fada* [ˈfadə] 'long' and *míle* [ˈmʲiːlʲə] 'thousand' [d] and [lʲ] begin the second syllable. This means that word-internal codas are restricted to sonorants [1a] and voiceless spirants [1b]. The non-appearance of voiced spirants in the coda position may be due to the fact that the voiced spirants [z] and [ɣ] have a

5.2 Word-final consonants in Irish

very limited distribution in the language, while [v] is probably best treated as a semivowel (it is often in free variation with [w]). However, plosive consonants are widespread in the language but they never appear in codas, i.e. *[ɑptə], *[blɑktə], are not well-formed Irish words. It is very clear, then, that Irish specifically limits the range of melodies that can appear in the coda by barring plosives from that position.

Plosives typically appear in initial and internal onsets [2a] and word-finally [2b], e.g.:

[2]
a.   bata ['bɑtə] 'stick'   cogar [kogər] 'listen!'
       tapa [tɑpə] 'speed'   gadaí [gɑ'diː] 'thief'
       dúdóg [duː'doːg] 'stump'   bábóg [bɑː'boːg] 'doll'
       cibé [kʲi'bʲeː] 'whatever'
b.   scuab [skuəb] 'sweep'   leib [lʲebʲ] 'fool'
       ciap [kʲap] 'annoy'   soip [sɪpʲ] 'wisp, gen. sg.'
       slat [slɑt] 'rod'   duit [dɪtʲ] 'to you'
       rud [rod] 'thing'   cuid [kɪdʲ] 'share'
       cnoc [knuk] 'hill'   mic [mʲɪkʲ] 'son, pl.'
       póg [poːg] 'kiss'   Nollaig ['noləgʲ] 'Christmas'

Thus, with the exception of the distributionally restricted voiced spirants [z, ɣ], practically any consonant can appear word-finally in Irish. If word-final consonants were to be treated as codas, then we would end up with two different types of codas: word-internal ones where plosives are disallowed, and word-final ones where they appear without any particular restrictions. This conclusion is hardly acceptable: codas are syllabic units and should have nothing to do with the position they occupy within larger units such as words. Alternatively, we would need to have some special reason why word-internal and word-final codas should be different. Since plosives freely occur in onsets word-initially and word-internally, while they never occur in word-internal codas, we have to conclude that their appearance word-finally indicates that they are onsets rather than codas. We can then make a general observation about Irish plosives, namely that they can appear in onsets only. The tentative theoretical conclusion that we can draw at this stage is that – contrary to traditional views on syllabification – word-final consonants behave as if they were onsets; to be able to make the claim that word-final consonants actually are onsets we need more arguments and more evidence.

Consider first word-final consonant sequences in Irish, which are limited to combinations of a sonorant and a plosive [3a], and of a fricative followed by a plosive [3b], e.g.:

[3]
a. corp [korp] 'body'　　　　　　oscailt [ˈoskəlʲtʲ] 'opening'
　　bord [boːrd] 'table'　　　　　long [luːŋg] 'ship'
　　féachaint [ˈfiaxənʲtʲ] 'looking'　stromp [stromp] 'stiffen'
　　páirc [paːrkʲ] 'field'　　　　　sagart [ˈsagərt] 'priest'
b. seift [ʃeftʲ] 'resource'　　　　Cáisc [kaːʃkʲ] 'Easter'
　　post [post] 'post'　　　　　　bocht [boxt] 'poor'
　　pléasc [plʲiask] 'explosion'

If word-final consonant sequences were to be treated as codas, we would be forced into another peculiar observation about Irish: what is a coda word-finally, must be analysed as a combination of a coda and a following onset word-internally. Recall that in [1] above we offer examples of sonorants and spirants in word-internal coda position, where in every case such sonorants or spirants are followed by a voiceless plosive. This is exactly the situation we encounter in [3]; to make this clear let us juxtapose a few examples of the possible combinations in the two positions.

[4]　　　　　　medial　　　　　　　　　　　　final
sonorant–plosive
torpa [ˈtorpə] 'clod'　　　　　　　　corp [korp] 'body'
gorta [ˈgortə] 'famine'　　　　　　　gort [gort] 'field'
rialta [ˈrialtə] 'regular'　　　　　　　oscailt [ˈoskəlʲtʲ] 'opening'
folca [ˈfolkə] 'flood, pl.'　　　　　　folc [folk] 'flood, sg.'
garda [ˈgaːrdə] 'policeman'　　　　　bord [boːrd] 'table'
rangaigh [ˈrauŋgəgʲ] 'classify'　　　　long [luːŋg] 'ship'

spirant–plosive
donachta [ˈdonəxtə] 'badness, gen.'　　donacht [ˈdonəxt] 'badness'
postaire [ˈpostərʲə] 'messenger'　　　 post [post] 'post'
Cásca [ˈkaːskə] 'Easter, gen.'　　　　 iasc [iəsk] 'fish'
seifte [ˈʃeftʲə] 'resource, gen. sg.'　　 seift [ʃeftʲ] 'nom.'

In the left-hand column words we find examples of coda–onset sequences of the general type, where the coda is a sonorant or a spirant while the onset is a plosive. Note that word-internally such sequences must be interpreted as **heterosyllabic**, i.e. belonging to different syllables. In the right-hand column we find the very same sequences which, however, would have to be treated as **tautosyllabic**, or belonging to the same syllable, since they would be treated as codas by a theory that identifies word-final consonants with codas. The fact that consonants in some words would have to change their syllabic status in closely related forms need not in itself be very surprising or disturbing: [k] and [t] are in the onset in *folca*, *donachta*, but in the alleged coda in *folc*, *donacht*, as one can legitimately claim that the syllabic status of consonants depends upon the availability of neighbouring nuclei. What is disturbing is the claim that the same consonantal cluster constitutes a coda–onset heterosyllabic combination word-internally but a tautosyllabic coda word-finally. A neutral stand would assume that if, say, [xt] is heterosyllabic word-internally, then it should have the same structure word-finally. In other words, single word-final consonants could be expected to behave as onsets, while final consonant sequences would be coda–onset sequences. Adopting this line of reasoning we have to conclude that word-final consonants are never codas. The very last consonant is an onset while the one preceding it is a coda. Since the existence of an onset presupposes a following nucleus, word-final consonants must be followed by nuclei which have no phonetic content, i.e. by empty nuclei. The representation of the words in the left- and right-hand column words in [4] will differ in that the final nuclei of the latter will be empty while those of the former will contain some vocalic melody. Consider the words *donachta* and *donacht*.

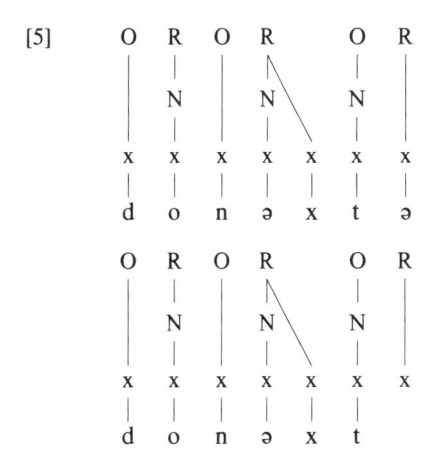

[5]
```
        O   R   O   R       O   R
        |   |   |   \       |   |
            N   N   \       N
            |   |    \      |
        x   x   x   x   x   x   x
        |   |   |   |   |   |   |
        d   o   n   ə   x   t   ə

        O   R   O   R       O   R
        |   |   |   \       |   |
            N   N   \       N
            |   |    \      |
        x   x   x   x   x   x   x
        |   |   |   |   |   |
        d   o   n   ə   x   t
```

These representations make it clear that syllabically the two forms of the word have the same structure: they only differ in that the final nucleus in one of them contains the melody [ə], while in the other it contains no melody whatsoever. Although melodically the position is empty, it still functions in the syllabic organisation of the word and hence, syllabically, the words are identical. In each of them the final consonant occupies the onset position. The distribution and syllable affiliation of consonants in Modern Irish are a challenge for the traditional identification of word-final consonants with syllabic codas. Obviously, the evidence supplied by a group of facts taken from one language is not in itself particularly compelling, and hence we will want to consider more languages and more data. Let us start by reviewing English word-final consonants and consonantal clusters; the situation is partially similar to what we have just seen in Irish but in certain ways somewhat more complex.

5.3 English word-final consonants and internal codas

Consider first true codas, i.e. word-internal consonants which are followed by an onset. Three groups of consonant types are possible in the coda position: sonorants, fricatives and plosives. The following onset is invariably occupied by an obstruent, either a plosive or a fricative. The possibilities are illustrated below.

[6] *sonorant coda–plosive onset*   *sonorant coda–fricative onset*
temper ['tempə]   rancid ['rænsɪd]
bandit ['bændɪt]   pilfer ['pɪlfə]
banter ['bæntə]   palsy ['pɔːlzi]
anchor ['æŋkə]   balsam ['bɔːlsəm]
alcove ['ælkəʊv]

fricative coda–plosive onset   *plosive coda–plosive onset*
aspen ['æspən]   chapter ['tʃæptə]
mister ['mɪstə]   October [ɒk'təʊbə]
rascal ['rɑːskəl]
laughter ['lɑːftə]

There are strong restrictions on what can appear in the coda position: as we have seen in the case of nasals, for example, these have to share their place of articulation with the following onset. There are other gaps in the list of combinations, however, which require a different explanation. What is particularly striking are the sequences involving plosives: as our examples indicate, the only plosives that can freely occur in the coda position are [p, k]. Given the fact that English has six such consonants – [p, t, k, b, d, g] – the restriction of the coda to just two of them constitutes a remarkable fact about English **phonotactics**, or the study of possible segment combinations. Note that there is nothing phonetically impossible about combining plosive sequences, and English does it regularly in morphologically complex forms: [gb] in *bugbear*, [bg] in *hobgoblin*, [gd] in *begged*, [dg] in *headgear*, [bd] in *robbed*, [db] in *good-bye*, [tk] in *outcast* etc. Such combinations, while commonplace at domain and word junctures, are never found domain-internally – in other words, the coda position admits no other plosives apart from [p, k]. This idiosyncratic phonotactic fact becomes even more surprising when we consider the word-final position, where all the plosives can readily be found: *sack*, *rib*, *bud*, *big*. In fact, word-finally all the plosives appear without restrictions, in the same way as they do in onsets. If word-final consonants were codas, we would need to say that phonotactically word-final codas are different objects from word-internal ones, a conclusion that is at odds with the very notion of a syllabic constitutent. Since word-final consonants show the same melodic possibilities as word-internal onsets, the simplest conclusion would again seem to be that such final consonants are onsets rather than codas.

The internal coda–onset clusters illustrated in [6] above have another intriguing property, namely they appear word-finally. In fact, leaving aside obvious sequences arising across domain junctures (e.g. [dz] in *cards* or [md] in *roamed*), these clusters constitute a large portion of all the word-final consonantal combinations of English. For ease of reference we repeat the internal coda–onset sequences and add examples of the same sequences found word-finally.

[7] *sonorant coda–plosive onset*   *sonorant coda–fricative onset*
  temper ['tempə]   hemp [hemp]   rancid ['rænsɪd]   once [wʌns]
  bandit ['bændɪt] end [end]   pilfer ['pɪlfə]   self [self]
  banter ['bæntə]   ant [ænt]   palsy ['pɔːlzi]   Naples [neɪplz]
  anchor ['æŋkə]   wink [wɪŋk]   balsam ['bɔːlsəm] false [fɔːls]
  alcove ['ælkəʊv] milk [mɪlk]

  fricative coda–plosive onset   *plosive coda–plosive onset*
  aspen ['æspən]   clasp [klɑːsp]   chapter ['tʃæptə] apt [æpt]
  mister ['mɪstə]   best [best]   October [ɒk'təʊbə] fact [fækt]
  rascal ['rɑːskəl] ask [ɑːsk]
  laughter ['lɑːftə] daft [dɑːft]

As the examples show, the word-internal coda–onset sequences also appear as final clusters. If we were to follow the traditional view and identify word-final consonants with codas, we would be forced into the same position again: word-final codas are different from word-internal ones. Note that sequences such as [nd] are never syllabified into a coda word-internally (e.g. *bandit*). They are always broken up between the coda [n] and the onset [d]; in fact, there are no word-internal codas like [nd] – sequences like [ndr], as in *foundry* ['faʊndri], conform to this regularity since the syllabic boundary falls between the nasal and the following consonantal cluster. Thus the same sequence [nd] would be ruled out as a coda internally in *bandit* but allowed finally in *end* and, conversely, word-final codas would have to be split into a coda–onset sequence internally. To maintain the unity of syllabic constituents, we need only say that what is a coda–onset internal sequence is likewise a coda–onset finally, no matter whether a phonetically pronounced vowel follows or not. In this interpretation the words *misty* ['mɪsti] – *mist* [mɪst] have the same syllabic structure and differ only in that the last nucleus has phonetic content – the melody [i] – in the former example but remains empty in the latter. The consonants in both cases are syllabified identically, as shown in the following diagrams, which in the relevant parts are identical to the Irish situation depicted in [5] above.

98   *More on codas*

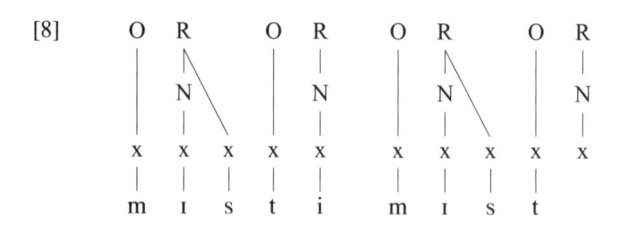

[8]
```
      O   R        O   R       O   R        O   R
      |  /\        |   |       |  /\        |   |
      |  N \       |   N       |  N \       |   N
      |  |  \      |   |       |  |  \      |   |
      x  x   x     x   x       x  x   x     x   x
      |  |   |     |   |       |  |   |     |   |
      m  ɪ   s     t   i       m  ɪ   s     t
```

The English internal and final coda–onset sequences allow us to make another generalisation about the phonological structure of the language. This concerns the appearance of long and short vowels in different positions. Vowels may be either short (non-branching) or long (branching) before single consonants both domain-internally [9a] and domain-finally [9b].

[9]
a.   ready ['redɪ]   sadist ['seɪdɪst]
      litter ['lɪtə]   litre ['liːtə]
      valid ['vælɪd]   tailor ['teɪlə]
      marry ['mæri]   Mary ['meəri]
      slobber ['slɒbə]   sober ['səʊbə]
b.   red [red]   raid [reɪd]
      lid [lɪd]   lead [liːd]
      but [bʌt]   bout [baʊt]
      bell [bel]   boil [bɔɪl]
      lot [lɒt]   late [leɪt]
      fat [fæt]   fate [feɪt]
      ash [æʃ]   leash [liːʃ]
      itch [ɪtʃ]   each [iːtʃ]

Before a sequence of two domain-internal consonants, i.e. before a coda–onset combination, branching nuclei are possible in highly restricted contexts. These basic possibilities are a coda fricative, e.g. *pastry* ['peɪstri], *oyster* ['ɔɪstə], or a coronal sonorant homorganic with the following onset, e.g. *manger* ['meɪndʒə], *shoulder* ['ʃəʊldə]. In other cases before a coda consonant, the vowel is short, e.g. *actor* ['æktə], *scripture* ['skrɪptʃə], *perceptive* [pə'septɪv], *limpid* ['lɪmpɪd], *finger* ['fɪŋgə] etc. We can interpret these facts by saying that with the exception of specified cases, the nucleus in English must be non-branching before a coda consonant. This, however, can only mean that word-final consonants do not occupy the coda position since, as [9b] documents, branching nuclei are perfectly acceptable before any final consonant.

By now we may have come to expect that when a word-final consonant sequence is identical to an internal coda–onset combination, similar effects follow. Thus, since before a true coda only short vowels occur – with specified exceptions – word-final codas followed by a consonant should exhibit similar results. This is

5.3 English word-final consonants and internal codas

indeed what happens, including the specified exceptions. We observed above that before a coda fricative or a coronal sonorant homorganic with the following onset – the *pastry–manger* cases – the nucleus can branch; the same 'specified exceptions' are attested word-finally, e.g. *haste* [heɪst], *range* [reɪndʒ], *child* [tʃaɪld]. Vowels are invariably short before other consonant combinations which word-internally function as coda–onsets, e.g. *limp* [lɪmp], *tank* [tæŋk], *self* [self], *act* [ækt]. In this context branching nuclei are impossible hence *[laʊmp], *[teɪŋk], *[siːlf], *[eɪkt] are not admissible single morphemes in English. We can thus repeat our earlier conclusion that word-final consonant clusters behave as if they were sequences of a coda followed by an onset. The phonological identity of the coda–onset internal combination with the word-final consonant sequence indicates that the final consonant is actually an onset, while the prefinal one is a rhymal complement (the coda).

What we have seen above are restrictions on branching nuclei in closed syllables, i.e. in rhymes containing a consonantal coda. The brunt of the argument was to show that a word-final consonant does not make the preceding syllable closed; rather such a consonant constitutes the onset of a syllable whose nucleus is melodically empty. The predominant tendency is for closed syllables to contain non-branching nuclei, i.e. short vowels. This constraint holds for monomorphemic words (single phonological domains) but is also attested in some morphophonemic alternations. We would like to consider these briefly now.

As we have seen, morphophonemic alternations are found when a given morpheme displays a changed phonetic form in combination with some other morpheme or morphemes. Thus, for example, the adjective *final* in isolation appears as [ˈfaɪnəl], but when combined with the noun-forming suffix *-ity* its stress shifts and its second vowel is changed to [faɪˈnæl], i.e. *finality* [faɪˈnæləti]. The patterns of morpheme combinations and possible morphologically complex words do not constitute the domain of phonology but rather of morphology and the lexicon. The alternations existing may be the result of changes which were operative in the language centuries ago and thus are not in any sense a direct result of the synchronic phonology of the language. However, if our phonological generalisations are correct and capture regularities prevailing in the language, then morphological alternations cannot be at odds with them. In this way we can regard morphological alternations as strengthening the validity of the generalisations we formulate. Thus, no matter when specific morphemes were combined and what historical changes they were subsequently subjected to, their current phonetic shape must conform to existing synchronic phonological generalisations. The scope of phonological regularities is, primarily, coterminous with the phonological domain, which need not and often does not coincide with what is a lexical word. However, when morphologically complex words entail alternations characteristic of simplex units, then they invariably are single phonological domains.

100 *More on codas*

With these observations in mind consider the alternations between branching and non-branching nuclei found in a number of related words: the final nucleus in the left-hand column words below is branching, whereas the corresponding vowel in the domain-internal (presuffixal) position is non-branching or short.

[10] receive [rɪ'siːv]   reception [rɪ'sepʃən]
      describe [dɪ'skraɪb]   descriptive [dɪ'skrɪptɪv]
      wise [waɪz]   wisdom ['wɪzdəm]
      five [faɪv]   fifty ['fɪfti]
      retain [rɪ'teɪn]   retentive [rɪ'tentɪv]

Note that the final consonant in the left-hand column words is an onset, which means that the preceding syllable is open and does not contain a coda; this is the context where the vowel can be long. In the right-hand column words, however, a sequence of a coda and an onset arises at a morpheme juncture and this means that the preceding syllable is closed. This is the context where, with the exception of forms of the *pastry–manger* type, branching nuclei tend to be disallowed. The alternations also involve vocalic qualitative differences and consonantal distinctions, but these are a matter for the lexicon rather than phonology: from the synchronic phonological point of view the relevant point is that closed syllables disfavour branching nuclei.

At this stage it comes as no surprise that similar alternations are also found when consonantal suffixes are attached to stems containing a branching nucleus.

[11] keep [kiːp]   kept [kept]
      leave [liːv]   left [left]
      thief [θiːf]   theft [θeft]
      five [faɪv]   fifth [fɪfθ]
      wide [waɪd]   width [wɪdθ]

The final consonantal cluster in the right-hand column words behaves in the same way as the cluster in the morphologically complex words in [10], i.e. the first consonant is a coda while the second one is an onset. A coda consonant closes the syllable and hence a long vowel is less likely to appear in its nucleus. The final consonant in *keep* etc. does not impose such a requirement, which follows from the fact that it is an onset in the same way as [p] in *keeper* is an onset, and hence a long vowel may precede it. As before, the nature of the qualitative alternations or consonant modifications is outside the purview of phonology.

The above discussion of the restrictions on the occurrence of consonants in different positions within a word and the concomitant limitations on the distribution of branching nuclei points in the same direction as the Irish consonant distribution: word-final consonants are onsets. If preceded by another consonant (within the same phonological domain) they have the same structure as word-internal sequences, hence in both cases they are interpreted as a combination of a coda and a following onset. This means, however, that we can talk about a coda only when there is a following onset. It is the onset which **licenses**, supports or sanctions the appearance of a coda. The onset itself in turn is licensed by a nucleus which may but does not have to be phonetically expressed. The structure of the coda then is the same word-internally and word-finally and can be represented as follows:

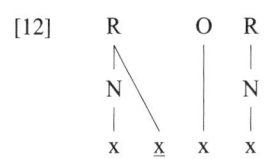

[12] R   O   R
      |\ | |
      N \ | N
      | \ | |
      x   x̲   x   x

The underscored x is the coda position. Note that the coda and the onset are invariably adjacent on the skeletal tier. This observation allows us to return to the notion of nasal place sharing which we discussed in the preceding chapter.

5.4 Nasal–obstruent place sharing continued

In chapter 4 we discussed at some length the sharing of the place of articulation between a nasal consonant and a following obstruent in a number of languages (examples like *simply* ['sɪmpli], *bandy* ['bændi], *finger* ['fɪŋgə] in English). In all the cases we considered the consonantal sequences which appeared word-internally, and we stressed that the sharing takes place when the nasal occupies the coda position which is immediately followed or – as we would now say – licensed by an obstruent in the onset. Thus the place sharing is found in the rhyme–onset combination, and the cases where no sharing is found can be interpreted as indicating that the phonetic consonant sequence is not a phonological sequence (e.g. *flimsy* ['flɪmzi]). In other words, the nasal and the following obstruent must be seen as being in separate onsets with a nucleus intervening. Some languages provide direct evidence for the reality of the nucleus, which in certain cases receives phonetic interpretation (recall the Polish examples like *słomka* ['swɔmka] 'straw, dim.' with a non-homorganic cluster and its gen. pl. form *słomek* ['swɔmɛk] where the nucleus separating the members of the offending cluster has melodic content).

The generalisation that nasal sharing crucially involves a rhyme and an onset is directly relevant to our discussion of the syllabic status of word-final consonants. If word-final consonants are indeed onsets, then a nasal preceding them should be syllabified into the rhymal complement position in exactly the same way as happens word-internally. The ensuing coda–onset combination should display place of articulation homorganicity, once again reflecting exactly the internal situation. This is indeed what happens in all the languages we have considered. In what follows we shall illustrate place sharing briefly, since it introduces no new factors into our analysis but confirms the conclusion that word-final consonants are onsets, and as such may be preceded by a rhymal complement in the previous syllable.

In English the attested domain-final nasal and obstruent sequences are homorganic, although there some language-specific complicating factors. Consider these examples

[13]
a.   stamp [stæmp]   bump [bʌmp]
     romp [rɒmp]   nymph [nɪmɟf]
     triumph [traɪəmɟf]
b.   tend [tend]   brand [brænd]
     abound [ə'baʊnd]   mount [maʊnt]
     font [fɒnt]   ant [ænt]
     dance [dɑːns]   tense [tens]
     bronze [brɒnz]   wrench [rent̠ʃ]
     punch [pʌnt̠ʃ]   plunge [plʌnd̠ʒ]
     whinge [wɪnd̠ʒ]
c.   brink [brɪŋk]   plonk [plɒŋk]
     rank [ræŋk]   dunk [dʌŋk]

In [13a] the shared place of articulation involves labiality or labio-dentality, in [13b] it is alveolarity or postalveolarity (the latter marked here as [n̠]), while in [13c] it is velarity – in brief, the clusters in question are homorganic. Viewed in this way the examples in [13] are not different from what is found domain-internally when rhymal complements are homorganic with following onsets (e.g. *tempo* ['tempəʊ], *dandy* ['dændi], *tango* ['tæŋgəʊ]). If we wish to maintain a single, syllable-based generalisation about nasal sharing in English, we need to conclude that the consonantal clusters in [13] constitute the same kind of syllabic structure finally as they do domain-internally, i.e. they are sequences of rhymal nasals followed by onset obstruents. This, of course, means that the final consonants of the words are onsets and, like onsets in general, they need to be sanctioned by a following nucleus. The final nuclei in these words happen to have no phonetic content and hence remain inaudible. English offers little direct evidence in the form of alternations which supports the existence of empty nuclei. What we have here is indirect evidence which is particularly significant as it emerges out of the logic of the system. The empty nuclei are a straightforward consequence of basic assumptions such as the one claiming that onsets must be licensed by nuclei.

Nasal sharing can be regarded as a uniform phonological regularity and in this sense there are no syllabification differences between the domain-internal and the domain-final position as far as the participating segments are concerned. Domain-final sequences do not tolerate anything which is not admitted internally. There are, however, certain differences between what can appear in the two positions, and although this does not undermine the main points we are making here, the differences are interesting from the point of view of the phonology of English as a whole and as such merit some discussion.

Notice that domain-finally certain consonantal combinations are not tolerated. These gaps are striking since they involve homorganic clusters of a nasal and a voiced plosive which are found domain-internally, namely [mb] and [ŋg]. While internally we find words like *lumber* ['lʌmbə], *gambit* ['gæmbɪt] or *finger* ['fɪŋgə], *bungalow* ['bʌŋgələʊ], the same sequences are impossible in the final position. Thus there are no words *[sæmb] or *[rɒŋg] with a pronounced final plosive. The only voiced plosive that can appear after a nasal domain-finally is a coronal, as in [13b]. When discussing the representation of the velar nasal in 3.2 we pointed out that the domain-final voiced velar plosive is suppressed after a homorganic nasal, yielding phonetically the simple nasal [ŋ], as in *king* [kɪŋ]. Such suppression is a language-specific operation and constitutes part of its synchronic phonology; in earlier English the voiced velar plosive was just as acceptable after a nasal as a voiceless one and even today, there are dialects of the language which do not follow this pattern, so that a word like *sing* is pronounced [sɪŋg] with an audible final plosive (see our discussion in 3.2). The impossibility of this combination in most varieties of the language is a phonological fact which turns out to be part of a more general tendency to disallow certain phonetic sequences. As noted above, apart from the absence of final [ŋg], there is also the inadmissibility of final [mb], which really means that the only voiced plosive tolerated domain-finally after a homorganic nasal is the coronal [d]. It is probably not an accident that a similar pattern can be observed when a lateral in the rhyme is followed by a voiced plosive in the onset: domain-internally the lateral can be followed by a labial (*elbow* ['elbəʊ]), a coronal (*shoulder* ['ʃəʊldə]) or a velar (*vulgar* ['vʌlgə]). Domain-finally the situation is radically different: the voiced coronal is amply attested after a lateral (*hold* [həʊld], *field* [fiːld]), the labial plosive seems to appear in just one word (*bulb* [bʌlb]), while the velar plosive is altogether unrecorded – a word like **dilg* [dɪlg] looks and sounds totally un-English. Viewed from this perspective, the restricted range of nasal plus plosive combinations domain-finally illustrated in [13] must be regarded as resulting from an independent phonological constraint operative in the language. The complications emerging from the operation of the constraint do not in any way undermine our main claim made in this chapter, namely that word-final consonants, rather than belonging to the coda, constitute onsets and are followed by nuclei without phonetic content. Nasal sharing domain-finally, to the extent that it is not disallowed by additional constraints, is not in conflict with this conclusion.

104   *More on codas*

The claim that nasal sharing is observed between a coda nasal and an obstruent in the following onset allowed us to provide an account of the cases where sharing is not observed between phonetically consecutive consonants, e.g. *flimsy*. It will be recalled that in such cases we postulate an empty nucleus separating the nasal and the following obstruent. Domain-finally we also find departures from the expected pattern. These include in the first place the very common cases where inflectional endings are attached to stems, e.g. *aims* [eɪmz], *aimed* [eɪmd] – in such examples, as we argued above, the ending is separated by a nucleus from the final consonant of the stem. In other words, the final consonant of the stem and the consonant of the ending are both independent onsets, and place sharing is neither possible nor required. There is, however, a handful of words, almost exclusively personal or place names, without any obvious internal morphological structure, which violate place sharing, e.g. *James* [dʒeɪmz], *Holmes* [həʊmz], *Thames* [temz], *Eames* [iːmz], *hames* [heɪmz] (the last word may be the plural of *hame* but it is also a lexicalised singular as shown by the regional expression *to make a hames of something*). These examples parallel certain similar and equally infrequent violations found domain-internally and by their infrequency confirm the reality of nasal sharing. It seems natural to view the failure of nasal sharing as due to the same phonological mechanism in both cases. Recall that in the case of words like *flimsy* an empty nucleus was posited between the nasal and the following spirant, which means that the two consonants both occupy onset positions, with no room for place sharing. Extending the same treatment to words like *James* we will claim that these, too, contain a nucleus which places the flanking consonants in onset positions and thus allows phonetic non-homorganic clusters. The representations of the words *flimsy, James* have the following shapes:

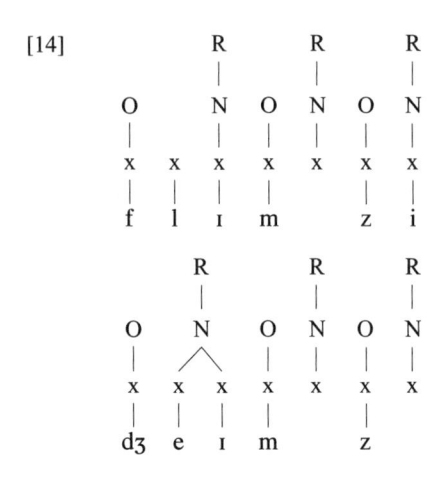

[14]
```
                R       R       R
                |       |       |
        O       N   O   N   O   N
        |       |   |   |   |   |
        x   x   x   x   x   x   x
        |   |   |   |       |   |
        f   l   ɪ   m       z   i

                R       R       R
                |       |       |
        O       N   O   N   O   N
        |      /\   |   |   |   |
        x   x   x   x   x   x   x
        |   |   |   |       |
        dʒ  e   ɪ   m       z
```

James is seen as containing two empty nuclei: one is required because it licenses the word-final onset, and one to explain the non-homorganicity of the nasal and the following obstruent. Note also that the related word *Jameson* has several possible pronunciations, one of them being [ˈdʒemɪsən] with the vowel [ɪ] filling the melody of the first of the empty nuclei above. The need to postulate an empty nucleus following the nasal in *James* and the fact that the corresponding nucleus in a related word has a melody can hardly count as an accident.

To sum up: English place sharing in nasal plus obstruent clusters is conditioned by exactly the same factors domain-finally as it is domain-internally. If a uniform analysis is accepted, then in both cases the obstruent must be assigned to the onset position. This, in turn, means that word-final consonants in such sequences are not codas but onsets, and thus strengthens the case for treating all final consonants, no matter whether preceded by a coda or not, as onsets and hence followed by empty nuclei.

After this extended discussion of nasal place sharing in word-final position in English we will deal with the situation in German, Dutch and Polish very briefly. From the point of view of the theoretical issue we are arguing, i.e. the non-coda status of word-final consonants, these three languages offer exactly the same type of evidence as does English. Thus a word-final nasal followed by an obstruent predominantly displays the same properties as it does domain-internally, where it is, indisputably, a coda. Nasal sharing can be described as a uniform regularity only when the consonants involved in it are syllabified in the same way in both positions. The examples below illustrate domain-final nasal sharing in German [15a], in Dutch [15b] and in Polish [15c].

[15]
a.   Hand [hant] 'hand'   Kind [kɪnt] 'child'
       ganz [gants] 'quite'   Wunsch [vʊnʃ] 'wish'
       Bank [baŋk] 'bank'
b.   ramp [ramp] 'disaster'   tand [tant] 'tooth'
       rund [rʏnt] 'cow'   bank [baŋk] 'bench'
       zink [zɪŋk] 'sink, imper.'
c.   dąb [dɔmp] 'oak tree'   sęp [sɛmp] 'vulture'
       band [bant̪] 'gang, gen. pl.'   rząd [ʒɔnt̪] 'government'
       rządź [ʒɔɲtɕ] 'rule, imper.'   chęć [xɛɲtɕ] 'willingness'
       drąg [drɔŋk] 'pole'   rąk [rɔŋk] 'hand, gen. pl.'

If we compare the final clusters in [15] with the examples of internal nasal place sharing discussed at length in the preceding chapter, we must conclude that [15] introduces nothing new. In fact, whatever combinations are attested finally are also found domain-internally.

The above examples are instructive in a somewhat indirect way: when we compare the internal and final sharing effects, we observe that while the final sequences are all subsumed under the internal ones, the reverse is not true. In all three languages the post-nasal obstruent is necessarily voiceless in word-final position, while internally both voiced and voiceless consonants are possible. While the range of effects might thus seem to be different in the two positions, a little familiarity with the languages reveals that the difference arises as a result of an independent constraint. German, Dutch and Polish display a reasonably widespread phenomenon whereby the word-final position does not tolerate voice distinction in obstruents; this means that all obstruents appearing word-finally are necessarily voiceless. The impossibility of voiced obstruents in this position is responsible for the restricted range of consonantal clusters with place sharing word-finally. What is crucial, however, is that place sharing and voicing distinctions are independent regularities of the three phonological systems – note that voicing or rather its impossibility is amply attested by examples where no nasal precedes, e.g. German *Wald* [valt] 'wood', Dutch *Madrid* ['madrɪt] 'Madrid', Polish *sad* [sat] 'orchard'. Word-finally the two independent regularities – nasal place sharing and the voicing restriction – meet and jointly affect the same phonological units. We conclude then that nasal sharing is a single phonological phenomenon, attested both domain-internally and domain-finally. The unified nature of the phenomenon strengthens the case for the onsethood of final consonants.

In the preceding pages we have looked at a few phonological regularities which indicate that consonants appearing in word-final position are different from typical word-internal codas. On the other hand, we have seen that they pattern with word-internal onsets in that they accept the same range of consonants and in that they have an identical effect on preceding nuclei. Thus the phonological role that word-final consonants play places them together with syllabic onsets. In chapter 7 we will see that some word-final consonantal clusters in Icelandic have to be analysed as branching onsets, a conclusion that may look initially surprising but which is in agreement with the view that onsets, and syllabic constituents in general are independent of the position they occupy within a word. Onsets, whether branching or not, have to be licensed by nuclei, hence if final consonants are onsets they must be followed by empty nuclei. A close study of the phonological data brings us to the conclusion that something that initially appears to be a coda is in fact a different syllabic constituent, namely an onset. In order to uncover the syllabic structure of words one must often go beyond mechanical procedures which interpret sequences of segments as syllabic units, and it is necessary to part with traditional assumptions or prejudices. We now turn to a different case which illustrates the same point, where something that looks as if it belongs to the onset actually behaves phonologically as if it were a different constituent.

5.5 Consonant sequences starting with [s]

Syllabification as a phonological operation consists in uncovering what constituent individual segments are assigned to. As we have seen, this is not a straightforward operation since certain elements of the syllabic structure may remain unexpressed phonetically. Thus the discovery of the syllable structure needs to go beyond the phonetic sequencing of segments and delve into the phonological consequences of specific syllabic configurations. In other words, the syllabic affiliation of segments need not be accessible to direct inspection but its impact is felt through its consequences. If words in languages consisted exclusively of strings such as [sælɪɣɒta] or [buðaχərɨ], i.e. if they were just alternating sequences of vowels and consonants, the question of syllable structure would either be trivial or it might as well not arise at all. In such a case vowels would have to be nuclei and consonants would have to be onsets. In other words, an intervocalic consonant – VCV – will always be in the onset position, where it is licensed by the second vowel; it could not be a rhymal complement since it would need to be licensed by a following onset. Apart from such simple options, syllabification is a significant phonological operation because in a number of cases its results cannot be predicted in a mechanical fashion. This is because syllable structure is intricately bound up with the phonological organisation of the language as a whole.

A case that illustrates this dramatically involves consonant sequences beginning with [s], which can be found in a variety of languages, e.g. English *still* [stɪl], French *scorbut* [skɔʁˈbyt] 'scurvy', Russian *stol* [stol] 'table', Irish *sparán* [spəˈrɑːn] 'purse' etc. European languages, in particular, abound in combinations of this type; it should additionally be noted that the spirant may be modified in various ways, mostly as regards palatality and voicing, e.g. English *shrew* [ʃruː], German *Sprache* [ˈʃpʁaːxə] 'language', Russian *zdorovyj* [zdʌˈrovɨj] 'healthy', Polish *ścisk* [ɕtɕisk] 'crowd' etc. In languages outside the Indo-European family such sequences are rare or not found at all: in Hungarian, for instance, they appear only in borrowings, e.g. *szkeptikus* [ˈskɛptikuʃ] 'sceptical', *sport* [ʃpɔrt] 'sport' etc. The infrequency of such combinations in the languages of the world may suggest that they are specific to Indo-European, and are in some sense exceptional.

Another intriguing characteristic of s+C(onsonant) combinations emerges once ' we attempt to interpret them in syllabic terms. An initial difficulty often noted in past syllabic studies is of a phonetic nature. It has been observed that a typical branching onset consists of an obstruent followed by a sonorant (which may be subject to additional conditions such as the ban on homorganicity). In this light, a sequence such as [sk] is an unlikely candidate for a branching onset since it consists of two obstruents.

As we have seen in the few examples above the s+C combinations are found at the beginning of words. A frequent assumption made in syllabic studies is that whatever precedes the first vowel in a word must be an onset, i.e. [tr] and [bl] are branching onsets in *treat* and *blaze* respectively. While this assumption yields the desired results in a number of cases, it is by no means necessarily true. There are languages which tolerate complex or exotic consonant combinations in word-initial position, but there is little evidence that these combinations are syllabified as onsets. In Polish initial [rt] is possible, e.g. *rtęć* [rtɛɲtɕ] 'quick silver', as is the improbable-looking string [drgn] in *drgnąć* ['drgnɔɲtɕ] 'shudder'. Domain-internally the former cluster is regularly syllabified as a coda–onset sequence. In *warty* ['vartɨ] 'worthy', for example, [r] constitutes the coda while [t] forms the following onset, thus conforming to the general requirement that a sonorant in the rhyme may be followed by an obstruent in the onset. The sequence [drgn] on the other hand does not appear in internal onsets, which would be a peculiar restriction since syllable structure should be in principle independent of the position of a cluster in the word. The most straightforward solution to this puzzle would be to claim that the sequences in question are not branching onsets but, arguably, combinations of onsets separated by empty nuclei. This conclusion means that we cannot mechanically identify word-initial consonants with the syllabic constituent onset, and it places on us the burden of establishing the syllabic structure of words on the basis of phonological evidence. If no automatic identification of word-initial sequences with onsets is possible, we cannot assume that s+C strings are necessarily onsets. Below we will consider evidence from a few languages which suggest that combinations of s+C are not branching onsets, but represent a different syllabic configuration. It should be borne in mind, however, that phonological evidence needs to be carefully sifted before its significance can be ascertained. Also, it is a well-known fact that languages very often fail to provide compelling evidence in support of a specific theoretical proposal, which makes the task of the phonologist more challenging. In our search for a syllabic structure for s+C sequences we start by looking at some facts of Italian.

5.5.1 Italian vowel length

Modern Italian vowels display alternations in length which depend on their position within the word. This type of dependence is found quite frequently in languages, although the factors determining the alternations may differ significantly (see chapter 7 for a detailed look at vowel length alternations in Modern Icelandic). In Italian long vowels can appear exclusively in internal stressed syllables. This is not a sufficient condition as additionally the vowels may not be followed by a rhymal complement (a coda); if a coda follows, the vowel is short. Examples of long and short vowels are provided below.

[16]
a. insipido [inˈsiːpido] 'insipid'
    figliolo [fiˈʎɔːlo] 'son'
    feroce [feˈroːtʃe] 'savage'
    casa [ˈkaːza] 'house'
    muro [ˈmuːro] 'wall'
    artefice [arˈteːfitʃe] 'craftsman'
    malefico [maˈlɛːfiko] 'harmful'
b. piccolo [ˈpikkolo] 'small'
    figlioccio [fiˈʎɔttʃo] 'godson'
    bocca [ˈbokka] 'mouth'
    campo [ˈkampo] 'field'
    ruzza [ˈruddza] 'argument'
    tristezza [trisˈtettsa] 'sadness'
    centro [ˈtʃɛntro] 'centre'

We can see that a stressed vowel followed by a single consonant is long; the single consonant must obviously be treated as the onset of the following syllable, hence the stressed syllable is open. When a sonorant occupying the rhymal complement position follows, or when a geminate consonant appears, the syllable is closed and its vowel is short. Thus a geminate consonant can be regarded as having the same structure as a coda–onset combination. Since a short vowel followed by a coda corresponds to two skeletal positions in exactly the same way as a long vowel, we may formulate the generalisation that in Italian an internal stressed rhyme must dominate two positions. If there is no coda consonant, the two positions will be taken by the nucleus, hence the vowel will be long; if a coda does appear, it occupies one slot, hence the preceding vowel must also make do with a single slot and remains short.

The above reasoning supplies us with a phonological test for the syllabification of internal consonant sequences: if a preceding vowel is short we would expect the first consonant of the cluster to be placed in the rhyme. Conversely, if the vowel is long it means that the consonant in question must belong to the next syllable. With this in mind, consider the examples below where a stressed vowel is followed by various consonant sequences.

[17]
a. quadro [ˈkwaːdro] 'square'
    sidro [ˈsiːdro] 'apple tart'
    pietra [ˈpjɛːtra] 'stone'
    zebra [ˈdzɛːbra] 'zebra'
    putrido [ˈpuːtrido] 'putrid'
    sopra [ˈsɔːpra] 'on'

b. basta ['basta] 'enough!'
triste ['triste] 'sad'
pesca ['pɛska] 'peach'
pesca ['peska] 'catch (of fish)'
ruspa ['ruspa] 'bury'
nostro ['nostro] 'our'

The significance of the evidence in [17] is straightforward: before a typical branching onset, as in [17a], the preceding stressed vowel is long. This is never the case before s+C, which can only mean that such clusters do not form an onset. Rather, the examples in [17b] form a match with those in [16b] where the first consonant of the cluster was invariably assigned to the rhyme of the syllable, hence its vowel could not be long. The same, it seems, must be said about the s+C sequences in [17b]: since the preceding stressed vowel is not long, this can only mean that it forms a branching rhyme with the consonant [s]. Thus internal s+C sequences assign their members to separate syllables, which conforms to the general requirement that within onsets two obstruents are not possible.

The syllabification within words whereby [s] is assigned to the rhyme rather than the onset is not particularly controversial, and the distributional restrictions on long vowels fully support it. However, sequences of s+C are also found in word-initial position, e.g. *scatola* ['skaːtola] 'box', *smarrire* [smar'riːre] 'lose', *specifico* [spe'tʃiːfiko] 'specific' etc., where there is no obvious rhyme to which the initial spirant [s] could be assigned. Could it be the case that it does form a branching onset with the following consonant initially? Could we then have different syllabification depending on the position in the word? To answer these questions we need to examine another problem of Italian grammar, namely the shape and distribution of articles.

5.5.2 Italian masculine articles and the s+C sequences

The definite masculine article in Italian displays a few different shapes which seem to be determined by the segment that begins the following word (a noun or a noun modifier). Oversimplifying somewhat the facts for the sake of clarity let us consider the definite article: it has the forms *il* [il], *lo* [lo] (and *l'* [l]) in the singular and *i* [i] or *gli* [ʎi] (*gl'* [ʎ]) in the plural. The variants *il*/*i* appear before a single consonant (18a) or a branching onset (18b):

[18]
a. il monte 'mountain'   i monti 'pl.'
    il cane 'dog'   i cani
    il soldato 'soldier'   i soldati
    il padre 'father'   i padri

b. il branco 'herd'   i branchi
   il plico 'file'   i plichi
   il granchio 'crab' i granchi
   il piato [pjaːto] 'trial' i piati

It should be noted in particular that a single initial [s] (*soldato*) selects the same variants as any other initial consonant appearing in the onset.

Before a vowel the definite article is *lo*, which appears in this form only in very artificial styles of speech where every word is pronounced separately; in connected speech the vowel of the article is dropped; in the plural the prevocalic variant is *gli*, occasionally simplified to just *gl'*.

[19] l'amico 'friend'   gli amici
      l'anno 'year'   gli anni
      l'italiano '(an) Italian' gli italiani – gl'italiani
      l'onore 'honour'   gli onori

We can say that the article apears in the shape *l'*/*gli* when the onset of the noun is empty. Consider now nouns beginning with our sequence s+C.

[20] lo scalo 'port'   gli scali
      lo studente 'student'   gli studenti
      lo sfoggio 'luxury'   gli sfoggi
      lo smacco 'insult'   gli smacchi
      lo slancio 'energy'   gli slanci

The article before the s+C combinations differs minimally from the variant appearing before vowel-initial nouns: as we have seen in [19], the vowel of the singular article is dropped before a vowel in the noun. In the plural the forms of the article before a vowel and before s+C are identical. It is important to stress that before branching onsets and before non-branching onsets containing just [s], the article has different shapes, as demonstrated in [18]. Since the initial s+C combinations behave differently from initial [s], we conclude that the [s] in the two cases occupies a different syllabic position, and specifically that the [s] beginning the words in [20] cannot be in the onset. The s+C sequences pattern with onsetless nouns. The question then arises as to what exactly the syllabification of such sequences is.

In our discussion of Italian vowel length above we concluded that domain-internally [s] before a consonant is a coda. The main reason for this was that the vowel preceding the cluster is invariably short exactly as before other coda–onset sequences. As we have just seen, initially [s] before a consonant is not an onset. If [s] in the s+C sequences must be analysed as a coda domain-internally, the most natural thing would seem to be to extend this interpretation also to the initial

112 *More on codas*

position. Since the nucleus has a coda consonant as its complement, we must assume that this holds for internal and initial position alike; internally there are no problems, since in words like *basta* (see [17b]) a vowel directly precedes the fricative [s]. If the consonant is to be a coda initially, it also must be preceded by a vocalic unit. The only difference is that the initial vowel has no melodic content, i.e. it is an empty nucleus.

We can summarise our discussion so far by plotting representations for the words *basta* and *scalo* which correspond to the classes of words where s+C is and is not preceded by a nucleus containing a melody.

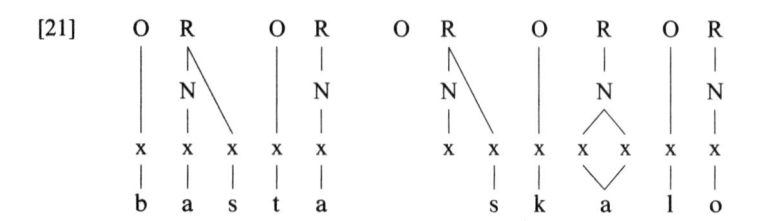

[21]

```
    O   R       O   R           O   R       O   R       O   R
    |  /\       |   |           |  /\       |   |       |   |
    |  N \      |   N           |  N \      |   N       |   N
    |  |  \     |   |           |  | \      |  /\       |   |
    x  x   x    x   x           x  x  x     x  x        x   x
    |  |   |    |   |           |  |  \    /           |   |
    b  a   s    t   a           s  k   a   l            o
```

The two problems in Italian we have discussed above indicate that the fricative [s] can appear in the onset by itself only, i.e. that it is not part of a branching onset. Both word-initial and word-internal combinations of [s] and a consonant have to be analysed as heterosyllabic or belonging to separate syllables. In both cases the fricative is a rhymal complement (a coda); the difference between the two positions reduces to whether the preceding nucleus has phonetic content, as is the case word-internally, or whether it is empty, the situation that prevails word-initially. Note also that this interpretation removes a theoretical problem we indicated at the outset, namely that a branching onset seems to comprise a sequence of two obstruents, instead of the expected obstruent–sonorant combination. This is no longer an option, since in every case the spirant forms part of the preceding rhyme, with or without a pronounced vowel. Needless to say, such a spirant does not have to be followed by a non-branching onset, as in the examples in [20], but may equally well be followed by a branching onset, e.g. *sgraffo* 'scratch', *splendore* 'splendour', *strada* 'road', *sprezzo* 'contempt' etc. What remains stable is the heterosyllabic nature of the initial [s].

A comment may be timely here about the empty nucleus in the initial position. We assume that it is silent in Italian, this being a specific phonological property of that language. In principle it could just as well be supplied with some melody, in which case there would be no initial s+C sequences but rather every such sequence would be preceded by a vowel. It can hardly be a coincidence that this is exactly what happens in a language closely related to Italian, namely Spanish. Initial s+C sequences do not exist in this language and where we would expect them on other grounds, they are accompanied by initial [e], e.g. *España* 'Spain', *esnob* 'snob', *escuéla* 'school', *eslovaco* 'Slovak', *escultor* 'sculptor' etc. (compare the corresponding Italian forms: *Spagna*, *snob*, *scuola*, *slovaco*, *scultore*). It appears that Spanish, in contradistinction to Italian (and other languages, including English), selects the option of filling the initial empty nuclei with a vocalic melody. It thus provides additional evidence for the reality of the initial nucleus, which in Italian can be defended only indirectly through phonological patterning. Crucially, however, the impossibility of branching onsets with [s] is equally true for Spanish and Italian: the languages merely select different ways of expressing this.

5.5.3 English s+C sequences: the evidence of yod

As we have mentioned above, direct phonological evidence for or against a specific syllabification of linguistic forms is not always easy to come by and sometimes may not be available at all. When no relevant evidence can be used, we need to rely on cases that are well supported and which invoke principles established independently. At times, such support may come from a different language, as in the case of the Italian–Spanish ways of handling the initial empty nucleus in the rhyme with the spirant [s]. Similarly, it may be useful to consider dialect variation in trying to decide an issue which cannot be solved on the basis of a single dialect. We will now consider one such case involving the evidence that the English glide [j] (yod) provides with reference to the syllabification of s+C sequences.

In RP the glide [j] can appear after most initial consonants in stressed positions. Thus we find numerous examples like those in [22].

[22] pure [pjʊə]   beauty ['bjuːti]   music ['mjuːzɪk]
      fury ['fjʊəri]   view [vjuː]   enthuse [ɪn'θjuːz]
      neutral ['njuːtrəl] tulip ['tjuːlɪp]   dune [djuːn]
      suit [sjuːt]   zeugma ['zjuːgmə]   lucid ['ljuːsɪd]
      kudos ['kjuːdɒs]   gewgaw ['gjuːgɔː]   humid ['hjuːmɪd]

There are some gaps, such as the impossibility of the palatal glide after a palatal consonant (e.g. *[ʃj]), or the striking absence of [rj] initially, hence *rule* is not likely ever to be pronounced *[rjuːl]. Such gaps are intriguing and they would have to be taken account of in an exhaustive study of English phonology; here it is enough to note that some varieties of British English admit yod after most single consonants. This is not contradicted by the fact that individual speakers may prefer a variant without yod, such as the frequently encountered *suit* [suːt] or *lucid* ['luːsɪd] – what is significant is that forms with the glide are found, something that could not be said about words like *rule*. Since single consonants are invariably onsets, it is natural to conclude that the glide [j] appears in branching onsets.

Let us now consider whether the glide can appear after uncontroversial branching onsets, i.e. sequences of an obstruent followed by a sonorant. The class of such onsets which could potentially be followed by [j] is restricted to those with [l] as the second member, since as we have already seen, single [r] cannot be followed by [j] initially. In such a case one would not expect to find a glide after a branching onset ending in [r]. This is confirmed by the impossibility of initial sequences such as [trj], e.g. *truce* is never pronounced *[trju:s]. What is more significant is the impossibility of [j] after an onset ending in [l], i.e. there are no pronunciations like the following:

[23] plural *['pljʊərəl]   blue *[blju:]
      clue *[klju:]   glue *[glju:]

Recall that yod can follow both a single plosive (e.g. *pewter* ['pju:tə]) and a single lateral (e.g. *lure* [ljʊə]) when these appear in the onset; what is impossible is its occurrence when a plosive and a lateral are combined. This prompts the conclusion that the glide cannot follow a branching onset.

Thus we reach our main concern, i.e. the syllabic status of preconsonantal [s] in words such as *stay* [steɪ]. If [s] formed a branching onset with the following consonant, the glide should be banned from appearing after such a sequence, since it is banned after other branching onsets. Consider however the data below.

[24] student ['stju:dənt]   stupefy ['stju:pɪfaɪ]   steward ['stju:əd]
      spume [spju:m]   spew [spju:]   spurious ['spjʊərɪəs]
      skew [skju:]   scuba ['skju:bə]   scutum ['skju:təm]
      smew [smju:]

In RP and most British dialects in general the glide is either required or at least possible (e.g. *scuba*). American English requires or tolerates it after non-coronals. In any event, the glide can appear after a sequence of s+C. This should not be possible if the s+C sequence were an onset, since, as we have just argued on the basis of examples in [23], yod cannot follow a branching onset. Additionally, RP admits the pronunciation with the glide in the words *slew* [slju:] and *sleuth* [slju:θ]. Although the number of such forms is very small, they are of overriding importance since they confirm that [sl] cannot be syllabified in an onset. Taken together the evidence points to the same conclusion as the Italian data presented earlier, namely that combinations of [s] with another consonant invariably belong to different syllables, i.e. such sequences are heterosyllabic. On the basis of Italian vowel length and definite article distribution we argued that the spirant [s] must be properly assigned to a rhyme with no melodic content in its nucleus. It is possible to apply

5.5 Consonant sequences starting with [s]

the same analysis to English – we can claim that in words beginning with phonetic s+C, there is an empty nucleus with the spirant as its complement, and the following consonant is the onset of the next syllable. Taking the word *student* as an example, we can offer the following representation of its syllabic and melodic structure:

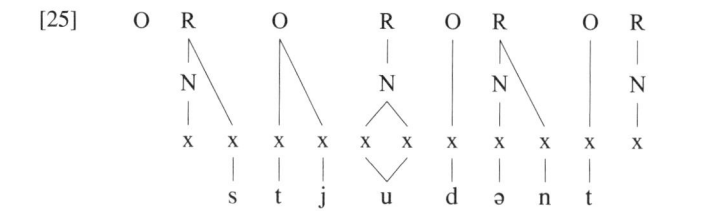

[25]

```
   O   R      O     R     O  R      O   R
   |\  |      |\    |     |  |\     |   |
   | \ N      | \   N     |  | \    |   N
   |  \|      |  \  |     |  |  \   |   |
   x   x      x   x x     x  x   x  x   x
   |   |      |   \/      |  |   |  |
   s   t      j   u       d  ə   n  t
```

As can be seen, our syllabic representation contains a nucleus both at the beginning and at the end of the word; in both cases the nucleus remains silent. Its appearance in the first rhyme is justified by the fact that a rhymal complement, i.e. [s] in this case, requires a nucleus. The reasons why [s] cannot be in the onset but must reside in the rhyme have been presented in the second part of this chapter. The final empty nucleus is necessary since the preceding onset must be licensed by it. The reasons why word-final consonants must be regarded as onsets were laid out in the first part of the chapter.

The interpretation of initial s+C sequences along the lines presented above removes a systematic obstacle to a uniform interpretation of branching onsets in English and other European languages. As we have seen, branching onsets consist of an obstruent and a following sonorant, which, foregoing other complications, means that this constituent can dominate two slots only. English, however, admits sequences of three consonants before the first vowel of the word; excluding those cases, discussed above, where the third consonant is [j], the combinatory possibilities can be seen in the following examples:

[26] spring [sprɪŋ]   splendour ['splendə]   string [strɪŋ]
      sclerosis [sklə'rəusɪs] scream [skri:m]   square [skweə]

The initial [s] can be followed by what is independently a branching onset, i.e. an obstruent and a sonorant [pr, pl, tr, kl, kr, kw]. If, following the arguments above, we believe that preconsonantal [s] must not be syllabified in the onset, then the three-consonant initial sequences in English (and elsewhere) are nothing but a mechanical combination of a rhymal complement and a well-formed two-element branching onset. The evidence of English initial [slj], corroborated by the facts of Italian, strengthens the conclusion that [s] cannot be the first member of a branching onset. We have argued that it must be a complement in a rhyme whose nucleus contains no vocalic melody.

5.6 Summary

In the preceding pages we have been concerned with the syllabification of selected word-final and word-initial consonant sequences. We have focused our attention on those consonant combinations that seem to call for a syllabic affiliation that departs from traditional practice, a practice which is guided by assumptions whose validity has seldom been called into question. One such assumption is that a consonantal sequence preceding the first vowel of a word is necessarily tantamount to the syllabic constituent 'onset'. Another is that the consonantal sequence following the last vowel of the word is the same as the syllabic 'coda'. We have tried to show that both these assumptions may be challenged: while the initial consonant sequence may but does not have to coincide with the onset, the word-final sequence is never identical to the coda. The way words begin and end in a language may only be suggestive of the possible syllable structures of that language. The syllabic constituents must be investigated through the study of the phonological effects they produce rather than through a mechanical chopping up of words into chunks.

On a more general level, syllabification provides evidence for the phonological regularities of the language; at the same time, syllabification itself can only be approached through such regularities. This formulation comes close to a vicious circle since it says that we study phonological regularities by invoking syllabification which is established by the regularities in question. The proximity to a vicious circle is something that cannot be avoided in linguistic argumentation but we should be aware of its existence and its pitfalls. The linguist has to establish both the structure and its regularities. Obviously the task would be easier if we could start knowing for certain what the structure is, if we could set off in full knowledge of, say, the syllabic organisation of a language and could just concentrate on discovering the regularities conditioned by that organisation. Unfortunately that is not the case: syllable structure is not given in advance. Even worse, what is given in the form of everyday intuitions, school training and the like is frequently superficial and misleading. Part of the phonological voyage of discovery is discarding some or perhaps most of the prejudices initially taken for granted.

In this chapter we have tried to shed a few such notions. Let us conclude by asking the simple question: how many syllables are there in the word *spring* in English? Everyday intuition, informed or perhaps simply formed by a particular type of education, would very likely prompt the answer: one. But this way of asking the question is simply another way of enquiring how many vowels are to be detected in the phonetic string [sprɪŋ]. The answer 'one' is harmless enough. It is probably useless enough just as well because it says very little apart from *I can hear one vowel*. By the same mechanism a speaker of Polish will give the same answer when asked about the number of syllables in the word *wzgląd* [vzglɔnt] 'consideration'. Speakers generally have limited, if any, direct access to the structure of languages; they can tell us that something is or is not a word of their language, sometimes they will tell us that something is a possible or an impossible word. Most of the opinions that speakers may venture about their languages are either downright simplistic or humorously naive – *In English stress tends to fall where it is easiest to pronounce*, the present writer was once instructed by an informed native speaker of English. Linguists must do their share of the work themselves. Passing the buck to the native speaker is unlikely to produce significant or permanent results.

5.7 Suggested further reading

On word-final consonants as non-codas see Giegerich (1985, chapter 2), Kaye (1990), Pigott (1991, 1999), Harris (1994, chapter 2), Harris and Gussmann (1998).

The Irish data are based on Ó Siadhail and Wigger (1975, chapter 2) and Ó Siadhail (1989, section 4.2).

The special status of s+C has been noted by most researchers, e.g. Selkirk (1982); the discussion of the issue in the present chapter is based on Kaye (1996).

For data on the Italian definite article, see Dressler (1985).

6

Some segmental regularities

6.1 Introduction

In the previous chapters we considered some of the basic notions relating to phonological representations and phonological generalisations. Crucial to them was the structuring of representations and the need to identify separate tiers within them. Each tier operates with units of its own (skeletal positions, melodies, syllabic constituents) which are connected with units of the other levels. An important concern in the theory of tiers is the presence of a unit at one level without any associated unit at a directly adjacent level, i.e. skeletal positions without attached melodies (empty positions), melodies unattached to positions (floating melodies) and syllabic constituents with no skeletal positions (empty onsets).

Phonological generalisations may hold for units at one level only. Often, however, what directly concerns one level will have consequences for units at other levels. Identifying and formulating generalisations involves making hypotheses about levels, units and interactions both between levels and between consecutive units at a given level. So far we have seen that phonological regularities embrace associations between levels, severed associations and conditions on adjacency including sharing relations.

In this chapter we will take a closer look at a few phonological phenomena in some detail. We will want to identify and capture the regularities which the data contain. When formulating the regularities we have to make assumptions that allow us to come up with reasonably satisfactory solutions. These assumptions should be held up for constant scrutiny – no description is possible without theoretical assumptions. On the other hand, theories are not God-given and necessarily true. As we saw in preceding chapters theoretical insights generally regarded as true are often accepted without questioning – recall the position of such 'generally obvious' concepts as the sound, the syllable or the word. For this reason the short case studies below, the phonological generalisations suggested and the theoretical implications should be taken as tentative rather than definitive. The reader is encouraged to question these on every occasion and to try and construct alternative interpretations, using the same set of data or taking other facts into consideration. While doing so the reader should be conscious of the theoretical implications a given solution may lead to or the questions it may raise.

The data below come from languages we have already looked at in other chapters (Turkish, English, Polish, Icelandic, German), and Russian enters the picture for the first time. The issues covered refer to what look like melodic interactions of vowels and consonants. We just look at a few cases here, so obviously the chapter is in no way an exhaustive survey of phonological regularities found across languages. Our objective is to see how data and theory shape each other, and what the trade-off between them is.

6.2 Turkish vowel harmony

Turkish vowels have already appeared in this book – in 2.4 we saw that long vowels can emerge as the result of optional compensatory lengthening. To deal with vowel harmony we need to take a closer look at all the vowels in the language; we will bypass long vowels which, apart from the compensatory lengthening contexts, also appear in a restricted way elsewhere. Basically Turkish has eight vowels: [i, y, e, œ, u, o, a, ɯ]. They are found in the following words: *it* [it] 'dog', *kürk* [kyrk] 'fur', *kese* [ke'se] 'pouch', *gör* [gœr] 'see', *kul* [kul] 'slave', *ot* [ot] 'grass', *at* [at] 'horse', *kısım* [kɯ'sɯm] 'part'. The first four vowels are front while the other four are back. Taking height as the criterion we distinguish four vowels as high, i.e. [i, y, u, ɯ], and four as non-high [e, œ, o, a]; [i, e, a, ɯ] are unrounded while [y, œ, o, u] are rounded.

A striking property of Turkish native vocabulary is that only certain vowels can co-occur with other vowels within any single word. Thus a word may have front rounded vowels only, e.g. *gönül* [gœ'nyl] 'heart', or back rounded, e.g. *çocuk* [tʃo'dʒuk] 'child', or front unrounded, e.g. *demir* [de'mir] 'iron'. However, certain other vowel sequences are severely restricted or totally ruled out. The appearance of front and back vowels within native morphemes is banned, although occasional loans can be found where this is tolerated, e.g. *otobüs* [oto'bys] 'bus'. The requirement that only specified vowels can follow other vowels within a word is referred to as **vowel harmony**. The existence of such harmony is of general significance for the language, which can be seen in the fact that when suffixes attach to stems, their vowels must adjust to stem vowels in particular ways. As a result, suffixes usually appear in more than one shape. To make this discussion more concrete, consider the two plural suffixes *-lar* and *-ler*.

120 *Some segmental regularities*

[1]
a. adam [a'dam] 'man'   adamlar [adam'lar]
    çocuk [tʃo'dʒuk] 'child'   çocuklar [tʃodʒuk'lar]
    ot [ot] 'grass'   otlar [ot'lar]
    kız [kɯz] 'girl'   kızlar [kɯz'lar]
b. el [el] 'hand'   eller [el'ler]
    it [it] 'dog'   itler [it'ler]
    müdür [my'dyr] 'director'   müdürler [mydyr'ler]
    söz [sœz] 'word'   sözler [sœz'ler]

The generalisation emerging from these examples is straightforward: the plural suffix appears as *-lar* after a back vowel in the stem, and as *-ler* after a stem front vowel. Note that it does not matter whether the vowel in the stem is rounded or unrounded, as the harmony apparently involves just agreement in frontness–backness. In other words, while consecutive nuclei can differ in height, e.g. *kızlar*, *itler* or rounding, e.g. *çocuklar*, *sözler*, they may not differ in frontness (backness). Frontness, then, is not subject to variation in consecutive nuclei. The fact that suffixal vowels share their frontness with the final vowel in the stem can be seen as due to a general rule of *frontness harmony*:

[2]   *Frontness Harmony*
    Within a phonological domain consecutive vowels share their frontness.

Frontness Harmony amounts to saying that the frontness/backness property is not an inherent property of an individual nucleus (in the way that height and rounding can be), but rather belongs to the phonological domain as a whole. Each non-empty nucleus within the domain must contain the same value for frontness or backness. Consider the representations of two words: *kızlar* and *müdürler*, where we disregard the syllabic structure and concentrate on the melody only.

[3]
```
    x   x   x x     x      x   x
    |   |   | |     |      |
    k  high z l  non-high  r
        _____/
             back

  x   x     x   x    x x     x     x x
  |   |     |   |    | |     |     |
  m round   d round  r l  non-high  r
      |         |
     high     high
       _____/_____/
              front
```

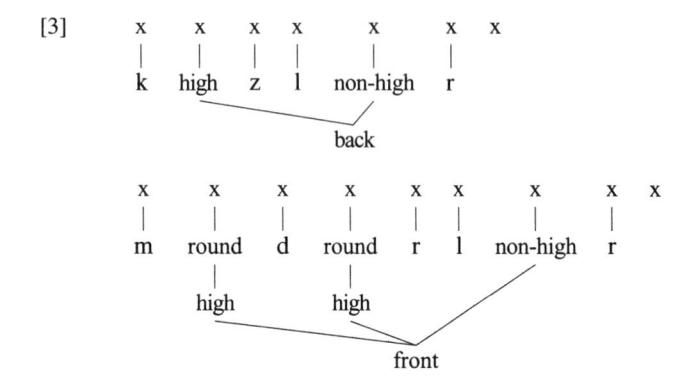

The representation makes it clear that the frontness/backness property belongs to all the nuclei within a given domain *at the same time*. There is no phonological sense of priority or dominance where the vowel(s) of the stem might be said to change or modify the vowel of the suffix. Given *Frontness Harmony*, well-formed Turkish words must be vocalically uniform with respect to the frontness/backness property; it is not the case that a front vowel *becomes* back or vice versa – vowels are what they are because words conform to the phonological patterns of the language, in this case, to the existence of frontness harmony. The fact that we find two forms of the plural suffix is a result of the phonological regularity (*Frontness Harmony*) which forces *-ler* to follow front vowel stems, and causes *-lar* to attach to stems with a back vowel. From this perspective there is no question as to whether one of the two variants is more basic: both of them must be assumed to exist in the morphology (or the lexicon) but *Frontness Harmony* ensures that the required one appears in the required shape when combined with other morphemes.

Frontness harmony represents one of the ways that vowel adjustment operates in Turkish. That *Frontness Harmony* does not exhaust the phenomenon can be seen when the genitive ending is attached to the singular and the plural of nouns in [1]. Consider [4].

[4]
a.   adamın [ada'mɯn] 'man'   adamların [adamla'rɯn]
           çocukun [tʃodʒu'kun] 'child'   çocukların [tʃodʒukla'rɯn]
           otun [ot'un] 'grass'   otların [otla'rɯn]
           kızın [kɯ'zɯn] 'girl'   kızlar [kɯzla'rɯn]
b.   elin [e'lin] 'hand'   ellerin [elle'rin]
           itin [i'tin] 'dog'   itlerin [itle'rin]
           müdürlün [mydyr'lyn] 'director'   müdürlerin [mydyrle'rin]
           sözün [sœ'zyn] 'word'   sözlerin [sœzle'rin]

The genitive suffix appears in four different phonetic shapes: [in, ɯn, yn, un], i.e. it contains a high vowel followed by the dental nasal. The vowel can be front or back, rounded or unrounded. We have already established a principle accounting for the front–back variation, namely *Frontness Harmony*: the genitive ending appears as [in] or [yn] when the preceding vowel is front, and as [ɯn, un] after a back vowel. Thus far the genitive suffix merely confirms what we know on other grounds. What needs to be accounted for is the rounding variation found on top of the front–back alternation. Additionally we would like to have a reason for the existence of four genitive variants in the singular but only two in the plural, if we assume that we are dealing with a single suffix.

An inspection of the forms in [4] reveals that the vowel of the suffix is round exclusively when the preceding vowel is round. This provides an answer to the

122 *Some segmental regularities*

second of our questions: since the plural suffix contains a non-round vowel, either [e] or [a], the following genitive suffix also contains a non-round one. The absence of a round vowel in the genitive plural is simply due to the fact that the plural suffix precedes the genitive.

The presence of a round vowel after another round one points to the existence of *Rounding Harmony*, similar to *Frontness Harmony*. Unlike *Frontness Harmony*, however, *Rounding Harmony* is not of general applicability, i.e. it is possible for vowels within a word to differ in rounding: the plurals of *çocuk* and *müdür* are a case in point, since the suffix contains non-round vowels: *çocuklar müdürler*. *Rounding Harmony* appears to prevail with high vowels only. The generalisation can be formulated as follows:

[5]   *Rounding Harmony*
        Within a phonological domain a high vowel shares its rounding with the preceding vowel.

Thus *Rounding Harmony* is restricted to high vowels only and its effects can be observed when the genitive suffix is attached to the singular, as in the left-hand column words in [4], where the high vowel of the suffix directly follows a round or non-round vowel in the stem. In the plural the genitive suffix follows the plural morpheme which has a non-round vowel, hence the genitive is also non-round. In other words, in *sözler* 'words' there is no rounding harmony because the vowel of the plural suffix is non-high.

The two types of vocalic harmony differ in their generality; as a result vowels in a word must agree in frontness but may differ in rounding. Consider the representations of the genitive singular and plural of *müdür* 'director', namely *müdürün*, *müdürlerin*.

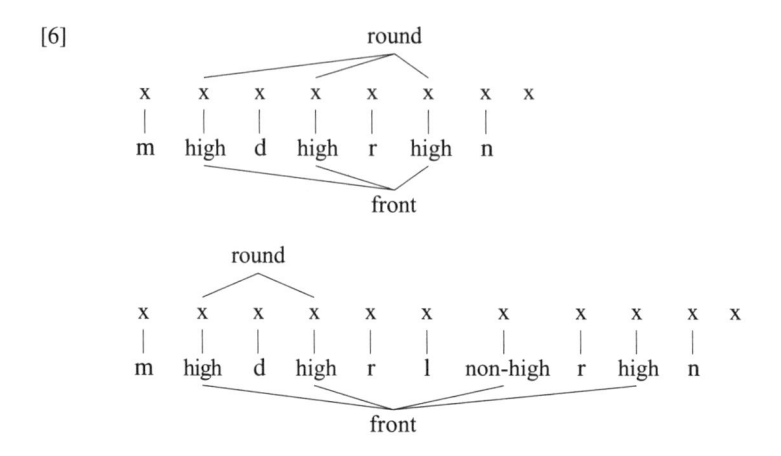

[6]
```
                    round
                 ‾‾‾‾‾‾‾‾‾‾‾
      x    x    x    x    x    x    x    x
      |    |    |    |    |    |    |    |
      m   high  d  high   r  high   n
                    ‾‾‾‾‾‾‾‾‾‾‾
                    front
```

```
              round
            ‾‾‾‾‾‾‾
   x    x    x    x    x    x    x    x    x    x    x
   |    |    |    |    |    |    |    |    |    |    |
   m  high   d  high   r    l  non-high  r  high   n
            ‾‾‾‾‾‾‾‾‾‾‾‾‾‾‾‾‾‾‾‾‾‾‾‾‾‾‾‾‾‾‾
                         front
```

In both cases all vowels within a given domain have the same value for frontness; in the first case the vowels are all high, hence they also agree in rounding. In the second case rounding agreement holds for the first two vowels because the second of them is high. The last high vowel in the domain is not rounded, just like the preceding vowel, thereby conforming to *Rounding Harmony*.

Turkish vowel harmonies illustrate the ways in which vowels in neighbouring nuclei can depend on each other. The existence of vowel harmony is a language-specific property and although it is commonly found in the languages of the world, it is by no means general: in Indo-European languages, for example, it is hardly found at all. Possibly, phenomena such as the various umlaut modifications in early Germanic languages could be regarded as the realisation of a tendency towards partial vowel harmony. Even in the languages where harmony appears on a general scale, its patterns can differ significantly: *Rounding Harmony*, which, as we have seen, is restricted to high vowels only in Modern Turkish, is more general in other Turkic languages, while it is completely absent in Old Turkish. Thus present-day *sözü* [sœ'zy] 'word, acc.', where *-ü* is the marker of the accusative, conforms, as expected, to both Frontness and Backness Harmony. The Old Turkish form was *sözi* [sœ'zi] with frontness observed but rounding disregarded; *Rounding Harmony* was established in the language after the Old Turkish period. The presence of a particular harmony and its scope are language-particular parameters which have to be determined independently for each language. Vowel harmony as a vocalic phenomenon has certain interesting implications for the structure of phonological representations. Note that the harmony sharing found among successive nuclei is completely insensitive to the presence of intervening consonants. The last pronounced vowel of *müdürler*, i.e. [e], shares its frontness with the other vowels in the word although it is separated from the immediately preceding one by the consonant sequence [rl]. This is generally the case in Turkish: vowels harmonise in the required fashion regardless of what consonants separate them. Although consonants and vowels follow each other in a sequence, vowel harmony involves vocalic elements only, as if the consonants were not there. Somewhat metaphorically, we can say that consonants are transparent to harmony or that vowels can see each other despite the intervening consonants. Translating this metaphor into a phonological notion we must conclude that vowels (and consonants) constitute separate levels or tiers, where members of a given tier are adjacent to each other. We can go even further: roundness and frontness have been shown to constitute independent parameters of harmony, which means that these two properties must also be seen to operate on separate subtiers within the melody. Although we cannot go into the issue much further here, it is clear that the melodic tier must be seen as broken up into or consisting of independent subtiers. Contemporary phonology has devoted a lot of research to the study of tier structure.

6.3 Vowel reduction in English

What we have seen in the discussion of Turkish vowel harmony is a case where the quality of a vowel is not freely variable but depends on the quality of neighbouring vowels. Thus while the first or root vowel can be either back or front, rounded or unrounded, the vowels in successive nuclei follow strict constraints on the occurrence and combinability of such properties. There are other ways of curtailing the freedom of individual vowels to occur within a word, restrictions which affect both the quality and – as we will see in the next chapter – the quantity of vowels. Here we will consider some restrictions in English conditioned by factors other than the neighbouring vowels. Discussing the phonology of English inflectional endings in 2.6 we referred briefly to the so-called strong and weak forms of certain words. Let us take a closer look at them now.

The class comprises a group of very common grammatical or function words, consisting of prepositions, articles, pronouns, conjunctions, some adverbs and auxiliary verbs, e.g. *at, for, the, them, she, and, to, but, there, does, are*, etc. These words assume somewhat different forms when they appear in stressed and unstressed position. When stressed in a sentence, or when pronounced in isolation, they display the same quantitative and qualitative possibilities as ordinary lexical words, i.e. the vowels can be short or long and can vary in height and backness (frontness). When unstressed in connected speech, these words lose some of their consonants and the vocalic possibilities are markedly reduced to just [ɪ, ʊ, ə]. Consider some examples

[7]	in isolation	in connected speech
	at [æt]	at home [ət 'həʊm]
	the [ðiː]	the apple [ðɪ 'æpl]
		the pear [ðə 'peə]
	and [ænd]	you and I ['juː ən 'aɪ]
		bread and butter ['bred n 'bʌtə]
	to [tuː]	he wants to eat [hiː 'wɒnts tʊ 'iːt]
		he wants to go [hiː 'wɒnts tə 'gəʊ]
	but [bʌt]	but you must [bət juː 'mʌst]
	them [ðem]	show them to me ['ʃəʊ ðəm tə miː]
		go with them ['gəʊ 'wɪð əm]
	she [ʃiː]	will she come [wɪl ʃi 'kʌm]
	for [fɔː]	for better or worse [fə 'betər ɔː 'wɜːs]
		wait for us ['weɪt fərʌs/frʌs]
	does [dʌz]	what does it mean ['wɒt dəz ɪt 'miːn]
	are [ɑː]	they are gone [ðeɪ ə 'gɒn]

When pronounced in isolation the words are said to appear in their strong forms while in connected speech they display weak forms. What needs to be emphasised here is the close connection that exists between certain phonetic shapes and word stress. In particular, the strong–weak distinction demonstrates that vowel quality, and to some extent also quantity, depends on the position of a nucleus within a word. In stressed positions we find all vowels with the exception of schwa [ə]; in unstressed positions, on the other hand, schwa is the dominant segment (although [ɪ, i] and [ʊ] can also be found, even if [ʊ] is rare). In general, unstressed positions can support fewer vowels than stressed ones. This is not to say that the asymmetry is absolute: vowels other than [ə, ɪ, i] can be found in unstressed positions, e.g. *syntax* [ˈsɪntæks], *kudos* [ˈkjuːdɒs], *contents* [ˈkɒntents], *phoneme* [ˈfəʊniːm], *placard* [ˈplækɑːd], *ballet* [ˈbæleɪ], *acorn* [ˈeɪkɔːn]. The number of such words is quite small as compared to those with schwa or [ɪ, i] in the unstressed position. The existence of strong and weak forms, although limited to a few dozen words, is very significant since these are some of the most basic words of the language, with a very high frequency of use. For this reason we will assume that the term **vowel reduction** denotes a productive phonological regularity in the language. It basically means that out of the set of nuclei appearing in stressed positions only a small subset is tolerated in unstressed ones, or, putting it another way, the unstressed position has its own melodic characteristics such as the appearance of schwa [ə] there. Somewhat metaphorically, the different vocalic qualities of the stressed positions get squeezed or reduced to a vowel which is normally described as having an indistinct quality: it is neither front nor back, neither high nor low. It occupies the central position in the phonetic vowel diagram. The articulatory possibilities available for producing vowels are reduced. This results in a limited inventory of segments which can appear in unstressed positions. Rather than thinking that any one vowel is specifically reduced to some other one, as was presumably the case in the historical development of the language, we can regard this phenomenon as resulting from a static generalisation which says that unstressed positions in English favour the vowels [ə, ɪ, i]. Of these [i] can only appear in word-final position. In other words, full vowels are more or less barred from unstressed position and restricted to stressed ones. Since schwa is, conversely, barred from the stressed position, we can regard it as the prototypical vowel of the unstressed position.

The requirement that unstressed positions in English support a limited number of vowels must be seen in the context of the complexity of English word stress. This, as is known, is not attached to any one particular nucleus, hence words of the same melodic composition can differ in where they place the stress, e.g. the verb *billow* [ˈbɪləʊ] vs. the preposition *below* [bɪˈləʊ]. Furthermore, when certain suffixes are attached to simplex words, the stress in the two words need not be in the same position, e.g. *stupid* [ˈstjuːpɪd] – *stupidity* [stjuːˈpɪdəti]. When the stress is placed on different syllables in morphologically related words, it frequently happens that the unstressed schwa in one word corresponds to some non-reduced vowel in the other. The vowels most often involved in such alternations with [ə]

126   *Some segmental regularities*

are the short non-high ones, i.e. [e, ɒ, æ, ʌ] as illustrated in [8a–d], although long vowels and diphthongs can also be found, as in [8e].

[8]
a.   [ə] alternates with [e]
      torrent ['tɒrənt]   torrential [tə'renʃəl]
      element ['elɪmənt]   elementary [elɪ'mentəri]
b.   [ə] alternates with [ɒ]
      phonology [fə'nɒlədʒi]   phonological [fɒnə'lɒdʒɪkəl]
      harmony ['hɑːməni]   harmonic [hɑː'mɒnɪk]
c.   [ə] alternates with [æ]
      validity [və'lɪdəti]   valid ['vælɪd]
      addition [ə'dɪʃn]   add [æd]
d.   [ə] alternates with [ʌ]
      autumn ['ɔːtəm]   autumnal [ɔː'tʌmnəl]
      subject [səb'dʒekt] 'vb.'   subject ['sʌbdʒekt] 'n.'
e.   [ə] alternates with a complex nucleus
      dramatic [drə'mætɪk]   drama ['drɑːmə]
      comedy ['kɒmədi]   comedian [kə'miːdɪən]
      protest [prə'test] 'vb.'   protest ['prəʊtest] 'n.'
      modern ['mɒdən]   modernity [mɒ'dəːnəti]
      crematorium [kremə'tɔːriəm]   cremate [krə'meɪt]

In certain cases alternations may involve more than one vowel: in *torrent – torrential* schwa alternates with [ɒ] in the first syllable and with [e] in the second; in *comedy – comedian* schwa alternates with [ɒ] and [iː]. In other words, different full vowels in stressed positions correspond to [ə], depending on where the stress is. To visualise the relations more clearly, consider the representations of the words *torrent* and *torrential*. In the diagrams below, the underlined emboldened **N** denotes a stressed nucleus.

[9]
a.
```
     O   R    O   R         O   R
     |   |    |   \         |   |
     |   N    |    N        |   N
     |   |    |    |\       |   |
     x   x    x   x  x      x   x
     |   |    |   |  |      |   |
     t   ɒ    r   ə  n      t
```

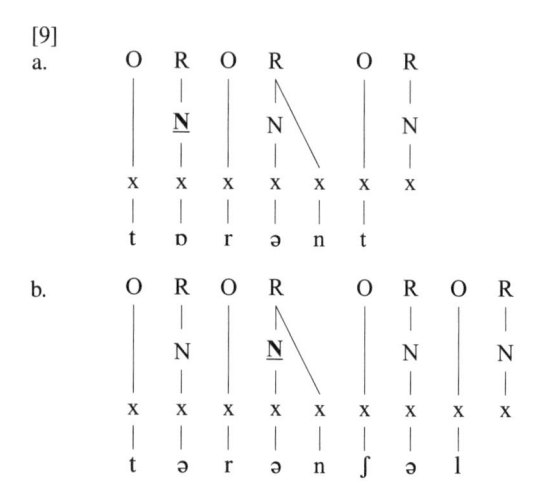

b.
```
     O   R    O   R         O   R    O   R
     |   |    |   \         |   |    |   |
     |   N    |   N         |   N    |   N
     |   |    |   |\        |   |    |   |
     x   x    x   x  x      x   x    x   x
     |   |    |   |  |      |   |    |   |
     t   ə    r   ə  n      ʃ   ə    l
```

6.3 Vowel reduction in English

Restricting ourselves to the first two nuclei we note that schwa in one corresponds to a full vowel in the other. The word *corresponds* should be taken literally, as there is no sense in which one vowel can be said to *become* another, any more than one can say that zero or nothing in [9a] becomes the suffix [əl] of [9b]. *torrent* and *torrential* are separate words, which must be entered as such in the lexicon of the language. Similarly we must say that the two words have separate phonological representations: what these have in common is the fact that full vowels appear in the stressed nuclei, and schwa in the unstressed ones. Their partial similarity is due to the fact that the words are morphologically related to each other, hence the phonological closeness, and the semantic affinity for that matter. From the synchronic point of view the two shapes ['tɒrənt] and [tə'renʃ] coexist in the language and their actual appearance is conditioned by the neighbouring suffixes, if any; thus ['tɒrənt] appears in isolation and when followed by the plural suffix *-s*, while [tə'renʃ] must be followed by the adjectival suffix *-al*, which may be followed by the adverbial *-ly*, i.e. *torrentially* [tə'renʃəli].

What, then, is vowel reduction? Despite the implications carried by the traditional term it is nothing more than a generalisation about the inability of unstressed syllables to support full vowels. Simultaneously it singles out the 'reduced' [ə] as the principal occupant of the unstressed positions. Thus schwa has to be recognised as an independent phonological segment in English, and not merely as the contextual realisation of some other 'full' vowel. It may be lexically related to a number of other vowels, as the cases of alternation show, but alternations are limited and in most instances schwa alternates with nothing, i.e. it remains stable. Consider the following words:

[10] obtain [əb'teɪn] rumba ['rʌmbə] America [ə'merɪkə]
 agent ['eɪdʒənt] London ['lʌndən] sofa ['səʊfə]
 consist [kən'sɪst] submit [səb'mɪt] parrot ['pærət]
 octopus ['ɒktəpəs] darken ['dɑːkən] chapel ['tʃæpəl]
 doctor ['dɒktə] talker ['tɔːkə] profound [prə'faʊnd]

The schwa which appears in these and numerous other words shows no lexical relatedness to anything, it is not involved in any alternations. If, as generally agreed, we bar spelling as a possible source of information about the phonological structure of words, the instances of schwa in [10] cannot be related to anything else. For this reason, schwa stands as a segment in its own right in English; the regularity referred to as vowel reduction restricts its occurrence to unstressed syllables only. This restriction is in itself no more puzzling than its converse, i.e. the fact that full vowels are by and large barred from unstressed positions. Vowel reduction simply says that the distribution of vowels is dependent upon stress.

Another problem which deserves mention in this context is the position of the vowel [ɪ] and its relatedness to schwa. Note first of all that this vowel can appear freely in both stressed and unstressed positions – words like *rigid* ['rɪdʒɪd], *prolific* [prə'lɪfɪk], *similarity* [sɪmɪ'lærəti] are common, and completely unremarkable. Among words which differ in the position of stress, there are some where the alternation [ɪ – ə] is possible [11a] and others where it is not [11b].

[11]
a.   rigid ['rɪdʒɪd]   rigidity [rɪ'dʒɪdəti], [rə'dʒɪdəti]
    physic ['fɪzɪk]   physician [fɪ'zɪʃən], [fə'zɪʃən]
    diplomat ['dɪpləmæt]   diplomacy [dɪ'pləʊməsi], [də'pləʊməsi]
b.   picture ['pɪktʃə]   pictorial [pɪk'tɔːrɪəl]
    diphthong ['dɪfθɒŋ]   diphthongal [dɪf'θɒŋgəl]

The alternations between [ɪ] in stressed and schwa in unstressed positions are far less consistent than those involving other vowels. There is quite a lot of variation as far as individual speakers are concerned, and the choice also depends upon the nature of the affix where the vowel appears. It has been observed that middle aged and young RP speakers distinctly prefer the forms with schwa, which seems to reflect a clear tendency towards generalising [ə] and eliminating [ɪ] from the unstressed position. Thus the suffixes *-ity*, as in *rigidity*, *validity*, and *-ness*, as in *strangeness*, *happiness*, are more common when pronounced [əti] and [nəs] than [ɪti] and [nɪs]. The inflectional endings *-ed*, *-es*, on the other hand, when pronounced with a vowel (see chapter 2), predominantly contain [ɪ] in RP, although in other varieties of English schwa may be the preferred option. The implication is that [ɪ] and schwa are independent phonological units; words such as *illusion* [ɪ'luːʒən] and *allusion* [ə'luːʒən] or *Lenin* ['lenɪn] and *Lennon* ['lenən] are, in general, kept distinct.

The tendency to replace unstressed [ɪ] by schwa is checked word-finally. Consider again the nominalising suffix *-ity*: in conservative RP this is pronounced [ɪtɪ], with two occurrences of the vowel [ɪ]. The predominant tendency among middle aged and young RP speakers is to replace the first [ɪ] by schwa and the second one by a short, tense [i], hence *validity* is most commonly pronounced [və'lɪdəti]. The final [ɪ] is never replaced by schwa and that is why the word is never pronounced *[və'lɪdətə]. The general replacement of final [ɪ] by [i] has been mnemonically termed *happy-tensing* as it takes place in *happy* ['hæpi]. Word-finally, then, we typically find either [ə] or [i] in unstressed syllables.

We conclude that schwa, although the principal occupant of the unstressed position in English at present, is definitely not the only one. It can be seen to be consistently expanding its influence there by replacing the vowel [ɪ] in non-final positions. The coexistence within the same dialect of both vowels indirectly attests to the independent position of schwa, which cannot be viewed as merely due to weakening, as has sometimes been claimed in the past.

6.3 Vowel reduction in English

Finally, let us note that in English schwa followed by a sonorant, in particular by [l, n, r], can alternate with a syllabic sonorant, marked by ˌ. This is illustrated below.

[12] torrential [tə'renʃəl] or [tə'renʃl̩]
      button ['bʌtən] or [bʌtn̩]
      memory ['meməri] or ['memr̩i]

The details of this regularity are complicated and involve idiosyncratic details – with some words the presence of schwa is hardly ever found in natural speech, e.g. *little* is normally [lɪtl̩] rather than *?[lɪtəl]. What is of direct interest for us is the equivalence between a pronounced vowel followed by a sonorant, and a syllabic sonorant unaccompanied by a phonetically present vowel. The very notion of the syllabicity of consonants suggests that the syllabic tier is independent of the melodic one, hence a vowel may be suppressed but the nucleus as a syllabic unit remains intact. In the case of English syllabic consonants we may assume that the melody of the sonorant is attached to the nucleus and the following onset at the same time. In [9b] we have a representation of the word *torrential* which is reproduced here for convenience as [13a]; in [13b] the alternative pronunciation is reflected, with syllabic [l̩] instead of schwa.

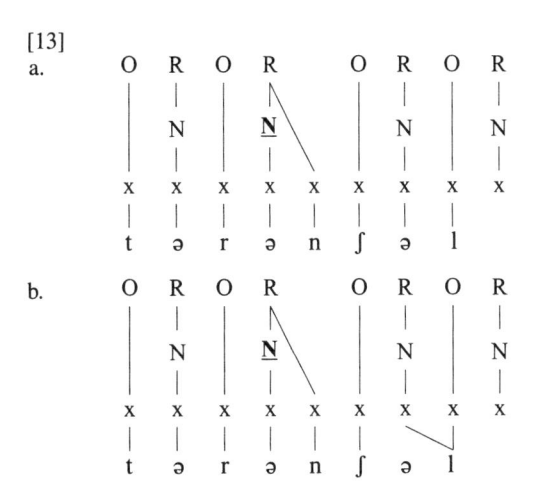

[13]
a. O   R   O   R   O   R   O   R
        | |\ | |
        N   N\   N   N
        | | \ | |
    x   x   x   x   x   x   x   x   x
    | | | | | | | | |
    t   ə   r   ə   n   ʃ   ə   l

b. O   R   O   R   O   R   O   R
        | |\ | |
        N   N\   N   N
        | | \ | |
    x   x   x   x   x   x   x   x   x
    | | | | | | ↘
    t   ə   r   ə   n   ʃ   l

The schwa in [13b] which is not associated to a skeletal position remains phonetically inaudible. Although in a certain sense the suppression of schwa is a case of vowel reduction *par excellence*, it reflects a different type of phonological regularity than vowels alternating with schwa in unstressed positions. Here we are dealing with a regularity which is phonologically conditioned in the sense that given one representation we can predict the other. Faced with the form [ɪg'zɑːmpl̩] we know that it must be related to [ɪgˈzɑːmpəl]; the traditional vowel reduction alternations, on the other hand, offer no way of predicting which full vowel an individual schwa will alternate with. In fact, in most cases, it will not alternate with anything. The information about the presence of schwa in the representation of a word is to be sought in the lexicon; related forms of words – morphological alternations – with full vowels corresponding to schwas are also present in the lexicon. The phonological generalisation of so-called vowel reduction in English is a statement about the distributional properties of specific vowels. It is a valid generalisation about the phonological structure of the language which has been established by the examination of the existing patterns of vowel distribution. Apart from being a static statement it does not effect any changes itself: no vowel is reduced to any other if only because in most cases we would not know what the source vowel could be (cf. the examples in [10]). This conclusion holds for English only, and is based entirely on the data of this language. As we will see in a later part of this chapter, vowel reduction in Russian has specific properties over and above the fundamental differences between vowels that appear in stressed and unstressed positions.

6.4 Polish nasal vowels

So far we have seen that neighbouring vowels may interact and also that their distribution may depend upon the position they occupy with respect to the stressed nucleus. It is to be expected that vowels will also relate to neighbouring consonants; a relatively simple case of such interaction comes from so-called nasal vowels in Polish. This is the only modern Slavic language with such vowels. Studies on the subject mention two nasal vowels, a mid front and a mid back one (spelt ę and ą respectively). Whether the two vowels are really nasal is something that needs to be determined, as do their phonological properties within the structure of Polish. Let us look at some facts first.

The phonetically nasal vowels [ɛ̃] or [ɔ̃] are the oral vowels [ɛ] and [ɔ] accompanied by nasal resonance – in other words, the configuration of speech organs needed for the oral vowel additionally includes the lowering of the soft palate which allows the air to escape through the nasal cavity. Vowel nasalisation is found when the oral articulatory gesture is synchronised with the nasal gesture for its duration. We encounter a typical instantiation of nasal vowels in French where *lait* [lɛ] 'milk' and *sort* [sɔʁ] 'fate' differ in the way just described from *lin* [lɛ̃] 'linen' and *bon* [bɔ̃] 'good'. Viewed in such terms, the Polish nasal nuclei qualify only partially for the label 'nasal vowels'. A striking characteristic of the Polish nasal nuclei is their diphthongal nature, with nasality spread unevenly over the oral gesture: it is only the second or semivocalic part that is nasal, while the

6.4 Polish nasal vowels

vocalic unit remains oral. A reasonably adequate transcription of the two nasal nuclei is [ɛʷ] for the front diphthong and [ɔʷ] for the back one; in the ensuing discussion we will use the terms *nasal vowel*, *nasal diphthong* and *nasal nucleus* interchangeably. Some examples of such nuclei are provided in [14]; both here and throughout this section we transcribe only the directly relevant parts of the Polish words to avoid unnecessary confusion.

[14]
a. w[ɔʷs] 'moustache'   m[ɔʷʃ] 'husband'   f[ɔʷf]el 'brat'
   wi[ɔʷz]ać 'bind'   d[ɔʷʒ]yć 'strive'   w[ɔʷv]óz 'valley'
   gał[ɔʷɕ] 'branch'   w[ɔʷx]ać 'smell, vb.'
b. t[ɛʷs]knić 'yearn'   w[ɛʷʃ]yć 'sniff, vb.'   w[ɛʷx] 'smell, n.'
   wi[ɛʷz]y 'bond, nom. pl.'   pot[ɛʷʒ]ny 'powerful'   g[ɛʷɕ] 'goose'
   wi[ɛʷz]ień 'prisoner'

The examples in [14a] contain the back nasal nucleus, and those in [14b] the front one. A further inspection of the examples reveals that in all cases the nasal nucleus is followed by a fricative consonant. Admittedly, the nasal diphthongs can also appear at the end of the word, although the number of such cases is limited, as they are employed exclusively as exponents of a few inflectional endings; the significance of this distribution will be made clear in the later part of the discussion and for the moment we will disregard it. What is true is that within lexical morphemes, the two nasal vowels are invariably followed by a spirant. What is more, they can never appear before any other consonant. What about the other consonants then? Supposing that for morphological reasons a nasal diphthong were to be followed by a non-spirant – what could we expect? To answer this question let us consider a few alternations involving nasal diphthongs in such contexts.

[15]
a. ksi[ɔʷʃ]ka 'book'   ksi[ɔŋk] 'augmen. gen. pl.'   ksi[ɛn̦dz]e 'dat. sg.'
                             ksi[ɛŋg]a 'nom. sg.'
b. mosi[ɛʷʒ]ny 'brass, adj.,'   mosi[ɔn̪ts] 'n.'
c. pot[ɛʷʒ]ny 'powerful'   pot[ɛŋg]a 'power'   pot[ɛn̦dz]e 'dat. sg.'
d. pieni[ɔʷʒ]ek 'coin'   pieni[ɔn̦dz]e 'money'
e. kr[ɔʷʒ]ek 'circle, dim.' kr[ɔŋk] 'idem'
f. ksi[ɛʷʒ]e 'priest, voc.'   ksi[ɛn̦dz]a 'gen. sg.'
g. r[ɔʷɕ]a 'hand, express.' r[ɔŋk] 'gen. pl.'   r[ɔnʃ]ka 'dim.'
h. ksi[ɔʷʒ]ę 'prince'   ksi[ɛɲtɕ]a 'gen. sg.'

In what follows we shall concentrate on the nasal element of the diphthong and shall disregard the occasional front–back vowel alternations (examples [15a – b, h]); these we consider to be outside the domain of phonological regularities. Nasal diphthongs appear regularly before a following fricative, as in the left-hand column above. This is in accordance with what we observed above and illustrated in [14]. When a non-fricative appears after the nasal nucleus as a result of some morphological regularity, the diphthong is not possible before it and instead a nasal stop is found. The middle column illustrates that the nasal stop is either velar, as in [15a, c, e, g], or palatal, as in [15h]. The right-hand column shows that the nasal can be either a dental stop [15a–f], or an alveolar one, as in [15g]. In this way we can see that a nasal diphthong, say [ɛʷ], is equivalent to a sequence of a vowel and a nasal stop consonant, i.e. [ɛŋ, ɛɲ, ɛṇ, ɛn].

The nasal stop can be seen to appear in the context of a following stop obstruent, either a plosive or an affricate – we then have a stop before a stop. The place of articulation of the nasal is the same as the following stop – the two consonants must be homorganic, i.e. they share their place of articulation. The homorganicity of a Polish nasal and a following plosive was discussed in 4.7 and 5.4 – it amounts to the claim that the two consonants are directly adjacent on the skeletal tier. A slightly expanded version of Polish nasal place sharing is presented in [16].

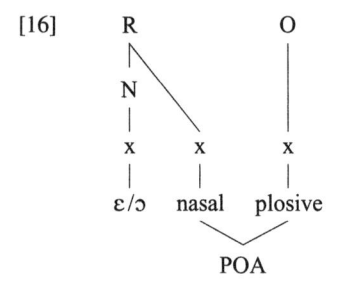

[16]
```
     R              O
    /|              |
   N |              |
   | \              |
   x  x             x
   |  |             |
  ɛ/ɔ nasal      plosive
        _____/
            POA
```

This representation states that if a nasal follows a mid vowel, then the following onset plosive and the nasal share their place of articulation.

We must turn now to the last outstanding issue in the interpretation of Polish nasal vowels, namely the melodic and syllabic structure of the nasal diphthongs [ɛʷ, ɔʷ]. These cannot be sequences of a nuclear vowel followed by a nasal consonant in the coda since then the nasal would need to be licensed by a following onset. However, as noted at the beginning of the discussion, nasal diphthongs are found not only before spirants but also, in a restricted number of cases, word-finally. Examples of prespirantal nasal diphthongs were offered in [14]; here are some cases of word-final diphthongs.

[17]   si[ɛʷ] 'reflexive pronoun'   mn[ɔʷ] 'I, instr. sg.'
       ci[ɛʷ] 'you, acc. sg.'   tob[ɔʷ] 'instr. sg.'
       trac[ɛʷ] 'I lose'   trac[ɔʷ] 'they lose'
       robot[ɛʷ] 'work, acc. sg.'   robot[ɔʷ] 'instr. sg.'
       jagni[ɛʷ] 'lamb'   drog[ɔʷ] 'dear, acc. sg. fem.'
       troch[ɛʷ] 'a little bit'   zreszt[ɔʷ] 'after all'

The nasal element of the diphthong cannot belong to the rhyme since there is no onset which would license it. It cannot belong to the onset of the next syllable, since then it would not make up a diphthong. The only remaining possibility is that the vocalic oral and the nasal element make up a single nucleus, i.e.:

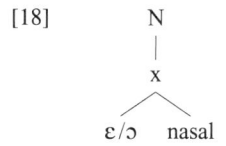

[18]
```
            N
            |
            x
           / \
         ɛ/ɔ  nasal
```

Nasal diphthongs are single, non-branching nuclei and for this reason we have selected the transcription with the raised nasal element, i.e. [ɛʷ̃, ɔʷ̃] rather than [ɛw̃, ɔw̃], which would imply a sequence of two independent segments. It is worth emphasising that oral and nasal elements are sequentially distinct, with one following the other, even though the nucleus is non-branching. Such complex, non-branching nuclei are called short diphthongs (recall the discussion in 2.3).

Being single nuclei, nasal diphthongs behave like all other vowels in that they can appear word-finally and do not need to be licensed by a following onset. Word-internally their occurrence is restricted to the neighbourhood of a following spirant. This, of course, means that nasal diphthongs are a vanishing species in Modern Polish, a conclusion which is in keeping with what is otherwise known about nasal vowels in the history of Slavic. As we mentioned at the outset, Polish is the only modern Slavic language which preserves nasal vowels to some extent. The extent is quite limited and even here there are indications that nasal vowels are unstable. In particular, the front vowel tends to lose its nasalisation in the word-final position. As a result all the left-hand column words in [17] have an alternative – and more natural – pronunciation without the nasal element, i.e.:

[19]   si[ɛʷ̃] 'reflexive pronoun'   or   si[ɛ]
       ci[ɛʷ̃] 'you, acc. sg.'   ci[ɛ]
       trac[ɛʷ̃] 'I lose'   trac[ɛ]
       robot[ɛʷ̃] 'work, acc. sg.'   robot[ɛ]
       jagni[ɛʷ̃] 'lamb'   jagni[ɛ]
       troch[ɛʷ̃] 'a little bit'   troch[ɛ]

The simplification of the front nasal diphthong is yet another step in the process of nasal vowel elimination. This happened in other Slavic languages and many regional varieties of Polish some centuries ago but standard Polish still preserves some of the properties of the old system. The representation of these diphthongs we suggest in [18] supplies some rationale for the elimination process: short diphthongs are complex structures and it is to be expected that they will

134   *Some segmental regularities*

undergo simplification. Before plosives such complex structures were broken up into rhyme–onset sequences as a result of a historical process a few centuries ago; in the modern language the complex structures are only tolerated prespirantally, and, to a limited extent, domain-finally. Thus nasal diphthongs and sequences of an oral vowel followed by a nasal consonant and a homorganic plosive are nasal vowels only in the historical sense; in the present-day language they require different representations. Because they can be traced back to a common historical source, it is unsurprising that they display a degree of interaction such as involvement in alternations illustrated in [15]. Such alternations cannot be taken as evidence that they are single units of representation any more than alternations between [aɪ] and [ɪ] in English (e.g. *wise – wisdom, dine – dinner*) support the claim that these nuclei should be regarded as phonologically related in the present-day language.

The example of the Polish nasal vowels shows that the interpretation of vocalic nuclei may depend upon the consonants surrounding them. Vowel–consonant interaction is a permanent and recursive phonological phenomenon found in the languages of the world. The specific nature of this interaction is language-dependent and needs to be studied individually for each language.

6.5   Obstruent sequences in Icelandic

In 3.3 we discussed preaspiration in Modern Icelandic, a phenomenon where the glottal fricative [h] precedes an unaspirated plosive in specified contexts. One of the contexts where this is manifested involves an expected or potential sequence of two identical aspirated plosives, i.e. a geminate. To illustrate, let us repeat a simple example.

The adjective *sætur* [saiːtʰʏr] 'sweet' contains the suffix of the masculine nominative singular *-ur* [ʏr]; the neuter singular ending *-t* [tʰ] is attached to the stem *sæt-*, hence we should expect to find there a sequence of identical consonants i.e. *sætt* *[saitʰtʰ]. This does not happen, and what we find is the form *sætt* [saiht], i.e. one where [h] precedes an unaspirated plosive, a configuration that is traditionally referred to as a preaspirated consonant. What is significant here is the fact that a geminate consisting of aspirated plosives is impossible, although unaspirated sequences are tolerated without any problems and transcribed as long consonants, e.g. *fæddur* [faitːʏr] 'born', *Sigga* [sɪkːa] 'fem. name', *labba* [lapːa] 'stroll'.

While sequences of identical aspirated obstruents are not permitted, we might want to ask whether dissimilar plosives can follow each other. Consider cases where the adjectival neuter nominative singular suffix is attached to stems ending in consonants other than [tʰ], bearing in mind that *-ur* is the ending of the masculine nominative singular. Alternations of short and long vowels should be disregarded for the moment as they will be discussed at length in the following chapter.

[20]   ríkur [riːkʰʏr] 'rich'   ríkt [rixt]
         mjúkur [mjuːkʰʏr] 'soft'   mjúkt [mjuxt]
         djúpur [tjuːpʰʏr] 'deep'   djúpt [tjuft]
         sleipur [sleiːpʰʏr] 'slippery'   sleipt [sleift]

The right-hand column neuter adjectives show that corresponding to the final plosive of the stem as seen in the masculine form – either [kʰ] or [pʰ] – we have a spirant, [x] and [f] respectively. What would otherwise be a sequence of two aspirated plosives is pronounced as a combination of a spirant and a plosive. Additionally, the plosive in such sequences is unaspirated which is presumably due to a general constraint disallowing aspirated plosives after consonants. Just as preaspiration effectively eliminates aspirated plosive geminates, the examples in [20] show that the language disallows aspirated plosive sequences; what is accepted is a spirant–plosive sequence. In terms of syllable structure the spirant–plosive sequence is a combination of a coda and a following onset. Facts like these lead us to the conclusion that the coda position cannot be occupied by an aspirated plosive. Rather, a **spirantisation** constraint must be assumed to be at work in Icelandic which places a fricative congener of a plosive in the coda position if a plosive follows in the onset. The existence of a constraint like this explains why plosives cannot occupy the rhymal position. Let us look closely at the representations of the two forms of our adjective in [20].

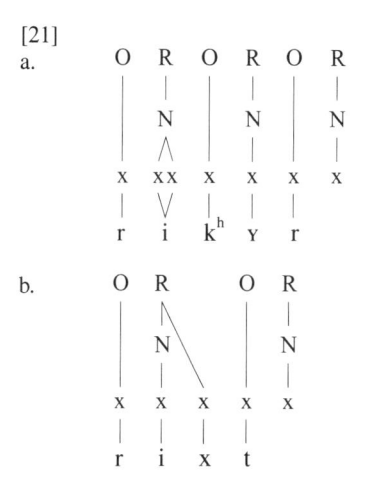

[21]
a.
```
       O   R    O   R    O   R
       |   |    |   |    |   |
           N        N        N
           /\       |        |
       x   x x  x   x    x   x
       |   \/   |_h  |   |   |
       r    i   k   ʏ    r
```

b.
```
       O   R        O   R
       |   /\       |   |
           N \      N
           |  \     |
       x   x   x    x   x
       |   |   |    |   |
       r   i   x    t
```

Note that the aspirated velar plosive [kʰ] marks the end of the stem in [21a]; syllabically it constitutes the onset, being licensed by the second nucleus in a word which has three nuclei. In [21b] there are only two syllables – the plosive marking the neuter gender occupies the second onset and is preceded by a velar spirant. The spirant corresponds to the velar plosive of the masculine form. The different syllabifications are motivated by the fact that the vowel is short in the neuter form and long in the masculine one – Icelandic vowel length will be discussed in the next chapter. The representations indicate that the alternations between aspirated plosives and voiceless spirants follow from the existence of the spirantisation constraint which bans plosive sequences in the language.

If the spirantisation constraint is general in the language, we should expect to see its effects outside the adjectival paradigm. This is indeed the case: one of the preterite suffixes is -*ti* [tʰɪ] which can be attached to stems ending in plosives. This results in alternations between a plosive in, say, the infinitive, and a spirant in past tense forms, as in [22].

[22] vaka [vaːkʰa] 'be awake'   vakti [vaxtɪ]
      reykja [reiːcʰa] 'smoke'   reykti [reixtɪ]
      lepja [lɛːpʰja] 'lap up'   lapti [laftɪ]
      kaupa [kʰœɪːpʰa] 'buy'   keypti [cʰeiftɪ]

As with the adjectives in [21], the relevant plosive occupies the onset position in the infinitive, while the consonant corresponding to it in the past tense is placed in the coda. Since the spirantisation constraint bans aspirated plosives in the coda, the spirantal congener of the plosive appears in its place. This is shown below.

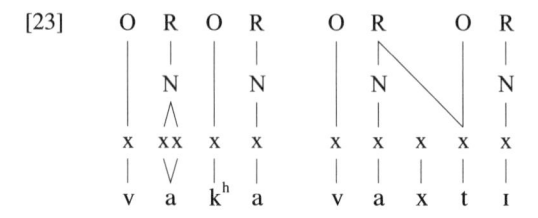

[23]
```
     O   R   O   R      O   R     O   R
     |   |   |   |      |   |\    |   |
     |   N   |   N      |   N \   |   N
     |  /\  |   |      |   |  \  |   |
     x  xx  x   x      x   x   x x   x
     |  \/  |   |      |   |   | |   |
     v   a  kʰ  a      v   a   x t   ɪ
```

The plosive–spirant relationship that the representations depict calls for some additional clarification. The two consonants have been called **congeners** since they are related in the sense of sharing a place of articulation: the [pʰ – f] pair are labial obstruents, while the [kʰ – x] pair are velar obstruents. There is a long-standing tradition in phonetic and phonological studies which views plosives as being stronger consonants than spirants, while voiceless (aspirated) plosives are regarded as the strongest of all consonants. The fact that aspirated plosives can appear in the onset position but are impossible as rhymal complements, may be interpreted to mean that the onset position is strong while the rhyme is relatively weaker. Spirants,

6.5 Obstruent sequences in Icelandic

being weaker than plosives, are tolerated in the rhyme. The change of a plosive into a spirant is consequently an example of weakening or **lenition**. However, *change* is fundamentally a historical or diachronic notion. Can we talk about the lenition of aspirated plosives as a synchronic phonological regularity in Modern Icelandic? The answer seems to be in the negative. Two brief arguments can be offered in support of this conclusion.

An inspection of the examples in [22], to which many more could be added, reveals that the past tense formation does not consist merely in the addition of a suffix accompanied by a putative spirantisation process, but also involves changes of the root vowels resulting in alternations like [ɛː – a] or [œiː – ei]. Such alternations, not unlike what we find in English examples such as *keep* [kiːp] – *kept* [kept], are unpredictable and the forms they appear in have distinct phonological representations. Since the shape of the infinitive has to be phonologically different from that of the past tense because of the vocalic unpredictability, there is no reason to assume that this different phonological shape should not include the consonants that are perceived as phonetically distinct. In other words, the stem in the past tense will end in a voiceless spirant and the plosive will be entirely absent from the representation.

The other argument is closely linked with this conclusion. Note that spirants can freely appear both in onsets and in codas. If the rhymal spirants were to come from plosives through lenition, this would mean that all such rhymal spirants are really plosives and would amount to an effective ban on spirants in rhymal positions. Such a conclusion would be peculiar, if not downright perverse, since what we do find in codas are precisely spirants. Alternatively, we could admit both spirants and plosives as possible in codas and stipulate that the latter are subject to the coda spirantisation. The problem here is that in most cases there would be no way of deciding whether in a given instance we are dealing with one or the other. To take an example, given words which show no alternations like *gifta* [cɪfta] 'marry' or *skipta* [scɪfta] 'change', we cannot know whether the spirant [f] is just a rhymal spirant or a plosive which has been lenited into a spirant. This would be similar to claiming that the schwa vowel in English words *parrot* ['pærət] and *sofa* ['səʊfə] has distinct representations or, put simply, is phonologically different in the two words. As we saw in 6.3 there are no reasons to think so – rather, words have to conform to the phonological regularities of the language as a whole. In the case of Icelandic this means that aspirated plosives are disallowed in the coda position while fricatives are possible there. This generalisation holds not only for native words but also for borrowings like those in [24].

[24]   doktor [dɔxtɔr] 'doctor'   lektor [lɛxtɔr] 'lecturer'
        Kopti [kʰɔftɪ] 'Copt(ic)'   kapteinn [kʰafteitn̥] 'captain'

138 *Some segmental regularities*

These examples show that lexical forms are well-formed if they conform to the existing phonological regularities. The specific regularity we have considered effectively banishes sequences of plosives from domain-internal positions in the language. The last reservation is necessary since plosive sequences may mechanically arise at word boundaries and within compounds. Consider the form *skiptapi* [scɪːp⁽ʰ⁾tʰapʰɪ] 'loss of a ship' where the medial consonantal cluster emerges at the juncture of two nouns: *skip* [scɪːpʰ] 'ship' and *tapi* [tʰaːpʰɪ] 'loss'; no matter whether domain structure is assigned to the constituent parts of the compound or not, its first part must end in an empty nucleus, which thus places the preceding plosive in the onset position with no violation of the spirantisation constraint.

A final point that we would like to make with reference to the Icelandic spirantisation is to indicate that the generalisation as we have formulated it – an aspirated plosive in the coda cannot precede another plosive in the onset – is not general enough and would need to be broadened in a comprehensive description of Modern Icelandic. It seems that the occurrence of rhymal plosives is also limited before onset spirants. As an example consider the ending *-s* marking the genitive singular of certain nouns and of masculine adjectives.

[25] bát [paːutʰ] 'boat, acc. sg.'   báts [paːut⁽ʰ⁾s] or [pausː]
      skip [scɪːpʰ] 'ship'   skips [scɪːp⁽ʰ⁾s] or [scɪfs]
      bak [paːkʰ] 'back'   baks [paːk⁽ʰ⁾s] or [paxs]
      slíkur [sliːkʰʏr] 'such'   slíks [sliːk⁽ʰ⁾s] or [slixs]

The genitives admit of two possible pronunciations. First there is the more careful or somewhat studied variant containing a sequence of a plosive and a spirant. Side by side we find variants with a spirantised congener of the relevant plosive preceding the spirant of the genitive; when the stem-final consonant is dental, a long spirant appears in the genitive, as when *báts* is pronounced [pausː]. The two possible forms call for somewhat different representations of the nouns in the genitive: if an empty nucleus intervenes between the stem and the genitive ending, then the final consonant of the stem will occupy the onset position without violating the spirantisation constraint; additionally the stem vowel will be long (of which more in the following chapter). If a consonant fills the coda position, then the preceding nucleus can only host a short vowel, and the final consonant of the stem must be a spirant. Consider the alternative representations of the genitive of 'ship'.

[26]
a.
```
      O   R       O   R     O   R     O   R
      |\  |       |   |     |   |     |   |
      N \ |       N   |     N   |     N   |
      |  \|       |  /\     |   |     |   |
      x   x   x   x  x x    x   x     x   x
      |   |   |   |  \ /    |         |
      s   c   ɪ      p                s
```

b.

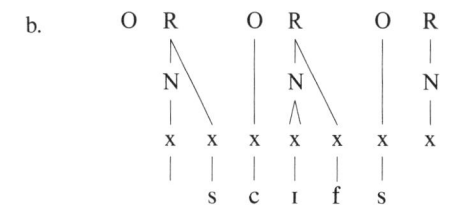

```
      O   R       O   R       O   R
          |\          |\          |
          N \         N \         N
          |  \        |\ \        |
      x   x   x   x   x   x       x
      |   |   |   |   |   |       |
      s   c   ɪ   f           s
```

The existence of two variant pronunciations may indicate that the genitive suffix is separated from the stem by a domain boundary in [26a]. In such a case the nucleus coming between the plosive [pʰ] and the fricative [s] of the ending would be domain-final. We do not have to take a stand at this point on what the domain structure of such forms is, since we are concerned with the coda spirantisation. What [26a] says is that the plosive does not violate the spirantisation constraint since it appears in the onset – whether the following nucleus is domain-final or domain-internal is immaterial as it has no bearing on the onsethood of the plosive. The plosive is in the onset on either interpretation.

On a more general level it is worth pointing out that the spirantisation constraint disallowing stop sequences in Icelandic has something in common with preaspiration and the optional spirantisation just discussed. In every case the rhymal coda position is allowed to support only a highly restricted set of melodies; specifically, preaspiration renders impossible a sequence of identical aspirated plosives (a geminate), spirantisation renders impossible a sequence of dissimilar aspirated plosives, and the optional aspiration disallows an aspirated plosive before a spirant. Each of these regularities has its own restrictions and peculiarities and for this reason we can only note that what unites them is a general tendency to rule out aspirated plosives from the rhyme of the syllable. The interaction between neighbouring consonants is crucially dependent upon their syllabic affiliation.

6.6 Russian vowel reduction

In 6.3 we presented an outline of problems relating to the so-called vowel reduction of English. Our conclusion was that synchronically there is little justification for any dynamic process of reduction; rather, stressed and unstressed nuclei are capable of supporting different sets of vowels. In particular, schwa tends to occupy unstressed positions to the exclusion of vowels which freely appear in stressed syllables. The addition of specific suffixes may result in stress being attached to different syllables, which in its turn leads to vocalic alternations between some stressed vowels and the schwa of the unstressed position, e.g. [æ – ə] in *add* [æd] – *addition* [ə'dɪʃn]. The decisive factor is the position of the stress rather than, for example, the nature of the surrounding consonants.

140 *Some segmental regularities*

We will now look at Russian and another case traditionally called *vowel reduction*, but one which involves both the position of the stress and the character of the neighbouring consonants. Before we look at the reduction itself we need to set the stage by presenting a few facts about Russian consonants and vowels.

Russian consonants fall into two broad classes: palatalised and velarised. The former, in accordance with the phonetic tradition, are transcribed by means of the diacritic ^{j} attached to the basic consonantal symbol, while the latter are normally devoid of any additional symbol. Thus a bilabial voiceless plosive is transcribed [p^j] when palatalised and [p] when velarised. Palatalised consonants are also impressionistically referred to as soft, and velarised ones as hard.

There are six vowels which can appear in stressed positions, namely the high vowels [i, u, ɨ] and the non-high vowels [e, o, a] – the middle one in each group is rounded. Examples are given in [27].

[27]
a. pit' [p^{j}it^j] 'drink, vb.'   dym [dɨm] 'smoke, n.'
   put' [put^j] 'path'   rot [rot] 'mouth'
   sad [sat] 'orchard'
b. pet' [p^{j}et^j] 'sing'   belyj ['b^{j}elɨj] 'white'
   tekst [t^{j}ekst] 'text'   den' [d^{j}en^j] 'day'
   sem' [s^{j}em^j] 'seven'
c. tercija ['tertsɨja] 'mediant'   centr [tsentr] 'centre'
   šest' [ʃes^{j}t^j] 'six'   celyj [tselɨj] 'whole'
   žest [ʒest] 'gesture'

There is a general regularity governing the appearance of some vowel–consonant combinations in Russian, namely the consonant preceding the front vowel [i] is palatalised, while that before [ɨ] is velarised. In other words, combinations such as [pi] or [p^{j}ɨ] are impossible. Before the other front vowel, i.e. [e] the situation is slightly more complex: the preceding consonants are predominantly palatalised [27b] although, as illustrated in [27c], velarised consonants can appear before [e] in unassimilated loans or when the preceding consonant belongs to the so-called hard group [ʒ, ʃ, ts] (a point that we will return to later on). Since palatalisation is achieved by the raising of the front part of the tongue towards the roof of the mouth, and velarisation by the raising of the back part of the tongue (towards the velum), we can conclude that palatalised or front consonants share their frontness with the front vowels [i, e], while velarised consonants share their backness with [ɨ]. This we shall refer to as the *Russian Frontness Sharing* constraint. It is not the case, however, that palatalised consonants may only be followed by front vowels. In fact, the vowels [u, o, a] may follow either palatalised or velarised consonants, e.g.:

[28]   tjur'my ['tʲurʲmɨ] 'prison, nom. pl.'   tur [tur] 'round, n.'
       nës [nʲos] 'he carried'   nos [nos] 'nose'
       djadi ['dʲadʲi] 'uncle, nom. pl.'   dast [dast] '(s)he will give'

What can be said then about the six **tonic**, or stress-bearing, Russian vowels is that only three of them are fully independent, in the sense that they are unconstrained by or unrelated to the nature of the preceding consonant. **Atonic** nuclei, i.e. those that lack stress, present a very different situation, since in addition to the high vowels [i, ɨ, u] we also find there the central ones [ə, ʌ], which differ in the degree of openness (half-close [ə] as against half-open [ʌ]). It is usually claimed that at least two atonic positions need to be distinguished, namely the directly pretonic position versus all the remaining ones. These include both pretonic syllables separated by one or more vowels from the stressed position, and also post-tonic vowels. Following velarised consonants we find [ʌ] in the directly pretonic position, whereas [ə] is further removed from the stress centre, or is final. Consider some examples.

[29]   paroxoda [pərʌ'xodə] 'steamship, gen. sg.'
       barabana [bərʌ'banə] 'drum, gen. sg.'
       golova [gəlʌ'va] 'head'
       xorosho [xərʌ'ʃo] 'good'
       skovoroda [skəvərʌ'da] 'frying pan'
       skovorody ['skovərədɨ] 'frying pan, nom. pl.'
       osnovat' [ʌsnʌ'vatʲ] 'found'
       alfavit [ʌlfʌ'vʲit] 'alphabet'

The last two examples indicate that the vowel [ʌ] is not restricted to directly prestressed position only, but also appears word-initially where otherwise [ə] would be expected. The exact sounds which appear in specific positions constitute the subject matter of a detailed phonetic description of Russian, a task that we are not interested in pursuing here. What transpires is that in unstressed syllables we find variants of non-high, unrounded, non-front vowels which either follow hard consonants or appear initially. Phonetic detail or the narrow transcription can be determined by considering these additional factors (the distance from the stressed vowel, or the presence of a preceding consonant) and need not be included in a phonologically oriented representation. For this reason we will adopt a simplified or broad phonetic transcription where unstressed vowels in words such as those in [29] will be uniformly represented by means of the vowel [a], i.e. [para'xoda, bara'bana, gala'va, xara'ʃo, skavara'da, 'skovaradɨ, asna'vatʲ, alfa'vʲit]. This conscious simplification is a procedure not different in kind from using the same symbol [ɪ] in English words like *bit* [bɪt] and *bid* [bɪd], even though it is uncontroversial that the two vowels differ markedly in length.

142 *Some segmental regularities*

Russian, and English, unstressed nuclei can support a smaller number of vocalic units than nuclei in stressed positions – this is **vowel reduction**. In English it is basically [ɪ] and [ə] that are found in pre- and post-tonic position; in Russian the data display a wider range of possibilities. As we have just seen, the unstressed vowel is typically [a] after a hard consonant, i.e. in actual fact it is a cluster of *a*-like sounds. In Russian, as in English, the crucial factor behind vowel reduction is the position of the stressed syllable within the word. Which vowel is stressed is determined by a complex of factors including the lexicon and the morphology of the language. It is only a stressed nucleus that can support the full range of vocalic possibilities of the language. Once stress is morphologically or lexically removed from a given nucleus, the range of melodies it can support is curtailed. This gives rise to alternations which in a language with a rich inflectional and derivational morphology illustrate the phonological reality behind vowel reduction with particular clarity.

As a starting point for our presentation, let us note that of the six Russian vowels four appear both in pre- and post-tonic position. When stress is moved away from any of [i, ɨ, u, a] these vowels remain unaffected in unstressed position (apart from certain details of the phonetic implementation, such as a slight shortening of the vowel, or centralisation and raising in the case of [a]). Let us consider some alternations involving different positions of stress but unmodified vowel quality.

[30]
a.   sila ['sʲila] 'strength'   silač [sʲi'latʃʲ] 'strong man'
       kislyj ['cislɨj] 'sour'   kisla [cis'la] 'fem.'
b.   dym [dɨm] 'smoke, n.'   dymok [dɨ'mok] 'puff of smoke'
       ryba ['rɨba] 'fish'   rybak [rɨ'bak] 'fisherman'
c.   pastux [pas'tux] 'herdsman'   pastuxa [pastu'xa] 'gen. sg.'
       grustno ['grusna] 'sadly'   grustna [grus'na] 'sad, fem. nom. sg.'
       tjur'my ['tʲurʲmɨ] 'prison, nom. pl.'   tjur'ma [tʲurʲ'ma] 'nom. sg.'
d.   staryj ['starɨj] 'old'   starik [sta'rʲik] 'old man'
       raz [ras] 'time'   razy [ra'zɨ] 'nom. pl.'

The high unrounded vowels [i, ɨ] must agree in frontness or backness with the preceding consonant in accordance with *Russian Frontness Sharing*. The back rounded vowel [u] does not conform to this regularity, hence in unstressed just as in stressed positions [u] can be preceded by a palatalised or a velarised consonant (as in [30c] above). We would expect that the vowel [a], which is neutral with respect to *frontness sharing*, would appear in its unstressed form not only after a velarised consonant (as in [30d]) but also after a palatalised one. This does not happen, as is shown by the following alternations:

[31]   mjagko ['mʲaxka] 'softly'   mjagka [mʲix'ka] 'soft, fem. nom. sg.'
       tjanet ['tʲanʲit] '(s)he pulls'   tjanut' [tʲi'nutʲ] 'to pull'
       mjaso ['mʲasa] 'meat'   mjasnoj [mʲis'noj] 'meaty'
       často ['tʃʲasta] 'frequently'   častota ['tʃʲista'ta] 'frequency'
       pjat' [pʲatʲ] 'five'   pjatak [pʲi'tak] 'five copeck coin'

It thus transpires that it is only [i, ɨ, u] that can unconditionally appear in stressed and unstressed positions. Additionally, [i] appears only after a palatalised consonant, and [ɨ] after a non-palatalised one. The vowel [a] in unstressed position can only appear after a non-palatalised consonant or word-initially. Corresponding to [a], after a palatalised consonant we find [i] in unstressed positions.

To understand the alternations in [31] we need to consider the unstressed vocalic position with a preceding palatalised consonant. In addition to [a – i] alternations after a palatalised consonant, we find also the vowels [e] and [o] displaying the same alternation.

[32]
a.   bedy ['bʲedɨ] 'misfortune, nom. pl.'   beda [bʲi'da] 'nom. sg.'
     les [lʲes] 'wood'   lesnik [lʲisʲ'nʲik] 'forester'
     čest' [tʃʲesʲtʲ] 'honour'   čestnoj [tʃʲis'tnoj] 'honoured'
     reki ['rʲeci] 'river, nom. pl.'   reke [rʲi'ce] 'dat. sg.'
b.   nës [nʲos] 'he carried'   nesla [nʲis'la] 'she carried'
     zvëzdy ['zvʲozdɨ] 'star, nom. pl.'   zvezda [zvʲiz'da] 'nom. sg.'
     tëmnyj [tʲomnɨj] 'dark'   temnet' [tʲim'nʲetʲ] 'grow dark'
     čoln [tʃʲoln] 'canoe'   čolna [tʃʲil'na] 'gen. sg.'

The evidence of [31] and [32] forces us to conclude that after palatalised consonants the vowels [a, e, o] are impossible in unstressed position; their place is taken by the high vowel [i]. This conclusion is valid not just for alternating forms like those above but holds good generally in the language: after palatalised consonants we find only [i] and [u] in unstressed position.

To complete the picture of unstressed vocalic melodies in Russian we need to consider a special case involving the consonant–vowel interaction alluded to at the outset of this discussion, namely situations when the consonant happens to be one of the phonetically hard obstruents [ʃ, ʒ, ts]. As we illustrated in [27c], repeated below as [33], these non-palatalised consonants can be followed by the front vowel [e].

[33]   tercija ['tertsɨja] 'mediant'   centr [tsentr] 'centre'
       šest [ʃesʲtʲ] 'six'   celyj ['tselɨj] 'whole'
       žest [ʒest] 'gesture'

As hard consonants they can naturally be followed by the back vowels [ɨ, u, o, a], e.g.:

144 *Some segmental regularities*

[34]
a. žizn' [ʒɨzʲnʲ] 'life' ošibka [aˈʃɨpka] 'mistake'
cypka [ˈtsɨpka] 'chick'
b. žutko [ˈʒutka] 'awfully' šuba [ˈʃuba] 'fur coat'
cugom [ˈtsugam] 'in tandem'
c. žox [ʒox] 'rogue' šov [ʃof] 'seam'
cokot [ˈtsokat] 'clatter'
d. žalko [ˈʒalka] 'pity' šag [ʃak] 'step'
capat' [ˈtsapatʲ] 'snatch'

This is the situation when the nuclei are stressed. When the stress is placed on some other syllable within the word, then the high vowels [ɨ, u] are unaffected, in the same way as they are unaffected after other hard consonants (cf. [30b–c]). The examples in [35] illustrate this for the vowels [ɨ, u].

[35]   žizn' [ʒɨzʲnʲ] 'life' živoj [ʒɨˈvoj] 'alive'
ošibka [aˈʃɨpka] 'mistake' ošibus' [aʃɨˈbusʲ] 'I shall make a mistake'
cypka [ˈtsɨpka] 'chick' cyplënok [tsɨˈplʲonak] 'chicken'
žutko [ˈʒutka] 'awfully' žutka [ʒutˈka] 'terrible, fem. nom. sg.'
šuba [ˈʃuba] 'fur coat' šubënka [ʃuˈbʲonka] 'shabby fur coat'
cugom [ˈtsugam] 'in tandem' cugovoj [tsugaˈvoj] 'team-horse'

The non-high vowels [e, o, a], however, are disallowed in unstressed position, a development that is unsurprising, since these vowels are banned from unstressed positions elsewhere, as we have seen. The back high unrounded [ɨ] corresponds to these vowels when unstressed; this is best seen in the following alternations:

[36]   šepčet [ˈʃeptʃʲit] '(s)he whispers' šepču [ʃɨpˈtʃʲu] 'I whisper'
šest' [ʃesʲtʲ] 'six' šestoj [ʃɨsˈtoj] 'sixth'
ceny [ˈtsenɨ] 'price, nom. pl.' cena [tsɨˈna] 'nom. sg.'
žëny [ˈʒonɨ] 'wife, nom. pl.' žena [ʒɨˈna] 'nom. sg.'
žëltyj [ˈʒoltɨj] 'yellow, nom. masc. sg' želta [ʒɨlˈta] 'nom. fem. sg.'
žarko [ˈʒarka] 'hot' žara [ʒɨˈra] 'heat'
šalost' [ˈʃalosʲtʲ] 'prank' šalit' [ʃɨˈlʲitʲ] 'play tricks'
car' [tsarʲ] 'tsar' carica [tsɨˈrʲitsa] 'tsarina'

The examples make it clear that the hard obstruents [ʃ, ʒ, ts] do not tolerate the vowel [a] in their immediate neighbourhood. Alternatively, we could claim that the unstressed vowel [a] does not license these hard consonants in the onset. On a more general level and in neutral terms, we could say that the melodic structure of the onset and the melody of the nucleus are strictly connected.

The vocalic possibilities for unstressed positions in Russian can be summarised in the form of the following statements:

[37]   after palatalised consonants: [i, u]
       after velarised [ʃ, ʒ, ts]:   [ɨ, u]
       after other velarised consonants: [ɨ, u, a]

It can be seen that the only unconstrained vowel is [u]; otherwise we find [i] after palatalised and [ɨ, a] after velarised consonants, in accordance with the *Russian Frontness Sharing* constraint. In this way *Frontness Sharing* is implemented more thoroughly in unstressed than in stressed syllables – recall that in the latter case all back vowels can be preceded by a palatalised consonant, as in [28]. The unstressed position, then, places more stringent requirements on the character of the consonant–vowel interaction. For one group of consonants – [ʃ, ʒ, ts] – the interaction is more strict than with other velarised consonants.

The so-called vowel reduction in Modern Russian is a telling illustration of the mutual dependence of vowels and consonants. We have seen that *Frontness Sharing* to a large extent makes the palatalisation of consonants and the frontness of vowels inseparable, but we have also seen how the melody of consonants determines the nature of the vowels in the nuclei which license these onset consonants. Both these conditions are directly dependent upon the position of the stressed syllable within the word. In this way it can be seen that in both Russian and English the vocalic inventory found in unstressed positions is considerably reduced compared to that found in stressed nuclei. English accepts [ə, ɪ] there while in Russian the selection of unstressed vowels is larger and partly connected with the quality of the preceding consonants.

6.7 German final devoicing

For our final example of segmental phonological regularities involving both vowels and consonants, we will consider the well-known case of what is traditionally called final devoicing in German. The German term *Auslautverhärtung* means literally *final hardening*, and reflects an insight concerning plosives in Germanic languages. Voice plays a limited role in Germanic, and a straightforward division of obstruents into voiced and voiceless, of the sort found in numerous other languages, does not adequately account for the data. As we saw in chapter 1, in English the non-aspirated plosives may be voiced in voice-friendly environments, typically between vowels. Thus the plosives in *sober* ['səʊbə], *ready* ['redi], *eager* ['iːgə] are fully voiced but in, for example, *bail* [beɪl], *dale* [deɪl] and *gale* [geɪl] only partly so, if at all. The same regularities hold for German, by and large. Detailed descriptions of individual Germanic languages with comprehensive accounts of the phonetic facts lead to the conclusion that the terms *voiced – voiceless*

146   *Some segmental regularities*

are not very felicitous and should be replaced by something more adequate. It has been suggested that the terms *fortis – lenis* reflect the phonetic reality better, hence rather than talk about devoicing we should study *fortition* (in the same way that we talked about *lenition* above). There is a lot to be said for this sort of change of terminology; in what follows, however, we shall be more concerned with the context of the regularity than its phonetic nature, and for this reason we will continue to use the familiar traditional terms.

Let us start by inspecting some of the unembellished facts normally associated with final devoicing in German. The examples in [38] illustrate words ending in a final obstruent and show what happens to the obstruent if an ending is attached to the word; only the relevant segments are transcribed.

[38]
a. Schi[f] 'ship'   Schi[fə]s 'gen. sg.'
   Bla[t] 'leaf'   Blä[tɐ] 'nom. pl.'
   hie[s] '(s)he was called'   hei[sə]n 'be called'
   Wer[k] 'work, n.'   wer[kə] 'vb.'
b. Lie[t] 'song'   Lie[dɐ] 'nom. pl.'
   Wei[p] 'woman'   Wei[bə]s 'gen. sg.'
   klu[k] 'clever'   klu[gə] 'nom. pl.'
   bra[f] 'good'   bra[və]s 'gen. sg. masc.'
   Gan[s] 'goose'   Gän[zə] 'geese'

The examples in [38a] are only meaningful when compared with those in [38b]: either voiceless word-final obstruents remain voiceless before a suffix beginning with a vowel, or else final voiceless obstruents correspond to voiced ones before a vowel-initial suffix. Since it is clear that intervocalically we can have both voiced and voiceless consonants, whereas word-finally only voiceless obstruents are admissible, it is the word-final position that is more restricted. Final devoicing refers to the impossibility of voiced obstruents appearing at the end of words and, concomitantly, to the existence of alternations between voiced and voiceless obstruents, as illustrated in [38b].

The requirement that final obstruents must be voiceless is enforced not only in absolute final position, i.e. before a pause, but also in connected speech even when the next word begins with a voiced consonant. Some examples are offered below.

[39]   das Lau[p b]rennt 'leaves are on fire' (cf. Lau[bə]s 'foliage, gen. sg.')
        es wir[t d]unkel 'it is getting dark' (cf. wer[də]n 'become')
        den Sie[k g]ewinnen 'win a victory (cf. sie[gə]n 'win')

Thus the word-final position does not support voiceless obstruents in German, which results in the identification of voiced and voiceless obstruents in that context.

6.7 German final devoicing

The suspension of a contrast in some positions has traditionally been called **neutralisation**. The neutralisation of voicing in German means that given a form such as [raːt], we cannot predict whether before the ending [əs] it will emerge as [raːtəs] or [raːdəs] – in fact both are possible: *Rates* 'advice, gen. sg.' and *Rades* 'wheel, gen. sg.' have the same nominative form, spelt *Rat* and *Rad* respectively.

In terms of the phonological model we have been developing in this book the word-final position is only superficially final. As argued in the preceding chapters, the final consonant in a word is universally in the onset position and is itself licensed by a following nucleus which contains no melody, i.e. by an empty nucleus. This view, when applied to the German data, translates into the claim that a final empty nucleus cannot license voicing in the preceding onset obstruent. Following the convention employed earlier we will indicate that a property is unlicensed by leaving it unattached to the rest of the melody; in the diagrams below we will also italicise it. Below we provide a representation of the word *Sieg* [ziːk] 'victory'.

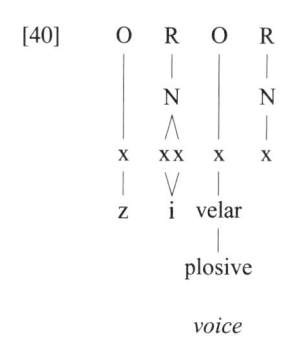

[40]
```
        O   R   O   R
        |   |   |   |
            N       N
           / \      |
        x  x x  x   x
        |   \ /  |
        z    i  velar
                 |
               plosive

               voice
```

An unlicensed property, although continuing to be part of the representation, is not pronounced and remains inaudible. The fact that a certain property is unlicensed in some contexts is an individual peculiarity of a given language or dialect. It is impossible to predict this peculiarity since the licensing of a certain property or the withdrawal of the licence is something that can change both in time and space.

The word-final withdrawal of licence for the voicing property can also account for the fact that in the morphological compounds that German abounds in, there can be no voiced obstruent at the end of the first element. Compare the first part of the following compounds with the same form before a vowel initial suffix:

[41] Hal[p j]ahr 'half a year'   Hal[bə]s 'half, gen. sg.'
      Flu[k r]ekord 'flight record'   Flu[gə]s 'flight, gen. sg.'
      Wil[t e]nte 'wild duck'   wl[də] 'wild, nom. pl.'
      Hau[s ai]ngang 'house entrance'   Hau[zə]s 'house, gen. sg.'

148 *Some segmental regularities*

Let us assume that compounds preserve the domain structures introduced by their constituent parts. The left-hand examples of [41] will each contain two such domains. Using conventional orthography the examples can be represented as in [42].

[42]   [[Halb] [Jahr]]   [[Flug] [Rekord]]
       [[Wild] [Ente]]   [[Haus] [Eingang]]

As can be seen, each of the parts of the compound is enclosed in a domain of its own and additionally, the whole compound constitutes a single domain. The fact that the first part of the compound necessarily ends in a voiceless obstruent is due to the withdrawal of voice-licence domain-finally. Hence *voice* remains inaudible in this position. The representation of the first part of the compounds here would not be different in any significant way from the one supplied for the word *Sieg* in [40].

Consider some further cases of voice alternations in German. In [41] we saw examples of the withdrawal of voice-licence before a domain-final empty nucleus but not before a nucleus containing a melody. Let us look at what happens when stems are followed by a consonant suffix.

[43]   Kin[də]s 'child, gen. sg.'   Kin[th]eit 'childhood'
       gel[bə]s 'yellow, masc. gen. sg.'   gel[pl]ich 'yellowish'
       Mäu[z]e 'mice'   Mäu[sl]ein 'little mouse'
       Far[bə] 'colour'   far[pl]os 'colourless'
       schrei[bə]n 'write'   schrei[pk]undig 'literate'
       wa[gə]n 'dare'   Wa[kn]is 'daring experience'
       Prei[zə] 'price, nom. pl.'   prei[sv]ert 'of good value'
       Schan[də] 'disgrace'   schan[tb]ar 'disgraceful'
       Hun[də]s 'dog, gen. sg.'   Hun[tç]en 'dog, dim.'

As can be seen, the final consonant of the stem emerges voiceless before consonant-initial suffixes. These suffixes are mostly, though not exclusively derivational. In some cases it is very difficult to decide whether we are dealing with a derivational suffix or an element of a compound, as in the case of the example *preiswert* 'of good value' in [43] with the suffix *-wert* which also functions as an independent word *wert* 'worthy'. The distinction between compounding and derivation is not easy to define, as morphology shows. From the point of view of German devoicing this may be an advantage: note that devoicing takes place before what are unquestionably the second parts of compounds (as in [40]) and before certain unquestionably derivational affixes. If we were to assume that all such affixes are separated from the preceding part of the word by a domain boundary, the phonological effects would follow automatically since – as we have seen – domain-final empty nuclei do not license voicing on the preceding onset obstruent.

6.7 German final devoicing   149

Words like *Kindheit* 'childhood' could be supplied with the following structured representation:

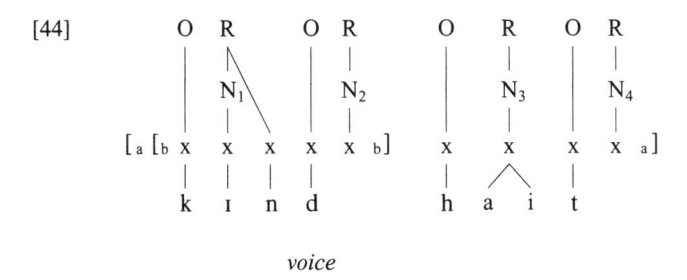

[44]   O   R   O   R   O   R   O   R
                  |\ | | |
                  N₁\   N₂   N₃   N₄
                  | \ | | |
             [ₐ [ᵦ x   x   x   x   x ᵦ] x   x   x   x ₐ]
                  | | | | | /\ |
                  k   ɪ   n   d   h   a i   t
                                 |
                                voice

The word constitutes a uniform domain, marked here by 'a' which comprises an internal domain 'b' and a derivational suffix. Since both N₂ and N₄ are directly followed by domain boundaries, they are domain-final. Nucleus N₂, domain-final for the domain 'b', is preceded by the plosive [d] – i.e. a cluster of properties including plosiveness, alveolarity and voicing – which, however, is perceived as voiceless. This is because N₂ is incapable of supporting or licensing voice.

This interpretation allows us to bring together the devoicing found at the end of words, like in [38b], and that encountered before certain suffixes, specifically before consonant-initial suffixes. This devoicing is, on our analysis, the failure of the voice property to be licensed by a domain-final empty nucleus; if consonant-initial suffixes are separated from their stems by a domain-boundary, then the devoicing word-internally and word-finally is due to the same constraint. This analysis finds some striking support but it also encounters certain problems, both of which deserve some attention.

Look at the following sets of alternations:

[45]
a.   üben ['yːbən] 'practise'   üblich ['yːplɪç] 'customary'
b.   über ['yːbɐ] 'over'   übrig ['yːbrɪç] 'remaining'
c.   Biler ['bɪldɐ] 'picture, nom. pl.' Bildnis ['bɪtnɪs] 'portrait'
d.   bilden ['bɪldən] 'shape'   Bilner ['bɪdnɐ] 'sculptor'

On the face of it we appear to be witnessing a contradiction: the voiced plosive is devoiced before the sonorant [l] ([45a]) but not before [r] ([45b]), while before the nasal devoicing either does ([45c]) or does not take place ([45d]). A closer inspection of the forms reveals, however, that this is precisely what we would expect given our interpretation of devoicing.

Note that in [45a] the suffix *-lich* is attached to a stem ending in a voiced consonant, i.e. the morphological structure of *üblich* must be presented as (üb)(lich). The devoicing of the stem-final consonant is due to the same mechanism which devoices the relevant plosive in *Kindheit* (see the representation in [44] above). In

150 *Some segmental regularities*

übrig on the other hand, the suffix is *-ig*, i.e. *übrig* is (übr)(ig), hence the plosive [b] does not find itself in the context which disallows voice licensing, i.e. before a domain-final empty nucleus; consequently it remains voiced. This is true despite the fact that the sonorant [r] itself is realised as a vowel domain-finally, as shown by *über* ['yːbɐ]. It might be argued that the plosive is separated from the sonorant by an empty nucleus, but since the nucleus is not domain-final it is not directly relevant to our concern here.

In *Bildnis* the consonant-initial suffix *-nis* is attached to a stem ending in a voiced consonant, which constitutes another *Kindheit* type of representation, with devoicing being a mechanical consequence of domain structure. In *Bildner* the agentive suffix *-er* [ɐ] is attached to the base *bilden* and hence the context for devoicing is not available. The words *übrig* and *Bildner*, with voiced plosives in the relevant places, are represented below. Note that in neither case is the potential target of devoicing followed by a domain-final empty nucleus.

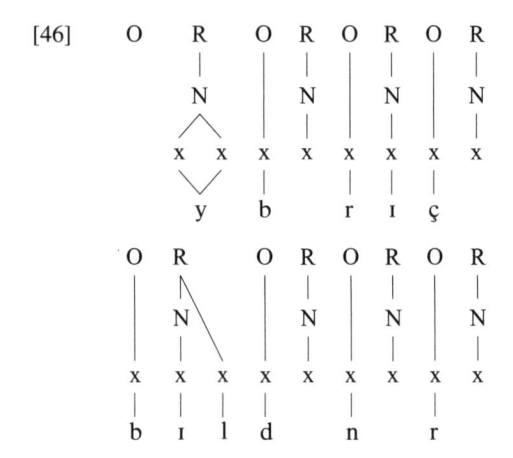

[46]

```
   O   R     O   R   O   R   O   R
   |   |     |   |   |   |   |   |
       N         N       N       N
      /\        |       |       |
   x  x  x   x  x   x   x   x
   \/        |       |       |
   y         b       r   ɪ   ç

   O   R     O   R   O   R   O   R
   |   |\    |   |   |   |   |   |
       N \       N       N       N
       |  \     |       |       |
   x   x   x   x   x   x   x   x
   |   |   |   |       |       
   b   ɪ   l   d       n       r
```

A slightly different regularity must be postulated for the following types of alternations:

[47]
a.   Adel ['aːdəl] 'nobility'   adlig ['aːdlɪç] (adl)(ig) 'noble'
     Schade ['ʃaːdə] 'harm'   schädlich ['ʃɛːtlɪç] (schäd)(lich) 'harmful'
b.   Nebel ['neːbəl] 'fog'   neblig ['neːblɪç] (nebl)(ig) 'foggy'
     Liebe ['liːbə] 'love'   lieblich ['liːplɪç] (lieb)(lich) 'lovely'
c.   Flügel ['flyːgəl] 'wing'   flüglig ['flyːglɪç] (flügl)(ich) 'winged'
     kluge ['kluːgə] 'wise, nom. pl.'   klüglich ['klyːklɪç] (klüg)(lich) 'wisely'

The reasons why there is no devoicing in the right-hand member of the first pair of each set of examples are the same as above: the plosive does not appear before a domain-final nucleus, which is what happens in the second pair of each set. The surface discrepancies that the right-hand column pairs seem to point to are only

6.7 German final devoicing

superficial and bypass a fundamental difference in their morphological structure. Note that in one case the [l] is part of the stem to which the suffix *-ig* is appended, e.g. *adel+ig*; there is no devoicing before this suffix. In the other case [l] is part of the suffix, e.g. *schäd+lich*, and devoicing follows.

A serious problem has been ignored so far, namely the restriction of devoicing to the context of consonant-initial suffixes. With vowel-initial suffixes, no devoicing takes place. This is shown in the examples below:

[48] Kin[t] 'child'   kin[dɪ]sch 'childish'
      Bil[t] 'picture'   bil[də]n 'shape, vb.'
      Hun[t] 'dog'   Hun[də]s 'gen. sg.'
      Die[p] 'thief'   Die[bə]rei 'thieving'
      Ban[t] 'volume'   Bän[də] 'nom. pl.'
      Ban[t] 'ribbon'   Bän[dɐ] 'nom. pl.'

At first blush it looks as if we might solve the problem by claiming that while consonant-initial suffixes are separated from the stem by a domain boundary, vowel-initial morphemes are attached directly to the stem. This solution would certainly work since if the stem-final consonant were to be followed by the vowel of the suffix, the context where licensing of the voice property might be withheld would never arise. Such a solution is totally ad hoc since there is no conceivable reason why all consonant-initial suffixes should be different from all vowel-initial suffixes. It is not impossible that some vowel-initial suffix could be attached directly to the stem without any intervening domain boundary. What we find implausible in the extreme is that all vocalic suffixes would have to follow one particular pattern while all consonantal suffixes would have to follow a very different one. Since being a consonant or being a vowel is a phonological rather than a morphological property, we ought to be able to provide a phonological account for what is happening. The morphology is responsible only for suffix attachment, not for the phonological effects which ensue.

Let us assume, then, that vowel-initial suffixes are also separated from their base by a domain boundary. In this way the representations of two derivatives based on the noun *Kind* [kɪnt] 'child', namely *kindlich* ['kɪntlɪç] and *kindisch* ['kɪndɪʃ], will have largely identical shapes:

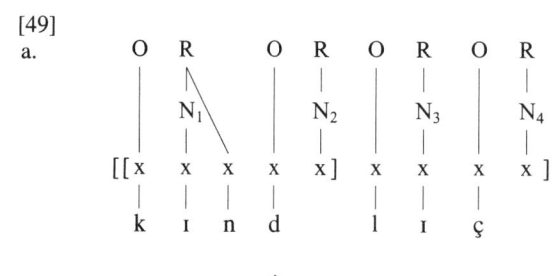

[49]
a.

```
      O   R       O   R   O   R   O   R
      |  /\       |   |   |   |   |   |
      |  N₁\      |   N₂  |   N₃  |   N₄
      |  |  \     |   |   |   |   |   |
    [[ x  x  x    x  x ]  x   x   x   x ]
      |  |  |        |    |   |   |
      k  ɪ  n        d    l   ɪ   ç

              voice
```

152 *Some segmental regularities*

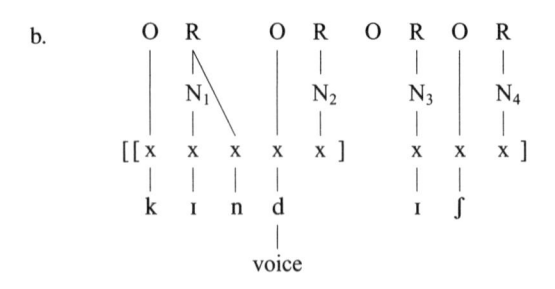

b.
```
        O   R         O   R     O   R   O   R
        |   /\        |   |     |   |   |   |
        |  N₁\        |   N₂    |   N₃  |   N₄
        |  |  \       |   |     |   |   |   |
        [[ x  x  x    x   x ]   x   x   x ]
        |  |  |  |            |   |   |
        k  ɪ  n  d            ɪ   ʃ
                 |
              voice
```

The phonological difference between these two representations consists in the presence of a positionless, i.e. x-less onset following the empty domain-final nucleus N₂ in [49b] in the word *kindisch*. What we have here is an empty nucleus followed by an empty onset, a configuration that seems to be anomalous. In our discussion of the French vowel elision in 4.3 we noted that a sequence of vowels without an intervening onset with a skeletal slot is something that tends to be eliminated. Here we have an even clearer case of what might need to be eliminated, namely two consecutive syllabic nodes (R – O) with no melody attached to either of them. If this is indeed an undesirable configuration, then we might have a way of tackling the phonological difficulty. Suppose that such unwanted or marked structures are eliminated by an operation we shall call **erasure**. This operation removes adjacent, melodically empty constituents (N₂ and the following onset) in [49b] yielding [50].

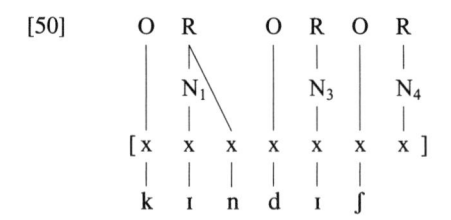

[50]
```
        O   R         O   R   O   R
        |   /\        |   |   |   |
        |  N₁\        |   N₃  |   N₄
        |  |  \       |   |   |   |
        [ x  x  x    x   x   x   x ]
        |  |  |  |   |   |   |
        k  ɪ  n  d   ɪ   ʃ
```

As a result, the stem-final plosive is no longer before a domain-final empty nucleus hence the context for devoicing is not met.

What is crucial is that we have established a link between certain phonological properties of the representation and the phonological effects that these properties induce. There is no need to resort to crude stratagems such as dividing suffixes into arbitrary groups on the basis of their alleged influence on the stem-final consonant. This had a particularly infelicitous consequence, as we saw, since the 'devoicing' suffixes would all – accidentally? – begin with a consonant. On a more general level we see once again that the connection between phonology and morphology is of a most indirect sort: morphology provides domains within which phonological regularities hold. This view of the interaction of phonology and morphology might be called the null hypothesis as it basically says that phonology is an autonomous component of the language. It relies on morphology only to the extent that the latter delimits areas where its generalisations hold. If we want to claim that there is a more intimate, or more complex, relation between phonology and morphology, we would have to provide strong evidence undermining the null hypothesis.

German final devoicing is thus seen to be crucially dependent upon the presence of a domain-final empty nucleus which is incapable of licensing voicing in its onset. This is a highly constrained condition which holds for the standard language, called *Hochlautung*. In some regional dialects the situation is somewhat different; we would like to consider one such case involving the northern dialects. Here the scope of the devoicing is broader than it is in *Hochlautung*. Compare the northern variants (left-hand column) with those of the standard dialect on the right.

[51]   ei[kn]en   ei[gn]en 'suit, vb.'
       re[kn]en   re[gn]en 'rain, vb.'
       A[tl]er   A[dl]er 'eagle'
       Or[tn]ung   Or[dn]ung 'order, n.'
       Do[km]a   Do[gm]a 'dogma'

Otherwise the northern dialects behave in much the same way as the standard language. The forms in [51] all contain sequences of a plosive and a sonorant which, arguably, are separated by an empty nucleus. Note that sequences such as [gn, dl] cannot function as branching onsets, hence the consonants must be assigned to separate onsets. This results in the following representation of the word *eignen* in the standard dialect:

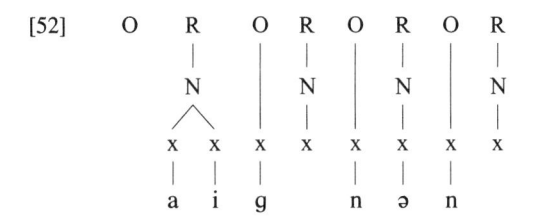

[52]   O   R   O   R   O   R   O   R
        | | | | | | | |
             N   N   N   N
            /\ | | |
        x   x   x   x   x   x   x   x
        | | | | |
        a   i   g   n   ə   n

It is clear why there is no devoicing here: the relevant plosive does not appear before a domain-final empty nucleus. The question arises as to what is responsible for the northern pronunciation. Since in the north all domain-final onsets are devoiced, and additionally those domain-internal ones which are followed by an empty nucleus, it might be suggested that the northern dialect is less restrictive in that any empty nucleus, not just a domain-final one, is incapable of supporting onset voicing. Alternatively we could say that in the north voice is supported exclusively by a nucleus with a melodic content. Whichever interpretation we settle upon it is clear that the distinction between the dialects reduces to a difference in the licensing potential of empty nuclei.

The German devoicing regularities show with particular clarity how phonological phenomena involve both phonological and morphological aspects of the representation. The latter are highly impoverished, merely entailing information about the placement of domain boundaries. It should be added, however, that the justification for domains is not a mechanical morphological procedure. We have tried to show in the preceding pages, just as we did in chapter 3, that the domains of phonological regularities do frequently coincide with the boundaries set by morphological procedures. Equally often, however, morphological boundaries are not reflected in phonological domain structure. Hence, although there is a considerable overlap between morphology and phonology, the primary source of evidence for phonological structure must come from phonology, just as the primary source of morphological evidence must be sought in morphology.

6.8 Summary

The preceding sections dealt with different aspects of the interactions between vowels and consonants and their theoretical implications.

The Turkish case was concerned with vowels which are non-adjacent as melodies within words, separated as they are by consonants. The vowels of this language display a restricted degree of mutual dependence, a dependence which is expressed in the form of backness and rounding sharing. The existence of these vowel harmony related regularities indicates that direct melodic adjacency is not a prerequisite for interaction. What is involved is not so much the adjacency of vowels as the adjacency of nuclei.

English vowel reduction shows that the appearance of certain vocalic melodies can be conditioned by their positioning with respect to stress, and that specific positions may be "reserved" for certain melodies. In this way the concept of a uniform or, simply, single vowel system in a language turns out to be either irrelevant or misleading, since the vowel system of unstressed syllables is different from that of stressed syllables. An undifferentiated inventory consisting simply of the vowels found in the language as a whole distorts the basic phonological asymmetry which exists between stressed and unstressed nuclei. Whether such an inventory has any useful role to play is an open question for which no immediately obvious answer suggests itself.

The same conclusion is given further substance by the other sets of data considered in this chapter. In Russian the so-called vowel reduction depends not only on the position of the nucleus with respect to stress but also on the melody of the preceding onset. This example and also the case of Polish nasal nuclei show that vowels interact with consonants in intricate ways. Polish nasal nuclei can only appear in specified environments and it is this dependence that is phonologically significant rather than the mere fact of their existence in the language. Similarly, Russian vowels are conditioned not only by stress but also by the consonantal environment. Once more, one can legitimately ask what significant information is contained in a list of all the vocalic elements found in Russian.

The Icelandic and German cases illustrated different ways in which specific syllabic positions may be melodically restricted. Icelandic bars aspirated plosives from the coda position, which suggests that onset melodies are incapable of licensing them. This is in agreement with the traditional view which regards aspirated plosives in Germanic as strong consonants; in fact, they seem too strong to be licensed by any onset consonant in Icelandic. The only obstruents which the coda position can support, i.e. the only obstruents which the following onset can license, are fricatives. German voiced obstruents are not licensed by the domain-final empty nucleus, which results in a different inventory of consonants being admitted domain-finally than, say, domain-initially. The more data we look at, the more elusive and less substantial the concept of a segment inventory becomes. The withdrawal of the licence for voicing in domain-final obstruents is a language-specific fact about the phonology of German. It is similar to the withdrawal of the licence for voiced plosives in a sharing relation with a preceding nasal which characterises certain dialects of English (see 3.2 above).

In this chapter we have seen again and again that phonological regularities manifest themselves through morphological alternations. However, alternations, although indicative of phonological regularities, can also be deceptive. For one thing they can be irregular, rare, defective and hence not very illuminating phonologically. Even worse, however, they are very often simply not available. Their role in a phonological analysis is thus at most ancillary, and neither their presence not their absence should form the focus of interpretation. Phonological regularities are invariably present in all the various arrays of vocalic and consonantal interactions, hence all these interactions are reliable sources of information. We have pointed out that morphology interacts with phonology in a most indirect fashion, by supplying domains within which phonological regularities hold. The so-called null hypothesis amounts to a strong, restrictive claim about the fundamental independence of phonology. Compelling evidence would be needed if it were to be challenged or undermined and replaced by a less restrictive hypothesis.

6.9 Suggested further reading

For distinctly different analyses of Turkish vowel harmony see Clements and Sezer (1982) and Charette and Göksel (1998). On vowel harmony in general see van der Hulst and van de Weijer (1995); on tier structure see Mester (1986).

Vowel reduction in English is discussed in various places by Chomsky and Halle (1968) and by Harris (1994); see also Gussmann (1991), Giegerich (1999, chapter 5). On *happy*-tensing see Wells (1982).

Russian vowel reduction is well illustrated in Shvedova (1980).

German voice-related phenomena have been studied in different frameworks by Rubach (1990), Hall (1992, chapter 2), Brockhaus (1995a) and Wiese (1996, section 7.3.1.).

Harris (1997) offers a proposal for dealing with the licensing possibilities of different positions within a representation.

More extensive surveys of phonological regularities can be found in Lass (1984) and Kenstowicz (1994).

7
Syllable structure and phonological effects: quantity in Icelandic

7.1 Introduction

In the preceding chapters we have introduced a cluster of notions connected with the phonological organisation of the language. We have seen that phonological units, apart from following each other in sequences, are structured internally into the skeleton and the melody, and also externally into larger chunks such as onsets and rhymes. Various modifications such as, for example, sharing arise as a result of the interactions of such phonological units in different combinations. This chapter will be devoted to an in-depth analysis of basically one problem in the phonology of Modern Icelandic, namely vowel quantity. We will try to see what the theoretical apparatus developed so far can do to cope with the facts of the language, and also what the facts of the language can tell us about the nature of phonological regularities. Although our main concern will be vocalic length or quantity, we will also need to look at a few other phenomena that are closely connected with it. This reflects the predominant situation in phonology, where very few regularities in the language can be analysed in complete isolation from other data. Normally, phonological regularities are connected in various ways and can only be properly appreciated and formulated when studied jointly. Needless to say, we cannot go into too many details here and for this reason the regularities other than those controlling vowel quantity will be presented briefly, and only to the extent that they are relevant to the discussion.

7.2 Preliminaries

Let us start by listing the main vowels and consonants of the language. As we pointed out in the previous chapter, such lists are of questionable phonological significance but they give some idea of the sounds of the language. Vowels are classified on the basis of the phonetic oppositions front – back, rounded – unrounded and high – mid – low. In Icelandic we find the following possibilities:

[1]	front, high, unrounded [i], e.g. *býr* [piːr] '(s)he lives'
front, mid, unrounded [ɪ], e.g. *syni* [sɪːnɪ] 'son, dat. sg.'
front, mid, rounded [y], e.g. *hundur* [hʏntʏr] 'dog'
front, low, unrounded [ɛ], e.g. *nema* [nɛːma] 'unless'
front, low, rounded [œ], e.g. *ör* [œːr] 'arrow'
back, high, rounded [u], e.g. *hús* [huːs] 'house'
back, mid, rounded [ɔ], e.g. *sofa* [sɔːva] 'sleep'
back, low, unrounded [a], e.g. *tala* [tʰaːla] 'speak'

Apart from the above monophthongs, there are five diphthongs, namely [ei, ai, au, ou, œi]. What is characteristic and striking about Icelandic diphthongs is that, just like monophthongs, they can be either short or long. We will return to this point presently. Examples are:

[2]	*gleyma* [kleiːma] 'forget'	*gleymdi* [kleimtɪ] 'I forgot'
ár [auːr] 'year'	*árs* [aurs] 'gen. sg.'
dæma [taiːma] 'judge'	*dæmadi* [taimtɪ] 'I judged'
lóð [louːð] 'weight'	*lóðs* [louðs] 'gen. sg.'
rauð [rœiːð] 'red, fem. nom. sg.'	*rautt* [rœiht] 'neut. nom. sg.'

Among consonants we encounter classes familiar from other languages. Thus the plosives consist of:

[3]	bilabial [p, pʰ], e.g. *blóm* [plouːm] 'flower', *penni* [pʰɛnːɪ] 'pen'
alveolar [t, tʰ], e.g. *dagur* [taːɣʏr] 'day', *tími* [tʰiːmɪ] 'time'
palatal [c, cʰ], e.g. *gæta* [caiːtʰa] 'look after', *kind* [cʰɪnt] 'sheep'
velar [k, kʰ], e.g. *gola* [kɔːla] 'breeze', *kalla* [kʰatla] 'call'

The fricatives consist of:

[4]	labio-dental [f, v], e.g. *fara* [faːra] 'go', *lofa* [lɔːva] 'promise'
dental and alveolar [θ, ð, s], e.g. *þoka* [θɔːkʰa] 'fog', *þýða* [θiːða] 'translate', *samur* [saːmʏr] 'same'
palatal [j, ç], e.g. *jötunn* [jœːtʰʏn] 'giant', *hjarta* [çar̥ta] 'heart'
velar [x, ɣ], e.g. *hugsa* [hʏxsa] 'think', *saga* [saːɣa] 'story'
glottal [h], e.g. *hissa* [hɪsːa] 'surprised'

The sonorants consist of the nasals [m, n, ŋ], the lateral [l] and the trill [r], which can also appear as voiceless [m̥, n̥, ŋ̊, l̥, r̥], e. g.:

[5]	*lamb* [lamp] 'lamb'	*lampi* [lam̥pɪ] 'lamp'
senda [sɛnta] 'send'	*panta* [pʰan̥ta] 'order, vb.'
fingur [fiŋkʏr] 'finger'	*banki* [pauŋ̊cɪ] 'bank'
ala [aːla] 'nourish'	*stúlka* [stul̥ka] 'girl'

Another notable feature is the absence of voicing among plosives: as just shown (see also 3.3 and 6.5), what distinguishes them is the presence or absence of aspiration. Also, the distribution of the voiceless fricatives [f, θ] is restricted mostly to initial position and to positions before a following plosive. Finally, since primary stress falls almost invariably on the first nucleus, as before it will be disregarded in our transcriptions. After this brief survey of the main segments of the language we are now ready to consider the question of vowel quantity in some detail.

Let us recall at the outset that a long nucleus comprises two skeletal positions, no matter whether it is a monophthong or a diphthong. Conversely, a short nucleus dominates a single slot, again irrespectively of whether a single or a complex melody is attached to it. Icelandic short diphthongs are, then, complex melodies attached to single slots (see [9] in chapter 2). In terms of the skeleton, a long nucleus is equivalent to a short one followed by a rhymal complement.

7.3 Open syllable lengthening

Icelandic vowels can be long or short in a way which is reminiscent of the Italian lengthening discussed in 5.6. According to standard textbooks stressed, i.e. normally initial nuclei are long in Modern Icelandic in one of the following situations:

[6]
a. they are word-final, e.g.:
 bú [puː] 'estate', *tvo* [tʰvɔː] 'two, acc. masc.', *fæ* [faiː] 'I get'
b. they are followed by a single consonant, e.g.:
 stara [staːra] 'stare', *lúða* [luːða] 'halibut', *færi* [faiːrɪ] 'opportunity, *kjöt* [cʰœːtʰ] 'meat', *hjón* [çouːn] 'couple'
c. they are followed by a cluster made up of [pʰ, tʰ, kʰ, s] and any of [j, v, r], e.g.:
 nepja [nɛːpʰja] 'bad weather', *apríl* [aːpʰril] 'April', *götva* [kœːtʰva] 'discover', *Ekvador* [ɛːkʰvatɔr] 'Ecuador', *flysja* [flɪːsja] 'peel', *luasra* [lœiːsra] 'loose, gen. pl.', *betri* [pɛːtʰrɪ] 'better'

A few initial comments are in order with respect to this traditional formulation. For one thing, the stressed vowel referred to in the statement does not have to be primarily stressed but may be secondarily stressed. Further, the claim that the sequence /kʰj/ is one of the clusters described in [6c] is probably unnecessary if we recognise the existence of the palatal plosive [cʰ]; the word *reykja* [reiːcʰa] 'smoke' has a long nucleus because it is followed by a single palatal plosive rather than a consonant sequence. Leaving aside these additions, we can note the problems that the listing in [6] reveals. The obvious task is to try and reduce the three different contexts to some kind of common denominator, apart from the requirement that the long nucleus must be stressed. We would like to be able to see why it is that the word-final position appears to induce the same behaviour as the context of a following single consonant or a specific consonant combination. Even more, we would like to enquire about the nature of the lengthening cluster and ask what it is that causes precisely these consonant combinations rather than any others to act as lengthening contexts. Put briefly, why is it that, say, [pʰr] causes lengthening but [lj] or [r̥p] do not?

To answer such questions we must try and identify the general conditions for the appearance of long nuclei. Of the contexts listed in [6], the first one seems the most straightforward: stressed vowels are long when they appear word-finally. Word-final syllables ending in a vowel are, of course, open, which prompts the conclusion that long vowels are found precisely in open syllables. Part of the context in [6b] provides direct support for this contention, namely, long vowels are also found before single internal consonants. This is completely unsurprising since single intervocalic consonants are syllabified in the onset of the second syllable and thus leave the first syllable open. The words *bú* [puː] 'estate' and *stara* [staːra] 'stare' can be represented as in [7].

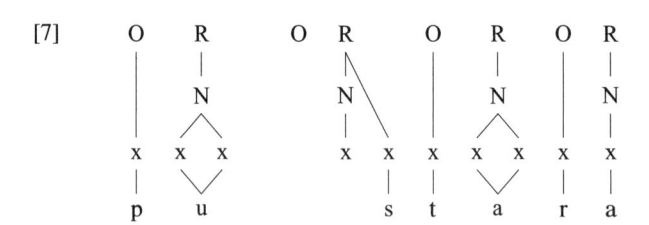

[7]

```
    O   R           O   R        O   R     O   R
    |   |            \  |        |   |     |   |
        N             N \        |   N     |   N
       /\             |  \       |  /\     |   |
    x  x  x        x  x   x   x  x  x  x   x   x
    |  \/           |      \  |  |  \/     |   |
    p   u           s       t  a  r         a
```

There are branching nuclei in both words. Either the branching is word-final, or else the next consonant belongs to the onset of the following syllable. Note also that in accordance with the conclusion in chapter 5 we syllabify initial, preconsonantal [s] as the complement of a rhyme whose nucleus is empty.

If our reasoning is correct, we would not expect to find long nuclei in closed syllables, such as before an internal rhyme–onset sequence. This is borne out by the facts; consider the examples in [8].

[8]
a. kambur [kampʏr] 'comb'   kampur [kam̥pʏr] 'moustache'
    henda [hɛnta] 'throw'   henta [hɛn̥ta] 'suit, vb.'
    rangur [rauŋkʏr] 'wrong'   sínkur [siŋ̊kʏr] 'stingy'
    mjólka [mjoul̥ka] 'milk, vb.' ólga [oulka] 'foam, vb.'
    hálfur [haulvʏr] 'half'   snerta [snɛrta] 'touch'
    harður [harðʏr] 'hard'   harka [har̥ka] 'severity'

b. hestur [hɛstʏr] 'horse'   ástar [austar] 'love, gen. sg.'
    flaska [flaska] 'bottle'   fiskur [fɪskʏr] 'fish'
    aspar [aspar] 'aspen, nom. pl.' geispa [ceispa] 'yawn'
    asni [asnɪ] 'donkey'   kvíslar [kʰvislar] 'branch, gen. sg.'
    hismi [hɪsmɪ] 'chaff'

The examples in [8a] contain typical rhyme–onset junctures, where the rhymal position is occupied by a sonorant and the onset is an obstruent. Since the syllable is closed by a sonorant, the preceding vowel is – in accordance with our predictions – non-branching, i.e. short. The stressed syllables in [8b] also contain a short nucleus, which indicates that the following consonant [s] must be syllabified as a rhymal complement. This is unsurprising if we take seriously the views presented in chapter 5, where we argued at length that the fricative [s] must be heterosyllabic with the following consonant. This means that in [8b] the fricative closes the syllable, hence a long vowel cannot precede it.

The combined evidence of unquestionably open syllables with a branching nucleus and unquestionably closed ones with a short vowel leads us to the conclusion that stressed rhymes in Icelandic must dominate two skeletal positions. The first skeletal slot is invariably assigned to the nucleus; the second will also belong to the nucleus if and only if no rhymal complement follows. The two structures which are possible for Icelandic stressed rhymes are charted below:

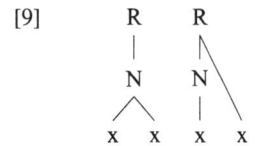

[9]   R   R
           | /\
           N   N \
          /\ | \
         x x   x   x

One way of interpreting the representations in [9] is to say that a vowel must be long if it is not followed by a coda consonant. This provides a partial answer to the question of where long vowels appear in Icelandic.

7.4 Word-final consonants and vowel length

Another context where vowels are long is the position before a single word-final consonant. In [6b] we saw two examples of this – more exemplification is offered below.

162 *Syllable structure and phonological effects: quantity in Icelandic*

[10] þak [θaːkʰ] 'roof' bát [pauːtʰ] 'boat, acc. sg.'
haus [hœiːs] 'head' ís [iːs] 'ice'
lit [lɪːtʰ] 'colour, acc. sg.' sæl [saiːl] 'blessed, fem.'
kot [kʰɔːtʰ] 'cottage' kvöl [kʰvœːl] 'torment'
kver [kʰvɛːr] 'booklet' heim [heiːm] 'world, acc. sg.'
ljós [ljouːs] 'light' bréf [prjɛːv] 'letter'
brún [pruːn] 'edge' brun [prʏːn] 'rush'

The evidence above makes sense within the approach to the syllable we adopt in this book. As argued extensively in chapter 5, word-final consonants are invariably onsets licensed by the following empty nucleus. For this reason all the words in [10] end in a pronounced onset consonant followed by a silent nucleus, which obviously means that the preceding syllable is open and its vowel must be long. Thus there is no difference in syllable structure between words of the type *þak* [θaːkʰ] 'roof' and *þaka* [θaːkʰa] 'gen. pl.' and the concomitant phonological effects will be identical. This is shown in the following diagram.

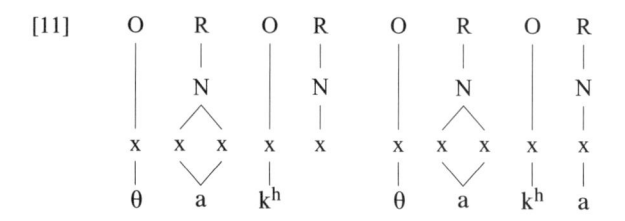

[11]
```
      O   R        O   R        O   R        O   R
      |   |        |   |        |   |        |   |
          N            N            N            N
         /\           |           /\           |
      x  x  x      x     x      x  x  x      x     x
      |   \/       |     |      |   \/       |     |
      θ    a      kʰ           θ    a       kʰ    a
```

The second nucleus – either empty or containing a melody – licenses the preceding onset, hence the first nucleus in both words must branch. We can see then that the regularity concerning Icelandic vowel length treats word-final consonants as onsets, which is exactly what we have come to expect on the basis of other phonological evidence.

This may be a good place to stress the relation between the interpretation of data and the assumed theoretical model. The claim that word-final consonants are onsets is a hypothesis, formulated independently of the Icelandic data. It constitutes part of a set of theoretical assumptions and hypotheses. In the formulation of any theoretical construct only a limited amount of evidence can be brought to bear and that is why it is necessary to test those assumptions against an ever increasing range of data from different languages. At times it proves necessary to modify or revise specific hypotheses, and occasionally we may be forced to abandon them altogether. It is important to realise that data cannot be analysed in a theoretical vacuum, and also that the theoretical apparatus must be subjected to constant verification and testing by assessing how it handles novel facts and complex problems. The phonological effects subsumed under Icelandic vowel length tally well with the hypothesis which views word-final consonants as onsets rather than codas.

7.5 Codas, onsets and vocalic quantity

It often happens that a consonantal ending is attached to a stem itself ending in a consonant – schematically a CVC stem is combined with a C ending. In such a case the first consonant may become a coda while the consonant of the ending is turned into an onset. Recall that codas must meet certain criteria to be licensed by onsets – in English for example they are typically sonorants: [l] qualifies as a coda if it is licensed by an obstruent in the onset, e.g. *filter* ['fɪltə]. On the other hand, a sonorant in the onset cannot license a preceding obstruent in the coda, hence the sequence [kl] in *eclipse* [ɪ'klɪps] will not be heterosyllabic but rather will form a branching onset. What we find in Icelandic is that the presence of a consonant-initial suffix frequently results in the formation of a well-formed rhyme–onset sequence; concomitantly, a short vowel is the only possibility in the preceding nucleus. It is not surprising, then, that the same stem can appear in different phonetic shapes – in other words, it has phonetic alternants, as shown below.

[12]　　heim [heiːm] 'world, acc. sg.'　　heims [heims] 'gen. sg.'
　　　　haus [hœiːs] 'head'　　　　　　hauss [hœisː] 'gen. sg.'
　　　　sæl [saiːl] 'blessed, fem.'　　　　sælt [sail̥t] 'neut.'
　　　　ljúf [ljuːv] 'dear, fem.'　　　　　ljúfri [ljuvrɪ] 'dat. sg.'
　　　　dæmi [taiːma] 'I judge'　　　　　dæmdi [taimtɪ] 'I judged'
　　　　talinn [tʰaːlɪn] 'counted, indef.'　taldi [tʰaltɪ] 'def.'
　　　　auga [œiːɣa] 'eye'　　　　　　　augna [œikna] 'gen. pl.'
　　　　kjósa [cʰouːsa] 'choose'　　　　　kjóstu [cʰoustʏ] 'imper.'
　　　　góð [kouːð] 'good, fem.'　　　　　góðra [kouðra] 'gen. pl.'

Although the number of similar morphological alternations in the language involving vowel length is quite considerable, the variation is governed by the same regularity: if the rhyme contains no consonantal complement, the nucleus is branching as in the left-hand column in [12]; if the rhyme ends in a consonant, the preceding nucleus is invariably non-branching, as in the right-hand column. Consider the representations of *heim* and *heims*.

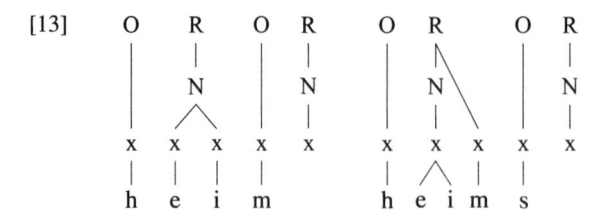

164   *Syllable structure and phonological effects: quantity in Icelandic*

[13]
```
   O   R      O   R      O   R       O   R
   |   |      |   |      |   \       |   |
   |   N      |   N      |   N\      |   N
   |  /\      |   |      |   | \     |   |
   x  x x     x   x      x   x  x    x   x
   |  | |     |   |      |   |  |    |   |
   h  e i     m          h   e  i    m   s
```

An important theoretical implication emerges from the Icelandic quantity alternations exemplified in [12] – [13], namely that syllabification is carried out independently of morphological structure. In the words in the right-hand column the vowels are short since they are followed by a rhymal complement and an onset. The coda consonant is the same as the final onset in the left-hand column words. The final right-hand onset is in fact the first consonant of an ending (in [13] the ending happens to be the genitive singular [s]). Since a sonorant and an obstruent such as [ms] can form a rhyme–onset sequence, they are syllabified as such, with a resulting short vowel. This shows that syllabification takes into account the melodic string and matches it with potential syllabic candidates; whether a given segment belongs to the stem or the ending is immaterial.

Likewise, if the consonant of the suffix is capable of forming a branching onset with the preceding consonant, the preceding syllable is open and consequently its nucleus must branch. Consider the forms in [14].

[14]   flata [flaːtʰa] 'flat, acc. sg. fem.'   flatrar [flaːtʰrar] 'gen. sg.'
       lík [liːkʰ] 'similar, fem.'   líkri [liːkʰrɪ] 'dat. sg.'
       ljót [ljouːtʰ] 'ugly, fem.'   ljótra [ljouːtʰra] 'gen. pl.'

The consonant [r] of the ending (*-rar, -ri, -ra*) combines with the stem-final plosive into a well-formed branching onset, which leaves the preceding syllable open, with its nucleus branching.

The absence of quantity alternations in [14], just as their presence in [12], is thus due to the same mechanisms of syllabification, whereby certain consonant sequences may and others may not appear in specific syllabic positions. The morphological status of the consonants in question is irrelevant. Further evidence for this can be seen in the following pair of adjectives:

[15]
a.   dapur [taːpʰʏr] 'sad, masc.'   dapran [taːpʰran] 'acc. sg.'
b.   fagur [faːɣʏr] 'fair, masc.'   fagran [faɣran] 'acc. sg.'

The final vowel [ʏ] of the masculine base is lost before vowel-initial endings in these (and other) adjectives. As a result the stem-final sonorant [r] finds itself next to an obstruent: when the obstruent is a plosive, a well-formed branching onset results and the preceding vowel is long [15a]; the voiced velar spirant [ɣ] cannot

7.5 Codas, onsets and vocalic quantity

appear in an onset with a following [r] – there are no words in Icelandic beginning with *[ɣr] – and hence it is assigned to the rhymal complement of the preceding syllable. Note that there are no morphological differences of any sort between [15a] and [15b]: the words differ in their melodic structure and consequently in their syllabification. Quantity follows as a mechanical consequence of syllabification.

As a final argument for the role of syllable structure in defining Icelandic quantity consider the following two classes of forms:

[16]
a.   kumra [kʰʏmra] 'bleat'   kumr [kʰʏmr] 'bleating'
      bölva [pœlva] 'curse'   bölv [pœlv] 'cursing'
      emja [ɛmja] 'wail'   emj [ɛmj] 'wailing'
b.   pukra [pʰʏːkʰra] 'be secretive'   pukr [pʰʏːkʰr] 'secretiveness'
      sötra [sœːtʰra] 'slurp'   sötr [sœːtʰr] 'slurping'
      snupra [snʏːpʰra] 'rebuke'   snupr [snʏːpʰr] 'rebuking'

The nouns in the right-hand columns are morphologically derived from the corresponding verbs. Verbs end in the suffix -*a* while the corresponding nouns end in an empty nucleus, which, in phonological terms, is a very minor change. This, however, means that syllabically the verbs and nouns have the same structure, as shown in [17] on the basis of the *kumra – kumr* pair.

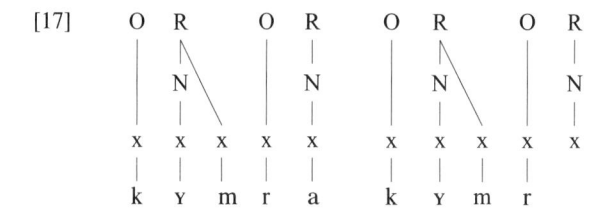

[17]
```
     O   R        O   R        O   R        O   R
     |   /\       |   |        |   /\       |   |
         N            N            N            N
         |            |            |            |
     x x x x     x    x x x x     x
     | | | |     |    | | | |     |
     k ʏ m r     a    k ʏ m r
```

The words in [16a] have a short vowel, which accords well with the view that the following consonantal sequence must be heterosyllabic: a sequence of two sonorants cannot form a branching onset. Consequently, the preceding vowel is short. In [16b] on the other hand the vowel is long before a well-formed branching onset both when the following – or final – nucleus contains a melody and also when it is empty. This goes to show that sequences of two word-final consonants are onsets when they meet the criteria of onsethood, i.e. when they constitute a specific combination of an obstruent and a sonorant. Whether the following nucleus is melodically empty or full has no bearing on the onsethood of a consonant or consonant sequence. The Icelandic case shows in the process that branching onsets appear not only word-initially and medially but that they are also perfectly possible word-finally.

Our discussion so far has covered long vowels in final syllables, before a single consonant, and before certain consonantal clusters. The unifying factor we have been able to discover in all these cases is the necessarily open nature of the stressed syllable. This is either because there is no consonant following, i.e. in the final position, or because the consonant or consonant cluster forms the onset of the syllable that follows. On the other hand, if the stressed syllable contains a rhymal complement (a coda), no long vowel is found there. The presence of vocalic length, then, depends upon the absence of a consonant in the rhymal position, and can be taken to reflect a general constraint prevailing in Icelandic which requires that a stressed rhyme must branch by dominating two skeletal positions. Vocalic quantity, then, is determined by the structure of the syllable.

If our conclusion is on the right track we should expect long vowels to appear regularly before branching onsets. However, case [6c] of the traditional context for vowel lengthening comprises the aspirated plosives [p^h, t^h, k^h] and the fricative [s] followed by any of [j, v, r] only; thus no unaspirated plosives or other spirants are mentioned there. The reasons for this are mostly historical in that generally in Modern Icelandic there are very few examples of single unaspirated plosives in the intervocalic, hence onset position; words like *edik* [ɛːtɪk^h] 'vinegar' are rare and mostly non-native. Just as rare are well-formed branching onsets involving non-aspirated plosives or spirants other than [s] in internal position; this is not to say that they are altogether absent, as shown below.

[18]   febrúar [fɛːpruar] 'February'   Madrid [maːtrɪt] 'Madrid'
       edrú [ɛːtru] 'sober'   Adríashaf [aːtrijashaːv] 'Adriatic'
       hebreskur [hɛːprɛskʏr] 'Hebrew'   Afríka [aːfrik^{h}a] 'Africa'
       vogrís [vɔːkris] 'stye (in the eye)' Labrador [laːpratɔr] 'Labrador'
       adrenalín [aːtrɛnalin] 'adrenalin'

The words in [18] behave exactly like those in the left-hand column of [16]: they have a long vowel before an obstruent followed by [r]. The only difference between them is that the group of plosives in [18] is non-aspirated. From a purely descriptive point of view we may note that the traditional formulation in [6] is simply not adequate as it does not cover all the known facts of the language. It could easily be rectified by the inclusion of the consonant sequences of [18] in the formulation in [6c]. This would merely increase the list of consonant sequences conditioning the appearance of long vowels, without making the set any less arbitrary. [6c] would now comprise [p^h, t^h, k^k, s] + [j, v, r] and also [p, t, k] + [r]. The unanswered (and unasked) question is why the [pr] of *febrúar* [fɛːpruar] requires a preceding long vowel but [lr], say, disallows it: *gulra* [kʏlra] 'yellow, gen. pl.' (cf. *gulur* [kʏːlʏr] 'nom. sg. masc.'). Since sequences of an obstruent followed by [r] are branching onsets, the examples in [18] simply show that vowels are long before a following branching onset, and thus they strengthen the case for the syllabic conditioning of vowel quantity in Icelandic.

Although words like those in [18] are not too numerous, they are particularly significant because they embrace loans, including place names. They testify to the reality of the constraint requiring stressed rhymes to branch: note that if such a constraint were not operative in the modern language, the appearance of long vowels in, for example, *adrenalín* [aːtrenalin] or *Madrid* [maːtrɪt] would be completely mysterious. Assuming that the words are borrowed from English and Spanish, there is absolutely no reason why the short [ə] of *adrenalin* [əˈdrenəlɪn] or the short [a] of *Madrid* [maˈðrið] should be replaced by Icelandic long [aː] rather than its short counterpart. The emergence of a long vowel in the target language – here Icelandic – corresponding to a short one in the source language – English or Spanish – indicates that the source language has nothing to do with the quantity of the vowel in the target language. Vowel quantity is governed by language-internal principles specific to the borrowing language. The cases of [18] actually bring additional evidence in favour of the syllable-based analysis of vowel length in Icelandic. In what follows we shall adopt as correct the position that if a stressed vowel is long, it must appear in an open syllable and conversely, if it is short, it must be closed with a rhymal complement. Since we now seem to know what factors control vowel length, we can take the facts concerning this phenomenon and try and see what they can tell us about syllable structure. This is a common practice in phonological analysis: one arrives at a generalisation on the basis of relatively clear evidence, and then one exploits the generalisation to learn more about the structure of the language, or else one uses that generalisation to deal with unclear or ambiguous cases. Our generalisation is that if a vowel is long, it cannot be followed by a coda. In what follows we shall see what vowel length can tell us about syllable structure in Icelandic.

7.6 Quantity as evidence for syllabification

Recall that in the traditional formulation vowels are long before obstruents followed by [j, v, r] (see [6c]). We have partially reinterpreted this as meaning that such clusters form branching onsets, a statement which may be in need of modification. In the light of the evidence presented in preceding chapters sequences of s+C are unlikely to be branching onsets. Let us inspect the Icelandic situation more closely, starting with the [sr] sequence.

The most common context for the occurrence of long vowels before [sr] involves certain endings of the adjectival declension: *-ri* 'dat. sg. fem.', *-rar* 'gen. sg. fem.'

and -*ra* 'gen. pl.'; occasional loans like *Ísrael* [iːsraɛːl] 'Israel' are also relevant. The adjectival forms are exemplified in [19].

[19] laus [lœiːs] 'loose'   lausri [lœiːsrɪ]   lausrar [lœiːsrar]   lausra [lœiːsra]
      hás [hauːs] 'hoarse'   hásri [hauːsrɪ]   hásrar [hauːsrar]   hásra [hauːsra]
      ljós [ljouːs] 'clear'   ljósri [ljouːsrɪ]   ljósrar [ljouːsrar] ljósra [ljouːsra]
      vís [viːs] 'certain'   vísri [viːsrɪ]   vísrar [viːsrar]   vísra [viːsra]
      fús [fuːs] 'eager'   fúsri [fuːsrɪ]   fúsrar [fuːsrar]   fúsra [fuːsra]

The evidence concerning vowel length clearly indicates that the consonant [s] does not belong to the first syllable and is not its rhymal complement; in other words, the sequence [sr] does not form a coda–onset combination. Logically, then, [s] itself must be the onset of the following syllable or at least part of it. The evidence concerning vowel length discloses nothing, however, about the status of the following sonorant [r]. Specifically, for the first vowel to be long the sonorant does not have to be in a single constituent with the spirant [s]; in brief, the syllabic affiliation of [r] has nothing to do with the branching nature of the preceding nucleus. In the previous chapter we gathered some evidence indicating that a sequence such as [sr] should not be analysed as a branching onset. Icelandic supports this position in a striking fashion.

If the sequence [sr] illustrated word-internally in [19] were a branching onset, we should expect to find examples of this cluster word-initially. This does not happen: in fact, there is not a single word recorded starting with [sr] in Icelandic. A gap of this sort can hardly be an accident. Note that we have specifically argued against identifying the word-initial position with a syllabic constituent (the onset), or the word-final position with the syllabic coda. In other words, just because some consonant combination appears at the beginning of the word does not mean that it is automatically a syllable onset. The reverse, however, cannot be maintained: if a certain consonant combination can be argued to be an onset on the basis of word-internal evidence, we expect to find it initially just as well. Since syllabic constituents are basically independent of their position within a word, the non-appearance and impossibility of [sr] initially shows that it is not a branching onset. Vowel quantity argues, as we have seen, against the cluster being a coda–onset combination, since then the preceding vowel would have to be short. What we are left with is the possibility that both members of the [sr] sequence must belong to separate onsets.

The separateness of the two onsets could be accounted for in two different ways. Taking into account the fact that [r] begins three distinct inflectional endings we might propose that the adjectival stem makes up a domain of its own and is hence separated from the ending by a domain boundary. The representations of the words *lausri*, *lausrar* would take the following shape.

7.6 Quantity as evidence for syllabification

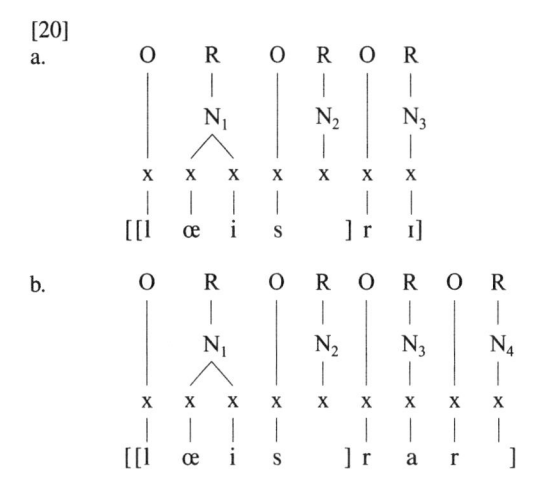

[20]
a.
```
         O   R       O   R    O   R
         |   |       |   |    |   |
         |   N₁      |   N₂   |   N₃
         |  /\       |   |    |   |
         x  x  x     x   x    x   x
         |  |  |     |   |    |   |
        [[l œ  i     s ] r    ɪ ]
```

b.
```
         O   R       O   R    O   R    O   R
         |   |       |   |    |   |    |   |
         |   N₁      |   N₂   |   N₃   |   N₄
         |  /\       |   |    |   |    |   |
         x  x  x     x   x    x   x    x   x
         |  |  |     |   |    |   |    |   |
        [[l œ  i     s ] r    a   r    ]
```

In both [20a] and [20b] the stem, as a separate phonological domain, ends in a vowel, which ensures that the preceding spirant [s] is in the onset and hence the first nucleus is branching. The endings -ri, -rar (and also -ra) form another domain together with the stem but are separated from it; this is indicated in the representation by the additional bracketing of the internal or stem domain.

An alternative representation of the forms would differ from this by assigning just a single domain to the whole word. In this way [20] would be replaced by [21].

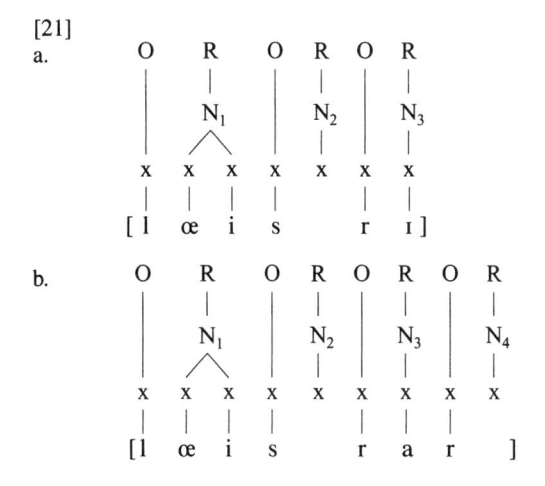

[21]
a.
```
         O   R       O   R    O   R
         |   |       |   |    |   |
         |   N₁      |   N₂   |   N₃
         |  /\       |   |    |   |
         x  x  x     x   x    x   x
         |  |  |     |   |    |   |
        [ l œ  i     s       r   ɪ ]
```

b.
```
         O   R       O   R    O   R    O   R
         |   |       |   |    |   |    |   |
         |   N₁      |   N₂   |   N₃   |   N₄
         |  /\       |   |    |   |    |   |
         x  x  x     x   x    x   x    x   x
         |  |  |     |   |    |   |    |   |
        [ l œ  i     s       r   a    r   ]
```

As in [20] the two consonants making up [sr] are in separate onsets, with an empty nucleus coming between them. This ensures that the conditions for the appropriate length of the stem vowel are met.

Given that the representations with and without internal domain structure have identical consequences, we may legitimately ask whether there is anything that allows us to choose between the two.

To try and answer this question we need to note that by separating the stem from the ending by an internal domain, we are in effect making a statement about the morphological isolation of both the stem and the ending. If a particular ending constitutes a morphologically independent unit, we would expect this to be visible whenever it is attached to a stem. In other words, we would expect stems other than those that end in [s] to display some phonological properties when pronounced in isolation and when combined with the ending. This, however, is not the case.

Compare the adjectives containing the ending of the masculine singular nominative -*ur* and the same stems preceding the three suffixes under discussion, i.e. -*ri* in the dative singular feminine, -*rar* in the genitive singular feminine and -*ra* in the genitive plural.

[22]

gulur [kʏːlʏr] 'yellow'
    gulri [kʏlrɪ]   gulrar [kʏlrar]   gulra [kʏlra]
glaður [klaːðʏr] 'glad'
    glaðri [klaðrɪ]   glaðrar [klaðrar]   glaðra [klaðra]
slæmur [slaiːmʏr] 'bad'
    slæmri [slaimrɪ]   slæmrar [slaimrar]   slæmra [slaimra]
vanur [vaːnʏr] 'accustomed'
    vanri [vanrɪ]   vanrar [vanrar]   vanra [vanra]
dýr [tiːr] 'expensive'
    dýrri [tirːɪ]   dýrrar [tirːar]   dýrra [tirːa]

The masculine singular examples all contain a long stressed vowel since they are followed by an onset consonant; in the remaining forms the stem-final consonant occupies the rhymal position because the preceding nucleus is non-branching. This means that the [r] of the ending is in the onset position. In other words in [22], unlike [19], the stem-final consonant is not in the onset and is not separated from the consonant of the ending by an empty nucleus. These examples show, then, that stems do not make up internal domains in the case of the three inflectional endings in Icelandic; were this so, the length of vowels in the stems of [22] would remain unaffected. With respect to the data in [19] we can claim that the linguistic reality is captured most adequately by the representations without an internal domain structure and with the two consonants [s] and [r] in separate onsets, i.e. those in [21]. We also know now that [sr] is not a branching onset; the fact that vowels are long before this cluster is simply due to the fact that the [s] is not a rhymal complement but an onset. As the discussion has revealed, it is a single slot onset, with the [r] being separated from it by an empty nucleus.

7.6 Quantity as evidence for syllabification

Before proceeding it is necessary to stress one important theoretical implication which emerges from our discussion so far. Consider again the forms in [22] like *gulur* [kʏːlʏr] – *gulri* [kʏlrɪ], and specifically the syllabic position of the stem-final consonant, in this case of the lateral [l]. As evidenced by the length of the preceding vowel, the stem-final consonant in the nominative masculine singular in the left-hand column is invariably in the onset, while in the remaining cases it is a rhymal complement. A diagrammatic representation reveals the difference clearly.

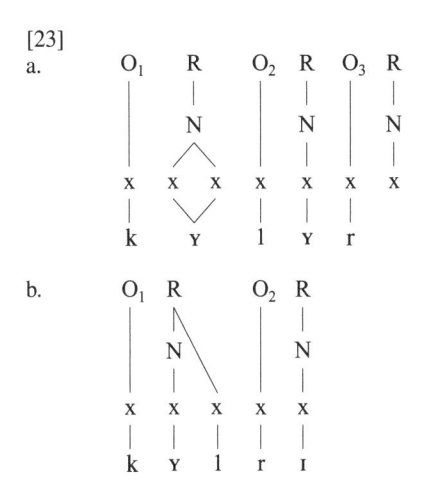

[23]
a.

```
        O₁   R        O₂  R      O₃  R
        |    |        |   |      |   |
             N            N          N
             /\           |          |
        x   x  x      x   x      x   x
        |   \ /       |   |      |   |
        k    ʏ        l   ʏ      r
```

b.

```
        O₁   R        O₂  R
        |   /|        |   |
            N\        N
            | \       |
        x   x  x      x   x
        |   |  |      |   |
        k   ʏ  l      r   ɪ
```

In [23a] the lateral occupies the second onset O₂ while in [23b] it is placed in the complement position of the first rhyme. Thus, depending on what follows, the same stem has two different syllabic representations with partly different phonological consequences. The Icelandic quantity effects show that melodic units of one and the same morpheme may have different syllabic affiliations depending on the context they find themselves in. Since [s] and [r] cannot form a branching onset or a rhyme–onset sequence, a nucleus has to intervene between them, and thus they both find themselves in separate onset positions. The sequence [lr], on the other hand, can be divided between a rhyme and a following onset, hence no additional syllabic structure needs to be supplied. It follows from this that syllabic structure results from the interplay of the syllabic possibilities of a language with the melodic composition of words; critically, it is not the case that individual morphemes need to maintain a uniform syllabic representation. We observe here further confirmation of the tentative conclusion in the preceding chapter as to the role which morphological considerations play in phonological analysis – a phonological interpretation must be based primarily on phonological evidence. Similarly we have also seen repeatedly that phonetic data alone provide an

172 *Syllable structure and phonological effects: quantity in Icelandic*

unreliable guide to phonological structure. In particular, a mere phonetic sequence is only a partial indicator of the phonological arrangement: while presumably a phonetic sequence C_1C_2 is unlikely to appear in a different linear order phonologically, i.e. as C_2C_1, it does, as we have seen, correspond to three possible structural configurations, namely a branching onset, a coda–onset combination and a sequence of two onsets. Since onsets and rhymal complements necessarily presuppose a licensing nucleus, we end up with the following three schematic representations for a C_1C_2 sequence. The actual shape a given phonetic sequence will display depends on the specific choices the language in question makes.

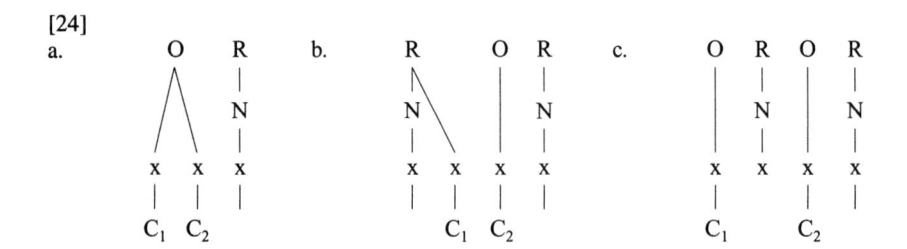

[24]
a.   O   R   b.   R   O   R   c.   O   R   O   R
        /\ | /\ | | | | | |
       / \ N   N \ | N | N | N
      /   \ | | \ | | | | | |
      x x x   x   x   x   x   x   x   x   x
      | | | | | | | | | | |
      C₁ C₂   C₁   C₂   C₁   C₂

The structures can be exemplified in Icelandic by: [tʰr] in *betri* [pɛːtʰrɪ] 'better' ([24a]), [rt] in *svartur* [svar̥tʏr] 'black' ([24b]), and [sr] in *lausra* [lœiːsra] 'loose, gen. pl.' ([24c]).

We will now continue our investigation of what Icelandic vowel length can tell us about the syllable structure of that language. We take it as established that stressed nuclei must branch if no coda follows; the question is to what extent this generalisation is useful in determining the syllabic status of consonant sequences. In the case of [sr] we have argued that the most plausible interpretation involves a sequence of two onsets. Let us now turn to the other sonorant consonant that appears after [s] in a lengthening context, namely [j]. As shown in [25], a nucleus preceding such a cluster is necessarily branching.

[25]   flysja [flɪːsja] 'peel'   dysja [tɪːsja] 'bury'
        gresja [krɛːsja] 'prairie'   Esja [ɛːsja] 'name of a mountain'
        grisjun [krɪːsjʏn] 'thinning out'

Additionally there is a small number of very common words beginning with [sj], e.g.:

[26]   sjúkur [sjuːkʰʏr] 'sick'   sjór [sjouːr] 'sea'
        sér [sjɛːr] 'oneself'   sjálfur [sjaulvʏr] 'self'

7.6 Quantity as evidence for syllabification

On the basis of such examples we might conclude that the cluster in focus forms a branching onset: the vowels which precede it are long and it can appear in the initial position. Alternatively, we might place the two consonants of the [sj] cluster in separate onsets with an intervening empty nucleus, thus paralleling the interpretation of the [sr] combination. Since in the previous chapter we saw plenty of evidence strongly arguing against the possibility of [s] appearing in branching onsets, this alternative might well be worth exploring.

Let us look at the way that other consonants combine with [j] both internally and initially. The examples in [27] omit sequences following a long nucleus, i.e. combinations in which the first part is an aspirated plosive or the spirant [s].

[27] temja [tʰɛmja] 'tame, vb.'   mjólk [mjouɭk] 'milk'
      venja [vɛnja] 'get used'   njóta [njouːtʰa] 'enjoy'
      hefja [hɛvja] 'begin'   fjalla [flatla] 'discuss'
      biðja [pɪðja] 'ask'   þjónn [θjoutn] 'waiter'
      kilja [cʰɪlja] 'paperback'   ljótur [ljouːtʰʏr] 'ugly'
      berja [pɛrja] 'beat'   rjómi [rjouːmɪ] 'cream'

The situation is quite straightforward in the left-hand column words with a short stressed vowel: the vocalic quantity shows that the following sonorant or voiced spirant is a rhymal complement, while the palatal spirant [j] is located in the following onset. There is another, more general consideration, which makes sequences of a sonorant followed by [j] quite implausible candidates for branching onsets: as we have pointed out several times before, usually branching onsets are formed by an obstruent followed by a sonorant. In this way general theoretical expectations are confirmed by the fact that the vowel preceding the cluster is short, and we conclude that the clusters are heterosyllabic, making up a coda–onset sequence.

What about the same sequences appearing word-initially, as in the right-hand column? As we have just seen, they are implausible as branching onsets on theoretical grounds and are definitely heterosyllabic when they appear domain-internally. Since they are never branching onsets internally, one might doubt whether they are syllabified into onsets initially. Choosing among the possibilities in [24], they can be either a rhyme–onset combination or a sequence of two onsets separated by an empty nucleus. Since internally sequences of a sonorant or a voiced spirant and [j] are a coda–onset structure, the simplest solution would be to extend this generalisation to the initial position. This would mean that the right-hand words in [27] are also heterosyllabic, with [j] being located in the onset. Arguably, the initial consonants are syllabically rhymal complements and hence are preceded by an empty nucleus. The words *temja* 'tame, vb.' and *mjólk* 'milk' can be represented as follows.

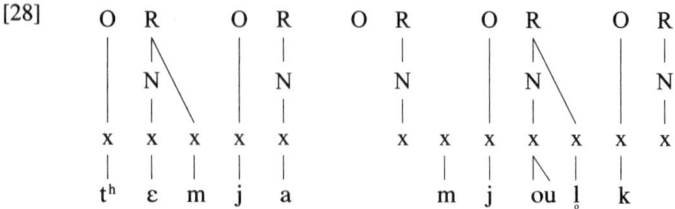

174 *Syllable structure and phonological effects: quantity in Icelandic*

[28]

```
 O   R      O R    O R    O   R      O R
 |  /\      | |    | |    |  /\      | |
 |  N \     | N    | N    |  N \     | N
 |  |  \    | |    | |    |  |  \    | |
 x  x  x    x x    x x    x  x  x    x x
 |  |  |    | |    | |    |  | /\ |  | |
 tʰ ɛ  m    j a           m  j  ou l̥  k
```

In no case does [j] appear in a branching onset – if anything, it occupies a separate onset itself. The evidence of examples like [28] fully supports this conclusion and would be true even if words like *mjólk* were to be represented with both initial consonants in separate onsets.

There is more evidence in favour of [j] appearing as the sole consonantal melody in a non-branching onset. It pertains to the ways in which consonants can be combined word-initially.

Initial consonant sequences consisting of three segments either begin with [s] or end in [j]. The former group is uninteresting from our point of view since words like those in [29a] can be analysed as beginning with rhymal [s] followed by a branching onset, as in [29b].

[29]
a. splundra [spluntra] 'shatter'   sprengja [spreiɲca] 'explode'
   straumur [strœi:mʏr] 'current'   sklokur [sklɔ:kʰʏr] 'saliva'
   skrifa [skrɪ:va] 'write'

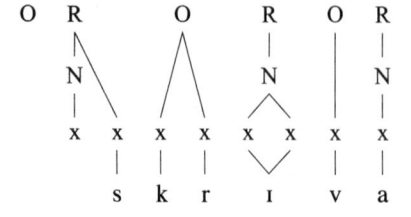

b.
```
  O     R       O   R    O R
 /\    /\       |  /\    | |
 N \  /  \      |  N \   | N
 |  \/    \     |  |  \  | |
 x  x x   x     x  x  x  x x
 |  | |    \/   |  |  |  | |
 s  k r    ɪ    v  a
```

Far more interesting are those cases where a well-formed branching onset is followed by another consonant, which invariably happens to be [j] ([30a]). In fact, Icelandic admits combinations of such three-member sequences with initial [s] which yield four consonant clusters ([30b]).

[30]
a. brjóst [prjoust] 'breast'   bljúgur [plju:ʏr] 'modest'
   prjón [pʰrjou:n] 'knitting'   drjúpa [trju:pʰa] 'drip'
   tré [tʰrjɛ:] 'tree'   krjúpa [kʰrju:pʰa] 'kneel'
   kljást [kʰljaust] 'fight'   gljá [kljau:] 'glisten'

	grjón [krjouːn] 'cereal'	flétta [fljɛhta] 'plait'
	frjáls [frjauls] 'free'	þrjótur [θrjouːtʰʏr] 'villain'
b.	strjáll [strjautl] 'sparse'	skrjáfa [skrjauːva] 'rustle'

If we continue to view branching onsets as maximally binary, i.e. consisting of two members, the examples in [30] are thus violations of this requirement and they need to be interpreted in such a way as not to constitute such a violation. We regard the fact that the necessary third member of such combinations (or fourth if the first is [s]) must be [j] as a non-accident. In other words, this fact reveals something regular and systematic about the structure of Icelandic. It could be proposed that the three consonant sequences in [30a] consist of a well-formed branching onset followed by an empty nucleus and an onset containing just [j]; the four-consonant sequences of [30b] would have a rhymal [s] preceding a branching onset and another onset with [j]. In both cases [j] would constitute an onset of its own. The representations of *brjóst* [prjoust] 'breast' and *skrjáfa* [skrjauːva] 'rustle' are supplied below.

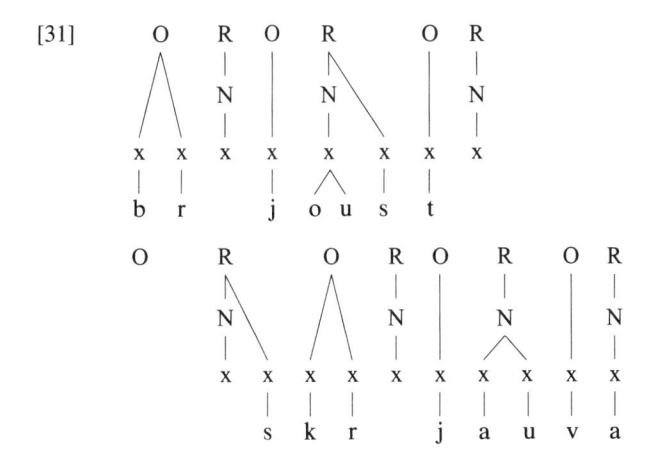

[31]

It is clear that the onset positioning of [j] in such forms dovetails with the structure we have proposed above for words like *temja*, *mjólk* (see examples in [27]). No violations of syllabic structure need to be recognised and no quantity complications arise when [j] is in the onset. Recall now that the [sj] sequences also require a preceding vowel to be long, as in *flysja* [flɪːsja] 'peel' (see [25] for more examples). The long vowel tells us that [sj] is not a possible coda–onset combination but that [s] must be in the onset; if we adopt the solution for the invariable onsethood of [j] just presented, we no longer need to regard [sj] as a potential branching onset, but it can be interpreted as a sequence of two onsets. This analysis would allow us to obtain all the required quantity effects without compromising what are

176   *Syllable structure and phonological effects: quantity in Icelandic*

reasonably well-established syllabification conditions. [32] applies this analysis to the word *flysja*.

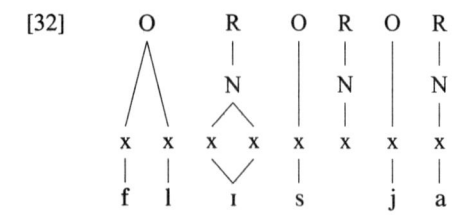

[32]

```
        O       R     O  R   O  R
       /\      |      |  |   |  |
              N      N      N
             /\
       x x   x x     x  x   x  x
       | |    \/     |      |  |
       f l     ɪ     s      j  a
```

Having gone this far, we can take a further step and claim that it is mandatory for all instances of [j] in the language to be in the onset. This would include not only the lengthening sequences consisting of an aspirated plosive and [j] ([6c]), but also all initial combinations of a plosive followed by [j], e.g.:

[33] nepja [nɛːpʰja] 'bad weather'   sitja [sɪːtʰja] 'sit'
      pjatla [pʰjahtla] 'rag'   björk [pjœr̥k] 'birch'
      tjald [tʰjalt] 'tent'   djúpur [tjuːpʰʏr] 'deep'
      fjölga [fjœlka] 'multiply'   vél [vjɛːl] 'machine'
      þjá [θjauː] 'plague'

The decision to extend the analysis to the forms exemplified in [33] may seem far-fetched. Note, however, that initial sequences of a sonorant plus [j] have to be interpreted as onset sequences with an intervening empty nucleus, partly because they do not conform to the structure of branching onsets, and crucially because they never form onsets internally, hence preceding vowels are always short (see [27]).

It is not clear how we should treat spirants other than [s]: the voiced spirants [ð, v] when followed by [j] are internally rhymal complements because of the shortness of the preceding vowel (see *hefja, biðja* in [27]). Initially we have [v, f, θ] before [j] and it is possible to treat them in a fashion parallel to what is found domain-internally, i.e. as coda–onset sequences. Alternatively they might be treated as onset sequences with intervening empty nuclei. We have no evidence to back up this conviction so possibly this part of the analysis needs to be more thoroughly researched. For the sake of argument we shall adopt the view that [j] always appears in a non-branching onset in Icelandic.

The evidence for the s+C sequences after a branching nucleus is progressively dwindling. There seem to be just two examples left illustrating this context, namely *tvisvar* [tʰvɪːsvar] 'twice' and *þrisvar* [θrɪːsvar] 'three times'; it might be possible to regard *-var* as a suffix which is separated from the root by a domain boundary. If we were to adopt this position, then the bases *tvis-* and *þris-* would have to have a long vowel in the same way as any word ending in a single consonant, since

7.6 Quantity as evidence for syllabification 177

that consonant is the final onset, which would leave the first syllable open (cf. the examples in [10]). In word-initial position the [sv] of *svara* [svaːra] 'answer', *svæði* [svaiːðɪ] 'area', *svefn* [svɛpn] 'sleep' etc. could be analysed in the same way as the initial sequence [sj], i.e. as two onsets with an intervening empty nucleus. The words *svepn* [svɛpn] 'sleep' and *sjúkur* [sjuːkʰʏr] 'sick' can be represented as follows.

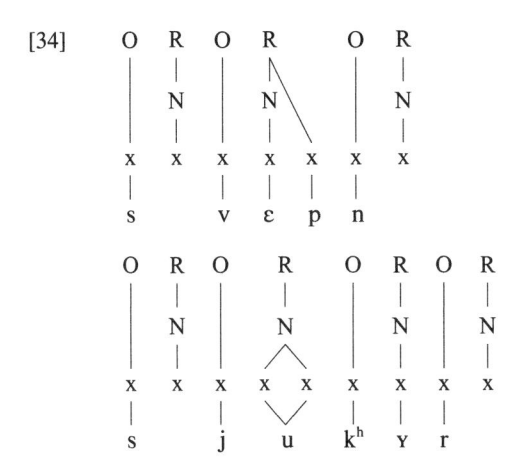

[34]

```
    O   R   O   R       O   R
    |   |   |   \       |   |
    |   N   N    \      |   N
    |   |   |     \     |   |
    x   x   x   x  x    x   x
    |       |   |  |    |
    s       v   ɛ  p    n


    O   R   O   R       O   R   O   R
    |   |   |   |       |   |   |   |
    |   N   N   |       N   |   N
    |   |   |  /\       |   |   |
    x   x   x x  x      x   x   x   x
    |       |  \/       |       |
    s       j   u       kʰ      ʏ   r
```

In the preceding discussion we have tried to explain why s+C sequences after long vowels are not branching onsets. We suggest that both [s] and the sonorants [j, v, r] are assigned to separate onsets; this accounts for the length of the preceding vowel and also allows us to come to grips with additional phonological facts, such as certain restrictions on the combinability of consonants, i.e. their phonotactic potential. We have arrived at these results because our view of syllable structure and of syllabification is not confined to the assignment of chunks of melodic material to successive constituents. Quite conversely, our approach is that the syllable structure needs to be discovered, and that existing phonological regularities, such as restrictions on vowel length or consonant combinations in Icelandic, help us to find this structure. Alternative solutions can certainly be entertained, but in evaluating them we must ask how they cope not just with quantity itself but with the whole complex of facts related to quantity in the language.

Summing up from a slightly different perspective, we can say that the s+C sequence after a long vowel in Icelandic is the result of two regularities. One of them bans [s] from appearing in branching onsets; as we saw in previous chapters, this is a general principle of phonology rather than anything specifically Icelandic. The other regularity refers to the nature of the coda–onset junctures, a point that needs to be addressed now.

7.7 Coda–onset contacts in Icelandic

Discussing the rhymal complement (the coda) and its relation to other constituents in chapter 5 we insisted that it has to be licensed by a following onset. Typically, rhymal sonorants are licensed by onset obstruents. Other combinations are also possible, such as for instance the combination of a rhymal obstruent with an onset obstruent (English [pt] in *chapter*), but these are normally subject to various restrictions (e.g. in English the reverse order of the two obstruents, yielding [tp], is not tolerated). The melodic possibilities of such syllabic **contacts** between a coda and a following onset are the domain of word phonotactics, a subject which needs to be studied individually for each language.

Returning to Icelandic, we note that the s+C sequence is not a possible contact when the C is [j, v, r]. This obviously follows from the fact that the preceding vowel is long, hence [s] is not a coda. No matter whether we interpret such clusters as branching onsets or onset sequences, [sj] etc. are not possible coda–onset contacts. [s] can be a coda before a specified onset only. Consider again the examples in [8b] repeated here for convenience as [35].

[35]   hestur [hɛstʏr] 'horse'   ástar [austar] 'love, gen. sg.'
           flaska [flaska] 'bottle'   fiskur [fɪskʏr] 'fish'
           aspar [aspar] 'aspen, nom. pl.'   geispa [ceispa] 'yawn'
           asni [asnɪ] 'donkey'   kvíslar [kʰvislar] 'branch, gen. sg.'
           hismi [hɪsmɪ] 'chaff'

An inspection of the onsets following the coda [s] in these examples reveals that this position is occupied either by a plosive or a stop sonorant. Generally, then, [s] is licensed in the coda by a stop in the onset. It is not licensed when followed by a continuant sonorant, as we have seen. This is why we interpret an initial s+stop as a coda–onset contact (see [29b, 31]), and an initial s+continuant sonorant as an onset sequence (see [34]). In other words, given a sequence of s+C there is in every case only one possible way of syllabifying it; the choice will depend upon the melodic structure of the C and the evidence supplied by phonological regularities such as quantity distribution.

A striking case of the interdependence between melodic and syllabic structure can be found when, for morphological reasons, an aspirated plosive comes to stand before the voiceless spirant [s]. The spirant represents the genitive singular ending of certain classes of masculine and neuter nouns and adjectives. The addition of the suffix admits a short vowel in some cases [36a] but not in others [36b].

7.7 Coda–onset contacts in Icelandic

[36]
a. heimur [hei:mʏr] 'world'   heims [heims]
   dýr [tiːr] 'animal'   dýrs [ti̥rs]
   dalur [taːlʏr] 'valley'   dals [tals]
   dagur [taːɣʏr] 'day'   dags [taxs]
   hús [huːs] 'house'   húss [husː]
   vanur [vaːnʏr] 'accustomed'   vans [vans]
   góður [kouːðʏr] 'good'   góðs [kouθs]
b. tap [tʰaːpʰ] 'loss'   taps [tʰaːpʰs]
   rit [rɪːtʰ] 'written work'   rits [rɪːtʰs]
   bak [paːkʰ] 'back'   baks [paːkʰs]

The right-hand column in [36a] shows that a sonorant or a spirant and another spirant make a well-formed coda–onset contact, with the consequence that the preceding vowel is short. All the examples in [36b] on the other hand violate the traditional formulations of the contexts where vowels can be long: sequences of a plosive and a spirant are not listed in [6c] as a length inducing context. One cannot resort to morphological conditioning since [36a] shows that vowels do not have to be long before genitival -s. Within our syllabic approach to Icelandic quantity, an aspirated plosive in the coda is precluded not only before a spirant in the onset but, as argued in 6.5, before any consonant – in brief, aspirated plosives never appear in codas. As a result both the aspirated plosive and the spirant [s] in [36b] have to occupy separate onsets and hence the nucleus must branch. There is, then, a basic difference between aspirated plosives and the voiceless spirant [s]: while the former are categorically ruled out as rhymal complements, the spirant is accepted there as long as the licensing onset is itself a stop (see [35]).

The melodic composition of segments is crucial to the determination of coda–onset contact possibilities. We have just seen that aspirated plosives can only appear in the onset. The same restriction does not hold for unaspirated plosives, which can occupy the coda position if licensed by a stop sonorant. In this way we see why sequences such as [pl, tl, kl, pn, tn, kn] are preceded by a short vowel.

[37] efla [ɛpla] 'strengthen'   efna [ɛpna] 'carry out'
    kalla [katla] 'call'   seinna [seitna] 'later'
    sigla [sɪkla] 'sail'   sagna [sakna] 'story, gen. pl.'

The different combinatory possibilities of aspirated and unaspirated plosives can be appreciated by comparing the word *taplaus* [taːpʰlœis] 'without loss' with *tafllaus* [tʰaplœis] 'without chess'. The aspirated plosive must be in the onset, which leaves the preceding syllable open and hence requires a branching nucleus; the unaspirated plosive is accepted as a rhymal complement before a lateral stop, which accounts for the shortness of the vowel.

The segmental possibilities of what we have called the contact position are determined in part by language-independent conditions and in part by language-specific restrictions; the impossibility of [nd] as a branching onset and the likelihood of it forming a contact combination illustrates the former situation, while the necessary onsethood of [j] or of aspirated plosives in Icelandic is an instance of the latter situation. In [38] we list briefly the most typical combinations found in Icelandic, some of which have been amply illustrated above. Note that in each case the stressed nucleus is non-branching, exactly as we have come to expect.

[38] coda–onset contact combinations in Icelandic
a. sonorant – obstruent
panta [pan̪ta] 'order, vb.', *gúrka* [gur̥ka] 'cucumber'
b. spirant – obstruent
taska [tʰaska] 'bag', *hefti* [hɛftɪ] 'notebook', *liðka* [lɪθka] 'make flexible', *sagði* [saɣðɪ] 'I said', *vaxa* [vaxsa] 'grow'
c. unaspirated plosive – sonorant
hefna [hɛpna] 'avenge', *elli* [ɛtlɪ] 'old age'
d. voiced spirant – sonorant
eigra [eiɣra] 'wander', *eðli* [ɛðlɪ] 'nature', *efri* [ɛvrɪ] 'upper', *faðma* [faðma] 'embrace'
e. [s] – sonorant stop
asni [asnɪ] 'donkey', *hismi* [hɪsmɪ] 'chaff', *veisla* [veisla] 'party'
f. sonorant – sonorant
hamra [hamra] 'hammer, vb.', *harma* [harma] 'lament, vb.', *hamla* [hamla] 'restrain', *ilma* [ɪlma] 'smell, vb.'

The above presentation is schematic and calls for further study. An attempt should also be made to collapse the different statements, since as formulated in [38a–f] they seem to be nothing but a list of unrelated conditions. We will refrain from conflating the conditions or formalising them here since the general point is quite clear: the classes of segments admitted into the coda or the onset slot in the contact are severely delimited. It is not the case that the rhyme can end in any consonant irrespectively of what follows. This is in no way necessary or obvious: since syllables are independent units, one would expect precisely the opposite to be true, i.e. the structure of one syllable should have nothing to do with that of the neighbouring syllable. Our investigation shows conclusively that this is not the case: when syllables are combined within a phonological domain, the nature of the coda has to be negotiated with the consonant appearing in the following onset. In other words, the coda consonant has to be licensed by the following onset. If licensing is not possible, an alternative strategy conforming to general principles of syllabification has to be devised. We have seen above one such mechanism, namely the projection of both consonants as onsets with an intermediate empty nucleus: recall the vowel length difference between *heims* [heims] 'world, gen. sg.' and *taps* [tʰaːpʰs] 'loss, gen. sg.' and the discussion surrounding the examples in [36]. There is another mechanism which forces forms to conform to the licensing possibilities. Consider the alternations shown in [39].

[39] bátur [pauːtʰʏr] 'boat'   báts [pauːtʰs] or [pausː] 'gen. sg.'
      litur [lɪːtʰʏr] 'colour, n.'   litka [lɪːtʰkʰa] or [lɪθka] 'vb.'
      ríkur [riːkʰʏr] 'rich'   ríks [rixs] 'gen. sg. masc.'
      vaka [vaːkʰa] 'be awake'   vakti [vaxtɪ] 'I was awake'
      kaupa [kʰœiːpʰa] 'buy'   keypti [cʰeiftɪ] 'I bought'
      dýpi [tiːpʰɪ] 'depth'   dýpka [difka] 'deepen'

The left-hand column words contain a stem-final aspirated plosive which, as we have established, can only appear in the onset in Icelandic. The stems come to stand before an obstruent representing some inflectional or derivational suffix; what is relevant is the syllabification of the two consonants at hand. *báts* and *litka* admit two pronunciations. In one, the aspirated plosive is projected as the onset with a concomitant preceding branching nucleus. This is the pattern discussed above and illustrated with the examples in [36b] where aspirated plosives are invariably onsets. The alternative variants are equally striking since corresponding to the [tʰs] and [tʰkʰ] of the first possibility we find a long [sː] and [θk] with a preceding short nucleus. In the remaining forms of [39] the onset plosive of the left-hand column corresponds to the spirant appearing before the obstruent of the ending; the nuclei are invariably non-branching. This is a general pattern in Icelandic which we discussed with respect to consonants in 6.5. Here we have an explanation for the regularity. The variants containing spirants before plosives in the right-hand column conform to the contact possibility formulated as [38b] above. If we have two plosives, then both of them must be onsets. Which of the alternatives is chosen, or whether both of them are licit appears to be a matter for the lexicon in the same way that the past of *dream* in English can be either *dreamed* or *dreamt*. What phonology does is to ensure that the forms of the language conform to constraints, both those of a universal nature and those which are at least partially language-specific, like [38].

7.8 Length in compounds

Our extended discussion of a single problem in Icelandic phonology – the length of nuclei – can, then, be seen to reduce to the presence or absence of a coda, and the nature of this coda, if present. Since this is a phonological regularity it is not surprising that its effects can be found within morphologically complex words, including compounds. Consider first two intriguing sets of words:

[40]
a. hvítur [kʰviːtʰʏr] 'white' hvítleitur [kʰviːtʰleitʰʏr] 'whitish'
 hvítvín [kʰviːtʰvin] 'white wine'
b. rauður [rœiːðʏr] 'red' rauðleitur [rœiðleitʰʏr] 'reddish'
 rauðvín [rœiðvin] 'red wine'

The long vowel in the first words is unsurprising: this is exactly what we expect before a single consonant, i.e. before an onset. The long vowels in the two remaining words in [40a] and the short ones in [40b] can only be explained by reference to what we have established about Icelandic: aspirated plosives must be projected as onsets, which leaves the preceding rhyme ready to accommodate a long vowel. The combination of a voiced spirant and a sonorant in *rauðleitur* is in accordance with the contact constraint [38d], while the presence of two spirants in *rauðvín* follows from [38b]. The morphological structure of the words in [40] is identical, and the examples thus show that the different phonetic effects follow exclusively from differences in the phonological structure, specifically the segmental make-up of the words, rather than from any morphological considerations.

We will now show that the same considerations are of a much more general applicability in compounding. Morphologically, compounds extend from fully lexicalised units with largely unpredictable meanings to novel formations with compositional semantics. The area of compounding is vast in Icelandic but we will merely consider the phonological aspects relating to stressed vowel quantity. We will look at compounds whose first part contains a long vowel in isolation, as this is the only context where differences can emerge.

[41]
a.
mið [mɪːð] 'middle'   aldir [altɪr] 'ages'   miðaldir [mɪːðaltɪr] 'Middle Ages'
gler [klɛːr] 'glass'   auga [œiːɣa] 'eye'   glerauga [klɛːrœiɣa] 'glass eye'
ljós [ljouːs] 'light'   ár [auːr] 'year'   ljósár [ljouːsaur] 'light year'
lofa [lɔːva] 'promise'   orð [ɔrð] 'word'   loforð [lɔːvɔrð] 'promise, n.'
b.
bak [paːkʰ] 'back'   poki [pʰɔːcʰɪ] 'bag'   bakpoki [paːkkpʰɔcʰɪ] 'rucksack'
hluti [l̥ʏːtʰɪ] 'part'   fall [fatl̥] 'fall'   hlutfall [l̥ʏtʰfatl̥] 'proportion'
djúp [tjuːpʰ] 'depth'   skyggn [skɪkn̥] 'seeing'   djúpskyggn [tjuːpʰskɪkn̥] 'profound'

7.8 Length in compounds

c.
haf [haːv] 'ocean'	gola [kɔːla] 'breeze'	hafgola [havkɔla] 'sea breeze'
hljóð [l̥jouːð] 'sound'	fræði [fraiːðɪ] 'science'	hljóðfræði [l̥jouðfraiðɪ] 'phonetics'
hljóð [l̥jouːð] 'sound'	líking [liːcʰiŋk] 'similarity'	hljóðlíking [l̥jouðlicʰiŋk] 'assimilation'
mál [mauːl] 'language'	fræði [fraiːðɪ] 'science'	málfræði [maulfraiðɪ] 'grammar'
vor [vɔːr] 'spring'	kuldi [kʰyltɪ] 'coldness'	vorkuldi [vɔr̥kʏltɪ] 'spring chill'
von [vɔːn] 'hope'	svikinn [svɪːcʰɪn] 'false'	vonsvikinn [vɔnsvɪcʰɪn] 'disappointed'
við [vɪːð] 'with'	ræða [raiːða] 'talk'	viðræða [viðraiða] 'negotiations'
kýr [cʰiːr] 'cow'	nyt [nɪːtʰ] 'use'	kýrnyt [cʰirnɪtʰ] 'cow's yield'

In [a] above the vowel is long when the word appears in isolation and as the first component of a compound. In syllabic terms this is completely unremarkable since the final consonant of the first component is in the onset, and hence the preceding stressed vowel appears in an open syllable. The difference between the word in isolation and in a compound is that in the former case the final onset is licensed by an empty nucleus, while in the latter it is supported by a vocalic melody.

The words in [b] show that the long vowel of the isolation form is preserved in compounds. If we tried to apply the traditional rules controlling vowel length as given in [6], these words would be problematic since a sequence of two or more obstruents (cf. *djúpskyggn*) should not admit a preceding long vowel. To salvage a formulation such as [6] additional principles referring just to compounds would have to be supplied. Within the syllabic approach we need to say nothing in addition to what has already been established, namely that aspirated plosives can only appear in the onset. When this principle is followed, it is obvious that the preceding syllable is open and its nucleus has to branch. No separate generalisations for simplex and complex words are necessary.

Similarly in [c] the appearance of a long vowel when followed by a final onset is familiar and predictable. The fact that the vowel is short in the first member of a compound can in every case be ascribed to the emergence of a well-formed coda–onset contact. A rhymal spirant can be licensed by an obstruent in the onset [38b], a voiced spirant can be licensed by a sonorant [38d], a sonorant is licensed by an obstruent [38a] or another sonorant [38f]. These generalisations hold for the word-internal position and also, as we can see, when single words become members of a compound expression.

The formation of compounds has its grammatical, semantic and phonological aspects. Looking at (some examples of) compounding from the phonological point of view, we observe that the process involves the syllabification of the melody in accordance with the principles of universal phonology, coupled with language-specific regularities. Universally, for example, a branching onset requires two skeletal positions of which the first is taken by an obstruent and the second one by a sonorant. In Icelandic, a language-specific regularity requires that aspirated plosives only appear in the onset. Universally, there are restrictions on the coda–onset domain which take a specific shape for individual languages; in Icelandic, for example, a voiced spirant in the coda can be followed by a sonorant in the onset. Finally, a short comment on empty nuclei is called for. Universally, onsets have to be licensed by nuclei, which may be devoid of any melodic content. Such empty nuclei appear when a consonant or consonant cluster is projected as an onset with no vocalic melody following it. Thus empty nuclei are enforced by the requirements of syllable structure, and their appearance is strictly determined by well-defined criteria. Given a sequence of two consonants, a branching onset or a coda–onset combination must be formed wherever possible; if neither of the two can be formed – because the melody consists of two plosives for example – then a nucleus must separate the two consonants. Under this interpretation, empty nuclei are one of the mechanisms available for ensuring the proper syllabification of words in a language.

7.9 Summary

This chapter has been entirely devoted to an in-depth analysis of one phenomenon in the phonology of Modern Icelandic. We have been interested in the conditions determining the length and shortness of stressed vowels in the present-day language. As is frequently the case in phonology, what starts off by being a trivial-looking minor problem develops into an intricate regularity or set of regularities with significant theoretical implications.

In the Icelandic case we formulated a simple condition connecting vowel length with rhyme structure: if the rhyme contains no consonantal coda, the nucleus must branch. We found evidence supporting this generalisation both within native vocabulary and also in loan-words, including proper names. Once we realised that vowel length is controlled by the openness of syllables we changed our strategy and set ourselves a new task. Assuming that a long vowel implies that there is no following coda, and that a short one necessarily entails one, we looked at more data in Icelandic in an attempt to find out what the quality generalisation can reveal about the structure of onsets, codas and coda–onset contacts. In this way we started by using phonological theory to help us understand a language-specific problem, and then exploited what we hoped were reliable results to probe further theoretical questions. Two issues emerged as particularly relevant: the status of final consonants and of coda–onset contacts.

Icelandic vowel quantity provides additional support for the claim that word-final consonants are onsets licensed by empty nuclei. What is singularly striking about Icelandic is the way it reveals that final consonant sequences can be branching onsets as long as they meet the general criteria for onsethood – recall the length distinction between *kumr* [kʏmr] 'bleating' and *pukr* [pʰʏːkʰr] 'secretiveness' in [16] above. Examples like these are particularly damaging for any description which resorts to merely counting the number of consonants following a stressed vowel. They are equally challenging to syllable theories which do not identify word-final consonants with onsets.

The coda–onset contacts are intriguing because they are in no way obvious or necessary. In other words, given traditional assumptions about syllable structure, which claim that the syllable is a self-contained unit, there is no reason to expect that the coda consonant can be in any way controlled by the nature of the following onset. Within the model of the syllable developed in this and the preceding chapters, the existence of coda–onset contacts is not surprising. As we argued at length in chapter 5, codas must be licensed by following onsets, hence codas do not exist unless there are onsets supporting them. The discovery of restrictions on coda–onset contacts follows naturally once the existence of such contacts has been recognised in the first place.

The formulation of the regularity governing Icelandic is in keeping with the framework developed in this book. As such, the analysis proposed here will probably not be found in exactly the same form elsewhere; readers wishing to study alternative descriptions should consult some of the references mentioned in 7.10 below. The present discussion has tried to show that even in dealing with ostensibly simple problems, we need to make far-reaching assumptions before we can arrive at a plausible interpretation. Before finishing, it is only fair to warn the reader that we are not finished with vocalic length in Icelandic. The next chapter looks at a particularly intriguing aspect of this subject.

7.10 Suggested further reading

Information on Icelandic vowel length can be found in a number of textbooks, e.g. Einarsson (1945), grammars, e.g. Kress (1982), and phonetic descriptions, e.g. Guðfinnsson (1946), Gíslason and Þráinsson (1993), and in dictionaries which provide phonetic transcriptions, e.g. Blöndal (1924), Bérkov and Böðvarsson (1962). There is also no dearth of partially or radically conflicting interpretations within different frameworks, e.g. Haugen (1958), Benediktsson (1963), Orešnik and Pétursson (1977), Árnason (1980, 1998), Gussmann (1985), Stong-Jensen (1992).

For syllable contacts see Vennemann (1988), Kaye, Lowenstamm and Vergnaud (1990), Harris (1994). On the relation between quantity and stress see Anderson (1984).

8
Segmental double agents

8.1 Introduction

In several places in the preceding chapters we have indicated that there may be a mismatch between the way a segment is specified as regards its phonological properties and the way it is pronounced. On the one hand we used the notion of the phonetic effect to refer to those aspects of sounds which are not due to any systematic phonological regularities but are in some sense accidental (see 3.5). On the other hand the reverse is also possible, when a segment may be specified for a property which is suppressed as a result of some constraint operative in the language, a case in point being German final devoicing, discussed in 6.7. In the latter case different phonological representations are articulated and perceived as the same physical or phonetic object. Looking at it from a phonetic perspective, this means that the same physical or phonetic object has a double – or perhaps multiple – phonological identity. In the present chapter we would like to take a closer look at such double agents, which are particularly challenging from the point of view of phonological analysis. The double (or multiple) identity of certain segments places upon the analyst the burden of proving their reality. The need to marshal strong and cogent arguments becomes particularly acute. Before considering some more complex cases let us have a look at a relatively simple instance taken from German.

In 6.7 we discussed the issue of German final devoicing and concluded that, in the standard dialect, domain-final empty nuclei do not license the voice property. The property, although not licensed, remains part of the representations. Thus a devoiced obstruent, although phonetically identical with a voiceless one, differs from it representationally in having a silenced or latent voice specification. A case in point is the pair of words *Bad* 'bath' *bat* 'I asked' both pronounced in the same way as [baːt]. The phonetic identity of the two words is not at stake; nor is the fact that the words are different grammatical and lexical units. It is, of course, perfectly possible for different words to be not only phonetically but also phonologically identical, as for instance the English [feə] in *my fair lady* and *Scarborough fair*. The question with reference to the final consonant in the German [baːt] is whether it is one and the same phonological segment in both words or whether it is a double agent, representing two distinct segments which just sound the same.

The evidence we wish to adduce comes from a regularity known as spirantisation, whereby word-finally the voiced velar plosive, apart from being devoiced, is also realised as the spirant [ç] after the vowel [ɪ]. Consider some examples:

[1]   Könige [ˈkøːnɪɡə] 'king, pl.'   König [ˈkøːnɪç] 'sg.'
      fertigen [ˈfɛʁtɪɡən] 'get ready'   fertig [ˈfɛʁtɪç] 'ready'
      lebendige [leˈbɛndɪɡə] 'lively, pl.'   lebendig [leˈbɛndɪç] 'sg.'

When the plosive [ɡ] finds itself in domain-final position (i.e. before the final empty nucleus), it has no license to support the voicedness property and hence is pronounced as [k]. This devoicing is accompanied by spirantisation of the plosive, resulting in [ç] if it follows the vowel [i]. Note that devoicing is independent of the spirantisation, so that we can have one without the other, e.g. *Zug* [tsuːk] 'train' (cf. *Züge* [tsyːɡə] 'pl.'). The plosive which is spirantised alternates with a voiced plosive, as shown in [1] above. Does this mean that the sequence [ik] is impossible in German? The answer is 'no' – there are quite a lot of words with that sound sequence but where the voiceless plosive does not alternate with a voiced one. Consider some examples:

[2]   Musik [muˈziːk] 'music'   Musiker [ˈmuːzikɐ] 'musician'
      Fabrik [faˈbʁiːk] 'factory'   Fabrikant [fabʁiˈkant] 'manufacturer'
      Blick [blɪk] 'glance, n.'   Blicke [blɪkə] 'nom. pl.'
      Grammatik [ɡʁaˈmatɪk] 'grammar'   Grammatiker [ɡʁaˈmatɪkɐ] 'grammarian'

The voiceless plosive in [2] does not participate in devoicing alternations. This shows that it differs from the voiceless plosive in [1] which has its licence for voicing withdrawn domain-finally – in plain language, the two [k]'s are different. We decided in 6.7 to represent devoiced consonants as containing a voicing specification which is not associated with the rest of the melody. Under this interpretation, voicing in [1], being unassociated, is not pronounced but is present in the representation. Its presence allows us to capture its specific phonological behaviour (spirantisation) as compared to the other voiceless plosive. It is in this sense that we talk of domain-final voiceless obstruents being double agents. More intricate examples of this phenomenon will be presented below.

8.2 Icelandic vowel length: an extension

Although we devoted the whole of chapter 7 to a discussion of Icelandic quantity relations, the issue has not been fully exhausted. In brief, we

188 *Segmental double agents*

decided that stressed rhymes must branch, hence if there is no rhymal complement, the vowel must be long. The important issues in individual cases include the placement of domain boundaries and the segmental possibilities of the rhyme. Of particular importance is the coda–onset juncture, which we formulated as a list of segmental possibilities, repeated below for convenience of reference.

[3] contact coda–onset combinations in Icelandic
a. sonorant – obstruent
panta [pan̥ta] 'order, vb.', *gúrka* [gur̥ka] 'cucumber'
b. spirant – obstruent
taska [tʰaska] 'bag', *hefti* [hɛftɪ] 'notebook', *liðka* [lɪθka] 'make flexible', *sagði* [sayðɪ] 'I said', *vaxa* [vaxsa] 'grow'
c. unaspirated plosive – sonorant
hefna [hɛpna] 'avenge', *elli* [ɛtlɪ] 'old age'
d. voiced spirant – sonorant
eigra [eiɣra] 'wander', *eðli* [ɛðlɪ] 'nature', *efri* [ɛvrɪ] 'upper', *faðma* [faðma] 'embrace'
e. [s] – sonorant stop
asni [asnɪ] 'donkey', *hismi* [hɪsmɪ] 'chaff', *veisla* [veisla] 'party'
f. sonorant – sonorant
hamra [hamra] 'hammer, vb.', *harma* [harma] 'lament, vb.', *hamla* [hamla] 'restrain', *ilma* [ɪlma] 'smell, vb.'

These contact combinations account for the shortness of the preceding vowel since the first of the consonants occupies the rhyme complement position.

In what follows we will look yet again at the various combinations of [s] and a consonant. In view of what was established in chapter 7 we expect that [s], when followed by one of the continuant sonorants [j, v, r] is invariably assigned to the onset of the syllable, hence the vowel of the preceding syllable is long, e.g. *Esja* [ɛːsja] 'name of a mountain', *tvisvar* [tʰviːsvar] 'twice', *lausri* [lœiːsrɪ] 'loose, dat. sg. fem.' In all other cases, the vowel before s+consonant is short; the consonant is either an obstruent or a sonorant stop [3b, e]. The reason why we have to return to Icelandic vowel length is that contrary to what one would expect, long vowels do appear before some s+consonant combinations. This is shown for five lexical items in [4].

[4]
a. *brosa* [prɔːsa] 'smile'
broslegur [prɔːslɛɣʏr] 'ridiculous'
brosmildur [prɔːsmɪltʏr] 'smiling'
brosleitur [prɔːslɛitʰʏr] 'smiling'
brosgjarn [prɔːscart̥n̥] 'funny'

b. laus [lœiːs] 'loose'
   lauslegur [lœiːslɛɣʏr] 'unfixed'
   lauslátur [lœiːslautʰʏr] 'promiscuous'
   lausmáll [lœiːsmaut̥l̥] 'indiscreet'
c. ljós [ljouːs] 'light, n.'
   ljóslegur [ljouːslɛɣʏr] 'bright, clear'
   ljóslaus [ljouːslœis] 'without light'
   ljósfræði [ljouːsfraiðɪ] 'optics'
   ljósmóðir [ljouːsmouðɪr] 'midwife'
d. hús [huːs] 'house'
   húslaus [huːslœis] 'homeless'
   húsmóðir [huːsmouðɪr] 'housewife'
   húslegur [huːslɛɣʏr] 'house-proud'
e. ís [iːs] 'ice'
   íslaus [iːslœis] 'free of ice'
   íslagður [iːslaɣðʏr] 'covered with ice'
   Ísland [iːslant] 'Iceland'
   íslenskur [iːslɛnskʏr] 'Icelandic'

If [s] is followed by either an obstruent [3b] or a sonorant stop [3e], it should be able to occupy the rhymal position and hence the preceding vowel should be short. The fact that in all the examples in [4] the vowel is long indicates that the spirant [s] itself occupies the onset position, thereby forcing the previous nucleus to branch. The question arises as to why [s] should be placed in the onset in [4] but not in the other cases, i.e. why it occupies the onset position in *íslaus* [iːslœis] 'free of ice' but not in e.g. *kvíslast* [kʰvislast] 'branch out'? Let us consider two suffixes which recur in our examples above, namely *-legur* and *-laus*, as [s] before these suffixes is in the onset.

One's initial reaction might be to say that the suffixes in question are separated from their base by a domain-boundary. In such a case the last consonant of the base would necessarily be in the onset as it would be followed by a domain-final empty nucleus. Consider a possible representation of *broslegur* [prɔːslɛɣʏr] 'ridiculous'.

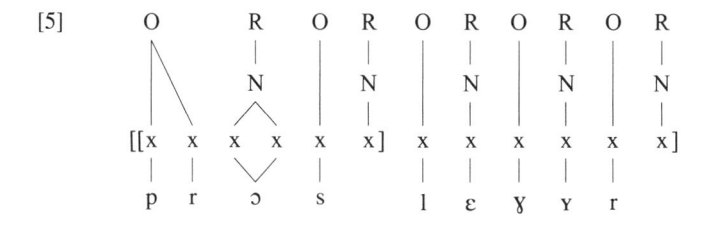

[5]
```
      O      R    O   R   O   R   O   R
     /\      |    |   |   |   |   |   |
    /  \     N    |   N   |   N   |   N
   /    \   /\    |   |   |   |   |   |
 [[x  x  x  x  x]     x   x   x   x   x]
   |  |  \/  |       |   |   |   |   |
   p  r   ɔ  s       l   ɛ   ɣ   ʏ   r
```

Separating suffixes like *-legur* by a domain boundary from the base might be further supported by examples such as those in [6], where the stressed vowel is long when the final aspirated plosive is followed by the suffix:

[6] sjúkur [sjuːkʰʏr] 'sick'   sjúklegur [sjuːkʰlɛɣʏr] 'sickly'
    skop [skɔːpʰ] 'humour'   skoplegur [skɔːpʰlɛɣʏr] 'comical'
    kátur [kʰauːtʰʏr] 'merry'   kátlegur [kʰauːtʰlɛɣʏr] 'funny'

The positing of a domain boundary might also salvage the traditional description of the context for vowel lengthening in Icelandic; in the preceding chapter we noted that traditionally vowels are long if they are followed by a cluster made up of any of [pʰ, tʰ, kʰ] and any of [j, v, r]. Obviously, examples such as those in the right-hand column of [6] constitute counterevidence to the traditional description, since [pʰ, tʰ, kʰ] are here followed by the lateral [l]. If, however, a domain-boundary were to fall between the plosive and the lateral, the difficulty would disappear. On the interpretation which we developed in the previous chapter the length of the vowel is due to the fact that in Modern Icelandic [pʰ, tʰ, kʰ] are invariably projected as syllable onsets. The question is which of the two interpretations is to be preferred, the syllable-based one or the suffix-dependent one.

The suffix-based analysis makes the explicit claim that the length of the preceding vowel is totally independent of the suffix since they are separated by the domain structure. If the base ends in a single consonant, then the consonant constitutes the final onset of its domain and the preceding vowel is long, exactly as in [5]. Unfortunately, this claim is not borne out by the facts of the language, since in addition to words conforming to the predicted patterns we also find numerous short vowels in the same environment. Consider these examples:

[7]
a. glaður [klaːðʏr] 'glad'   glaðlegur [klaðlɛɣʏr] 'cheerful'
    lofa [lɔːva] 'praise, vb.'   loflegur [lɔvlɛɣʏr] 'praiseworthy'
    dagur [tːaɣʏr] 'day'   daglegur [taɣlɛɣʏr] 'daily'
b. tómur [tʰouːmʏr] 'empty'   tómlegur [tʰoumlɛɣʏr] 'cheerless'
    fín [fiːn] 'elegant, fem. sg.'   fínlegur [finlɛɣʏr] 'delicate'
    ár [auːr] 'year'   árlegur [aurlɛɣʏr] 'annual'
    sæl [saiːl] 'happy, fem. sg.'   sællegur [sailːɛɣʏr] 'happy-looking'

Before trying to account for these facts we will now show that exactly the same regularities hold for the other of the two suffixes we have singled out, namely *-laus*. In [8a] and [8b] we offer examples where the vowels preceding the suffix are short.

[8]
a. frið [frɪːð] 'peace, acc. sg.'   friðlaus [frɪðlœis] 'restless'
    líf [liːv] 'life'   líflaus [livlœis] 'lifeless'
    hug [hʏːɣ] 'heart, acc. sg.'   huglaus [hʏɣlœis] 'cowardly'

b. fum [fʏːm] 'nervousness' fumlaus [fʏmlœis] 'quiet, composed'
    von [vɔːn] 'hope' vonlaus [vɔnlœis] 'hopeless'
    mál [mauːl] 'speech' mállaus [maulːœis] 'speechless'
    klór [kʰlouːr] 'chlorine' klórlaus [kʰlourlœis] 'without chlorine'

The evidence of the suffixes is overwhelming: at the juncture of the base and the suffix, consonant sequences arise which conform to the coda–onset contact combinations which we have independently established for Icelandic. Thus we have clusters of a voiced spirant followed by a sonorant [7a, 8a] or a sonorant sequence [7b, 8b], in agreement with [3d] and [3f] respectively. Since these are well-formed coda–onset combinations, the preceding vowel can only be short. The suffixes form single phonological domains with the preceding morphological base. The claim that adjectives in *-legur*, *-laus* might be interpreted along the lines outlined in representation [5] must be rejected out of hand.

There is more evidence strengthening this conclusion. Among the examples in [4] there are some complex forms whose first vowel is long before s+consonant. Consider these forms again and compare them with others of a similar morphological but different phonological structure.

[9]
a. brosmildur [prɔːsmɪltʏr] 'smiling' gjafmildur [cavmɪltʏr] 'generous'
b. brosgjarn [prɔːscartn̩] 'funny' góðgjarn [kouðcartn̩] 'gracious'
c. ljósfróði [ljouːsfraiðɪ] 'optics' málfræði [maulfraiðɪ] 'grammar'
d. húsmóðir [huːsmouðɪr] 'housewife'
    ljósmóðir [ljouːsmouðɪr] 'midwife' formóðir [fɔrmouðɪr] 'female ancestor'
e. Ísland [iːslant] 'Iceland' Írland [irlant] 'Ireland'
    Grænland [grainlant] 'Greenland'
    hérland [hjɛrlant] 'here, in this country'

The evidence of the different compounds in the right-hand column converges with that of the derivatives in [7] and [8]: whenever the last consonant of the first element forms a well-formed coda–onset combination with the first consonant of the second element, the preceding vowel is short. Since the consonants constitute a coda–onset sequence, no nucleus can intervene, hence no domain structure separates them. With respect to the length of vowels before s+consonant we have to conclude that *s is special*. There are some s's which occupy the rhymal position and hence the preceding vowel is obviously short (see [3e]), whereas others appear in the onset, hence the preceding nucleus must branch (examples in [4]).

The special status of [s] consists in the fact that unlike all other consonants it *systematically if unpredictably* admits of double syllabification. A word of clarification is necessary at this point. By means of comparison consider the lateral [l] in words like *latur* [laːtʰʏr] 'lazy' and *valdur* [valtʏr] 'responsible': in the former word the lateral will obviously appear as the onset if only because there is nothing that could compete with it for this position. In *valdur* on the other hand the lateral can appear as the rhymal complement since it is followed by an obstruent (see [3a]); it could only occupy the onset position if we had evidence for a following empty nucleus. The situation with s+consonant is different, in that only in some cases are we forced to recognise a following empty nucleus so that [s] can occupy the onset position. Put differently, there are words where [s] – just like the aspirated plosives [pʰ, tʰ, kʰ] – must appear in the onset. *broslegur* is a case in point: it has the representation we suggested in [5] but without internal domain-structure:

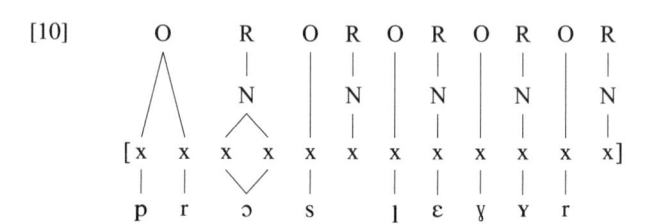

[10]
```
        O      R     O  R   O  R   O  R   O  R
       / \     |     |  |   |  |   |  |   |  |
      /   \    N     |  N   |  N   |  N   |  N
     /     \  / \    |  |   |  |   |  |   |  |
    [x  x  x  x  x   x  x   x  x   x  x   x  x]
     |  |  \  /  |   |  |   |  |   |  |   |  |
     p  r   ɔ    s   l  ɛ   ɣ  ʏ   r
```

The word *veisla* [vɛisla] 'party' must be represented with [s] in the rhyme:

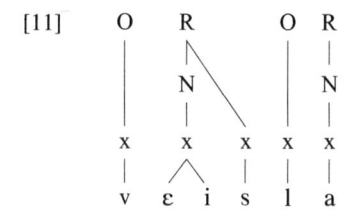

[11]
```
        O      R          O  R
        |     / \         |  |
        |    N   \        |  N
        |    |    \       |  |
        x    x  x  x      x  x
        |    | / \ |      |  |
        v    ɛ  i  s      l  a
```

The question suggests itself as to what enforces the two different syllabifications of what is obviously the same phonetic segment. This is a question we cannot go into here, as we would need to determine precisely the properties responsible for the aspiration of plosives and the voicing of spirants. What is beyond doubt is that the phonetic sequence [sl] in some cases requires the preceding nucleus to branch, and in others does not. In those cases where it is preceded by a long vowel, it is reminiscent of voiceless aspirated plosives, while following a short vowel it patterns with voiced spirants [3e]. Crucially, then, the Icelandic [s] is ambiguous in the phonological effects that it is accompanied by. Since phonological effects are not metaphysical phenomena but are produced by specific properties, we can only surmise that the Icelandic [s] is a double agent: in some words it displays properties which are not present in others. What these properties are can be established by a detailed study of the language in question. Our aim here has merely been to demonstrate the existence of the phonological diversity behind phonetic identity. The evidence of the preceding pages shows that Modern Icelandic recognises two phonological objects corresponding to what is perceived and articulated as phonetic [s].

8.3 Russian labial fricatives

Modern Russian obstruents can be either voiced or voiceless but their distribution is subject to certain restrictions. Just like German, Russian does not tolerate voiced obstruents before a pause, which results in frequent alternations of voiced and voiceless consonants. Consider some examples.

[12]   xleb [xlʲep] 'bread'   xleba ['xlʲeba] 'gen. sg.'
         drug [druk] 'friend'   drugu ['drugu] 'dat. sg.'
         trav [traf] 'grass, gen. pl.'   trava [tra'va] 'nom. sg.'
         muž [muʃ] 'husband'   muža ['muʒa] 'gen. sg.'
         mozg [mosk] 'brain'   mozgom ['mozgam] 'instr. sg.'
         nadežd [na'dʲeʃt] 'hope, gen. pl.' nadežda [na'dʲeʒda] 'nom. sg.'
         trezv [tʲrʲesf] 'sober, masc.'   trezva [tʲrʲiz'va] 'fem.'

The point is clear: a voiced obstruent cannot appear in word-final position before a pause. In this Russian agrees completely with what we find in German. Thus the domain-final empty nucleus fails to license voicing in the preceding onset in both languages. Where Russian and German part ways is in connected speech. In German the failure of word-final position to support voicing is observed categorically, i.e. no matter what follows. Consider the noun *Tag* [taːk] with a final voiceless plosive (as against its genitive singular *Tages* ['taːɡəs] with an internal voiced one): the voicelessness of the plosive is preserved in *der Tag beginnt* [deːɐ 'taːk bə'ɡɪnt] 'the day begins', which results in the juxtaposition of a voiceless and a voiced consonant [kb]. A situation of this sort is impossible in Russian where combinations of obstruents must agree in voicing. This means that, unlike German, Russian sequences of word-final and word-initial obstruents in connected speech must be either uniformly voiced or uniformly voiceless.

The voice uniformity of obstruent clusters, known under the traditional term of **voice assimilation**, accounts for a number of alternations in consonants in Russian: no matter whether they are voiced or voiceless intervocalically, when they are word-final they assume the voicing of the consonant beginning the next word. This is shown below.

194 *Segmental double agents*

[13] xle[b]a 'bread, gen. sg.'   xle[p] [k]upil 'he bought bread'
      jazy[k]a 'tongue, gen. sg.'   jazy[g] [b]udet 'the tongue will be'
      moro[z]a 'frost, gen. sg.'   moro[s] [sʲ]ilnyj 'heavy frost'
      bra[t]a 'brother, gen. sg.'   bra[d] [g]ovorit 'brother speaks'
      rja[d]y 'row, nom. pl.'   rja[t] [pʲ]ervyj 'front row'
      p[s]a 'dog, gen. sg.'   pjo[z] bʲ]ežit 'the dog runs'
      r[v]a 'ditch, gen. sg.'   ro[f] [p]ustoj 'empty ditch'

In our terms, the situation can be described as the imposition of the voice property by the second consonant on the first. This sort of imposition, or **spreading**, merely denotes that there can be no voice disagreement in obstruent clusters and serves to account for the existing alternations. One can imagine the spreading as an association established between the final consonant of the first word and the voice specification of the second. The fact that the same morpheme in a different phonological or morphological environment is pronounced differently follows from the existence of voice spreading (voice assimilation). However, this phonological regularity is nothing but a way of capturing the fact that in Russian obstruent clusters are uniform with respect to voicing, with the last consonant setting the tone for the whole cluster.

This voice uniformity is observed not only at word boundaries but also within words. Word-internal obstruent sequences conform to the same regularity which we have just observed at word junctures. As a result, consonants may display different voice qualities if they are separated by a pronounced vowel, as shown in [14a]. It is crucial, however, that when no vocalic melody intervenes between two consonants, these cannot differ in voicing, as in [14b].

[14] a. xle[bʲets] 'small loaf'   b. xle[pts]a 'gen. sg.'
          poe[zdok] 'journey, gen. pl.'   poe[stk]a 'nom. sg.'
          kni[ʒok]a 'book, dim. gen. pl.'   kni[ʃk]a 'nom. sg.'
          [vʲesʲ] 'whole, masc.'   [fsʲ]o 'everything'
          pro[sitʲ] 'ask'   pro[zʲb]a 'request, n.'
          ta[kof] 'such, masc.'   ta[gʒ]e 'also'

The generalisation at work seems quite straightforward: sequences of obstruents word-internally fully conform to the voice-uniformity requirement. The voice property of the last member of the cluster spreads to the preceding consonants, a condition that also affects loan-words, e.g. *fu*[db]*ol* 'football', *ane*[gd]*ot* 'anecdote', *e*[gz]*amen* 'examination'. We can conclude that both word-internally and at word junctures obstruent sequences share a single voicing specification.

There exists a striking departure from the Russian voice uniformity condition: the labio-dental spirants [f, v], in both their palatalised and velarised form, behave in a partly different way from other obstruents. The problem can be briefly illustrated by the adjective *moskovskij* [masˈkofscij] 'Moscow, adj.' with the morphological structure *moskov+sk+ij*. Here we have the voiceless spirant [f] before the voiceless cluster [sc], exactly as expected. However, in the base noun *Moskva* [mas'kva] 'Moscow' we find the voiceless cluster [sk] preceding the voiced spirant [v], hence a cluster which is not uniform with respect to voicing. This is generally true for Russian. In domain-final position and before a voiceless obstruent both within a word and at word junctures labio-dental fricatives behave exactly as any other obstruent. We have seen some examples of this above, which we repeat, with some additions, in [15].

[15]   tre[sf] 'sober, masc.'   tre[z'v]a 'fem.'
                                              tre[zʲvʲ]et' 'sober up'
        kro[fʲ] 'blood'   kro[vʲ]i 'gen. sg.'
                                              kro[v]avyj 'bloody'
        kro[fʲ] [kʲ]ipit 'blood is boiling' kro[vʲ] [d]vorjanskaja 'noble blood'
        ro[f] [p]ustoj 'empty ditch'   r[v]a 'ditch, gen. sg.'
                                              ro[v] [g]lubokij 'deep ditch'
        [fsʲ]o 'everything'   [vʲ]es' 'whole, masc.'
        [fsʲ]elennaja 'the universe'
        morko[fʲ] 'carrot'   morko[vʲ]i 'gen. sg.'
        morko[fk]a 'carrot, dim.'   morko[v]ok 'gen. pl.'
        la[fk]a 'shop'   la[v]očka 'dim.'

Here the behaviour of the labio-dental spirants is completely unremarkable; before a voiced obstruent either within the same word or in the next word, the labial spirant is voiced. Word-finally and before a voiceless obstruent it is voiceless.

The situation is very different when an obstruent precedes the voiced labio-dental spirants [v, vʲ]. Two cases need to be distinguished: at word boundaries and word-internally. As we have seen above (see the examples in [13]), word-final obstruents are voiced before a voiced obstruent beginning the next word. There is no voicing when the next word begins with a vowel, a sonorant **and** [v, vʲ]:

[16]
a.   poe[st] [i]dët 'the train goes'
        do[ʃtʲ] [i]dët 'it is raining'
        bra[t] [r]abotaet 'the brother works'
        vra[k] [nʲ]e spit 'the enemy is not asleep'
        kro[fʲ] [lʲ]ëtsja 'blood is flowing'
b.   uža[s] [v]ojny 'horror of war'
        vku[s] [vʲ]ina 'the taste of wine'
        svi[st] [vʲ]etra 'whistle of the wind'
        goro[t] [v]zjat 'the town has been taken' (cf. goro[d]a 'town, gen. sg.')
        sapo[k] [v]aš 'your boot' (sapo[g]om 'boot, instr. sg.')

In [16a] we have examples showing that word-final devoicing is found also before a following vowel or consonantal sonorant. The examples in [16b] show exactly the same with respect to the voiced spirants [v, vʲ]: these two sounds do not behave like obstruents which spread their voicedness to the final consonant of the preceding words, but rather like sonorants by failing to influence the voice quality of the preceding obstruent. Thus voiced labio-dentals pattern with sonorants as far as their phonological behaviour is concerned.

Another context where an obstruent does not have to agree with a following voiced labio-dental is word-internally. Some examples are offered in [17].

[17]   o[tvʲ]et 'answer, n.' not *o[dvʲ]et   Mo[skv]a 'Moscow' not *mo[zgv]a
       [tv]oj 'your, masc.' not *[dv]oj   [tsv]et 'colour' not *[dzv]et
       [svʲ]inec 'lead, n.' not *[zvʲ]inec   [xv]ost 'tail' not *[ɣv]ost

The cases where the voiced labio-dental follows a voiceless obstruent constitute a violation of the voice uniformity condition which otherwise seems generally operative in Russian. In fact, the labio-dental can follow either a voiced or a voiceless obstruent [18a] in very much the same way as all other sonorants [18b].

[18]
a.   [tv]oj 'your'   [dv]ojka 'a two'
       [svʲ]er''verify, imper.'   [zvʲ]er''animal'
       [kv]artira 'flat, n.'   [gv]ardija 'Guards'
b.   [pl]ač 'weeping'   [bl]at 'protection'
       [sn]op 'sheaf'   [zn]oj 'intense heat'
       [sm]ejat'sja 'laugh'   [zm]eja 'snake'
       [pr]ačka 'laundress'   [br]at 'brother'

An inspection of these examples leads us to the same conclusion as with the juncture (de)voicing: [v], although pronounced as a labio-dental spirant, patterns phonologically with sonorants. The expression 'patterns with' is a circumlocution: to say that a segment can 'pattern with' sonorants is simply to say that it is a sonorant itself. We must, then, nail our colours to the mast and say that in some contexts what sounds like a spirant is a sonorant. Just as Icelandic [s] displayed ambiguous behaviour with respect to the length of the preceding vowel, the Russian labio-dental spirant is also ambiguous and thus it qualifies for the category of double agent. At times it is an obstruent in that – like all obstruents – it undergoes devoicing and assimilates the voice of the following obstruent both domain-internally and across boundaries. The relevant examples are: *kro*[fʲ] (cf. *kro*[vʲi]), *la*[fk]*a* (cf. *la*[vo]*očka*) and *kro*[vʲ] [d]*vorjanskaja*. At other times it is a sonorant which conditions the devoicing of a preceding obstruent across word boundaries and fails to transmit voicing to the preceding obstruent word-internally, e.g. *sapo*[k] [v]*aš*, *Mo*[skv]*a*.

We can easily specify the contexts in which the labio-dental is an obstruent and those in which it is a sonorant. We are dealing with a true spirant word-finally and before another obstruent melody; in all remaining cases the consonant is a sonorant. Remembering that sonorants include vowels it is, of course, possible to formulate the contexts starting with the sonorant: the labio-dental is a sonorant before another pronounced sonorant and elsewhere it is an obstruent. The restriction to 'pronounced' sonorants is necessary since word-final consonants are followed by an empty nucleus, which must also count as a sonorant, albeit without phonetic content. Whichever formulation we adopt, the result is clearly the same: what is phonetically a labio-dental spirant must in some cases at least be seen as a phonological sonorant. As a sonorant it is not involved in voice alternations, which are typically found with obstruents. In this sense whenever we find voice alternations between $[f^{(j)} - v^{(j)}]$ we can be sure that the alternating members are obstruents. The failure to be involved in or to condition such alternations indicates that what sounds like a spirant is in reality a sonorant.

The Russian labio-dental consonant comprises two very different phonological objects whose identity is revealed through their susceptibility or resistance to phonological processing. Although there are additional questions which should be asked in this context, we will merely note that our objective has been to bring to light the existence of such phonological double agents. The Russian case, just like the Icelandic and German ones before, strongly supports the need to recognise phonological diversity behind phonetic identity. The task facing the analyst in such instances is to find evidence justifying the division of what appears to be phonetically the same segment(s).

8.4 Polish dorsal obstruents

Another candidate for a phonological double agent can be found in Polish. In what follows we will be interested in the three velar obstruents [k, g, x] and in their palatal congeners, transcribed as [c, ɟ, ç]. The special object of our interest will be the voiceless velar spirant [x] and the voiceless palatal spirant [ç]. Three front vowels will play a role in our discussion, namely the high front [i], the retracted half close [ɨ] and the half open [ɛ].

The vowels [ɨ] and [ɛ] function as independent inflectional endings and they also mark the beginning of a number of other endings. When they are attached to stems ending in a non-velar consonant, nothing happens. Below we illustrate this for the adjectival stem *bos-* [bos] 'bare-footed'.

[19] bo[sɨ] 'masc. nom. sg.'   bo[sɛ] 'nom. pl.'
      bo[sɨ]m 'masc. dat./loc. sg.' bo[sɛ]mu 'masc. dat. sg.'
      bo[sɨ]ch 'gen. pl.'   bo[sɛ]go 'masc. gen. sg.'
      bo[sɛ]j 'fem. gen. sg.'   bo[sɨ]mi 'instr. pl.'

198   Segmental double agents

If the same endings are attached to stems ending in velars, some striking phenomena come to light. Let us start with the velar spirant and a stem like głu[x]- 'deaf', which behaves in the same way as the adjective illustrated in [19], i.e. the consonant freely combines with a following vowel:

[20]   głu[xɨ] 'masc. nom. sg.'   głu[xɛ] 'nom. pl.'
        głu[xɨ]m 'masc. dat./loc. sg.'   głu[xɛ]mu 'masc. dat. sg.'
        głu[xɨ]ch 'gen. pl.'   głu[xɛ]go 'masc. gen. sg.'
        głu[xɨ]mi 'instr. pl.'   głu[xɛ]j 'fem. gen. sg.'

The velar spirant regularly combines with the front vowels in the same way as all other non-velar obstruents. Against this background, the behaviour of the velar plosives is quite striking. First of all, the front retracted vowel [ɨ] is basically impossible after a velar stop; thus, barring a few marginal and highly marked exceptions, sequences such as [kɨ] or [gɨ] are not found in Polish either morpheme-internally or at morpheme boundaries. Instead of [ɨ] one finds the front close vowel [i]. Secondly, velar plosives basically do not appear before front vowels either stem-internally or at morpheme boundaries; stem-final velars before endings beginning with front vowels are realised as the palatals [c, ɟ]. Let us take adjectival stems ending in a velar plosive and place them in the contexts illustrated above in [19] – [20]. The velar plosives are found before the ending -a of the feminine nominative singular: wiel[k]a 'big', dro[g]a 'dear'.

[21]   wiel[ci], dro[ɟi] 'masc. nom. sg.'   wiel[cɛ], dro[ɟɛ] 'nom. pl.'
        wiel[ci]m, dro[ɟi]m 'masc. dat./loc. sg.' wiel[cɛ]mu, dro[ɟɛ]mu 'masc. dat. sg.'
        wiel[ci]ch, dro[ɟi]ch 'gen. pl.'   wiel[cɛ]go, dro[ɟɛ]go 'masc. gen. sg.'
        wiel[ce]j, dro[ɟɛ]j 'fem. sg. gen.'   wiel[ci]mi, dro[ɟi]mi 'instr. pl.'

The evidence of alternations combined with the existence of palatal velars before front vowels morpheme-internally points to the existence of *Frontness Sharing* in Polish: front vowels when following velar plosives spread their frontness onto the plosives. A fronted velar denotes a phonetically palatal stop, i.e. either [c] or [ɟ]. The regularity is quite uncontroversial and reflects a general assimilatory tendency. What is surprising, however, is the fact that it is only velar plosives that display it while the velar spirant fails to do so (cf. the examples in [20]). Thus the velar spirant differs in two ways from the velar plosives: (i) it can be followed by the retracted vowel [ɨ] and (ii) combinations of the velar spirant with a following front vowel do not observe *Frontness Sharing*.

In fact the situation is slightly more complex than this. While it is true that the plosives cannot, and the spirant can appear before the retracted vowel [ɨ], it is not true that the spirant must be followed by that vowel – in its palatal version [ç] it may precede the vowel [i]. In other words, the velar spirant, unlike the velar plosives, may but does not have to observe *Frontness Sharing*. Above in [20] we have seen cases where it does not do so at morpheme boundaries, and in this it differs from the velar plosives in the same position. In [22] below we offer examples showing that the velar plosive can be followed by the retracted vowel domain-internally, and that it fails to conform to *Frontness Sharing* before the vowel [ɛ].

[22]
a.   [xɨ]bić 'miss, vb.'   po[xɨ]lony 'reclining'
    [xɨ]try 'cunning'   [xɨ]mn 'hymn'
    [xɨ]drant 'hydrant'   [xɨ]dra 'hydra'
b.   [xɛ]łpliwy 'boastful'   [xɛ]mia 'chemistry'
    [xɛ]bel 'plain'   [xɛ]rbata 'tea'
    [xɛ]roiczny 'heroic'

These examples show that the velar spirant differs from the velar plosives also domain-internally. There are other examples, however, where *Frontness Sharing* is observed by all velar consonants; consider the alternations involving two native suffixes, namely the feminine noun-forming suffix *-ini* [23a] and the derived imperfective suffix *-iw* [23b]. The addition of these suffixes to a base ending in a velar results in *Frontness Sharing* being observed.

[23]
a.   proro[k] 'prophet'   proro[ci]ni 'fem.'
    bo[g]a 'god, gen. sg.'   bo[ɟi]ni 'goddess'
    monar[x]a 'monarch'   monar[çi]ni 'fem.'
b.   klas[k]ać 'applaud'   oklas[ci]wać 'imperfective'
    ska[k]ać 'jump'   (pod)ska[ci]wać 'imperfective'
    przyle[g]ać 'adhere'   przyle[ɟi]wać 'imperfective'
    przebła[g]ać 'conciliate'   przebła[ɟi]wać 'imperfective'
    zako[x]ać 'fall in love'   zako[çi]wać 'imperfective'
    podsłu[x]ać 'overhear'   podsłu[çi]wać 'imperfective'
    rozdmu[x]ać 'blow out'   rozdmu[çi]wać 'imperfective'

Similarly, morpheme-internally both [çi] and [çɛ] are perfectly possible, e.g.:

[24]   [çi]chot 'giggle'   [çi]storia 'history'
    we[çi]kuł 'vehicle'   [çi]nina 'quinine'
    [çɛ]na 'hyena'   [çɛ]rarchia 'hierarchy'
    [çɛ]ronim 'personal name'

The importance of such examples cannot be overemphasised. The complete failure of *Frontness Sharing* before the front vowels of the endings in [20] or domain-internally in [22b] cannot be explained as resulting, for example, from the absence of the palatal congener of the velar spirant in the Polish system. As [23] and [24] show, the sound [ç] is regularly found in native and foreign words both before front vowel endings and domain-internally. If we assume that *Frontness Sharing* holds for velar consonants, then the conclusion must be that some of the

200 *Segmental double agents*

segments we have called the velar spirant [x] are simply not velar. Note that there is no reason why *Frontness Sharing* should fail in certain words but not in others. Likewise there is no reason why [x] – unlike the two velar plosives – should allow a following [ɨ] in some cases ([20], [22a]), but disallow it in others and thus behave like the plosives. The segment [x] covers two types of phonological objects, of which only one is a velar and accordingly behaves like the other velars. In other words, [x] is what we have called a phonological double agent.

There can be little doubt that when [x] patterns with the velar plosives, it is also a velar consonant. These are the cases illustrated in [23] and [24] when velars disallow a following retracted vowel and when they observe *Frontness Sharing*. In words where the retracted vowel is allowed [20, 22a] and where *Frontness Sharing* is not observed [22b] we are dealing with a spirant which is not velar. The obvious question which suggests itself is: if it is not velar, then what is it? Two tentative answers can be suggested. The first is that it is possible to have phonological segments without full specification – recall our discussion of so-called phonetic effects in 3.4 – 3.5. If we follow this line of thinking we can claim that in Polish there is a voiceless velar spirant and a voiceless spirant, both of which are rendered phonetically as [x]. In such a case the velar spirant would be the phonetic effect of a phonological voiceless spirant unspecified for place of articulation. Alternatively, we could speculate about the non-velar spirant being for example the glottal [h], an interpretation which has some phonetic support: an increasing tendency has been observed among Polish speakers for the glottal spirant to replace the velar one; for example, words like *chata* 'cottage' can be heard pronounced either [xata] or [hata]. No matter which of the two analyses we may want to select, the main point remains unaltered: the phonological properties of segments are determined not only by an inspection of their phonetic characteristics but also by considering the way they behave in the system of a language. If there is a conflict between the phonetic and phonological evidence, it is the latter that gets the upper hand. As we have seen repeatedly above, the phonological properties of a segment may be disguised or merged with those of other segments. The task of a phonological analysis is to go beyond the mere listing of phonetic facts; double agents demonstrate that phonetic properties may disguise significant differences in phonological behaviour. Our last example of this comes from the vowels of Modern Welsh.

8.5   Welsh vowels

The dialect of North Wales contains three high vowels [i, ɨ, u], three mid ones [ɛ, ə, o] and one low vowel [a]. With the exception of [ə] they can all be long, but Welsh quantity is not our concern here; it has been argued elsewhere that, in a manner not very different from Icelandic, the length of nuclei in Welsh can be determined by considering stress and the consonantal neighbours of a vowel. In [25] we illustrate the basic vowels of North Welsh.

[25] cig [kiːg] 'meat'
 sych [sɨːχ] 'dry'
 crwn [krun] 'round, masc.'
 iselder [iˈsɛldɛr] 'lowness'
 sydyn [ˈsədɨn] 'sudden'
 cron [kron] 'round, fem.'
 caniad [ˈkanjad] 'song'

A characteristic property of Welsh is the fact that the schwa vowel [ə] cannot appear as the last vowel of a word, apart from a few monosyllabic function words. Thus *[səð] or *[ˈturnə] are not possible words in Welsh; schwa is regularly found in the non-final position, both stressed and unstressed, e.g.:

[26] cysgu [ˈkəskɨ] 'sleep, vb.'   ysgafn [ˈəskavn] 'light, adj.'
 cymeriad [kəˈmɛrjad] 'reputation'   Cymraeg [kəmˈraːg] 'Welsh'

Additionally, schwa alternates with the high vowels [ɨ, u] in a number of words by means of a regularity that Welsh grammarians have termed *Vowel Mutation*. Its operation can be seen in the following sets of alternations:

[27]
a. bryn [brɨn] 'hill'   bryniau [ˈbrənjɛ] 'pl.'
 tyn [tɨn] 'tight'   tynnu [ˈtənɨ] 'pull, vb.'
 cryf [krɨːv] 'strong'   cryfder [ˈkrəvdɛr] 'strength'
 sych [sɨːχ] 'dry'   sychder [ˈsəχdɛr] 'drought'
b. cwm [kum] 'valley'   cymoedd [ˈkəmoð] 'pl.'
 bwrdd [burð] 'table'   byrddau [ˈbərðɛ] 'pl.'
 trwm [trum] 'heavy'   trymaidd [ˈtrəmɛð] 'sultry'
 crwn [krun] 'round, masc.'   crynion [ˈkrənjon] 'pl.'

The left-hand column words all contain a single pronounced vowel, either [ɨ] or [u]. If an inflectional or derivational suffix is attached to them, the root nuclei find themselves in prefinal position where these vowels are not acceptable. Instead the vowel [ə] appears in the stressed nucleus. Similarly, if a suffix is attached to longer words whose last vowel is [ɨ], schwa appears in its place before the suffix, e.g.:

[28] cybydd [ˈkəbɨð] 'miser'   cybyddion [kəˈbəðjon] 'pl.'
 mynydd [ˈmənɨð] 'mountain'   mynyddoedd [məˈnəðoið] 'pl.'
 sydyn [ˈsədɨn] 'sudden'   sydynrwydd [səˈdənruið] 'suddenness'

We can see then that schwa, which is barred from word-final nuclei, replaces the two high vowels in prefinal position. Modern Welsh provides numerous instances of alternations involving these vowels in exactly such contexts as those above, which allows us to conclude that we are dealing with a productive phonological regularity. The process of vowel replacement lies at the heart of Welsh Vowel Mutation which, in synchronic terms, constitutes the Welsh equivalent of Russian and English vowel reduction: some vowels are barred from specific positions, and other vowels take their place there. What these vowels are and how the positions are to be defined are problems for the phonology of individual languages. Our reasoning would lead us to expect that in Welsh the vowels [ɨ, u] are not found outside the final position, but this conclusion is not true in absolute terms.

The back rounded vowel [u] appears prefinally in a handful of borrowings like *swper* ['supɛr] 'supper' and, more interestingly, when the final nucleus also contains [u]; if a suffix is attached to such a form, schwa replaces both instances of [u], e.g.:

[29]   cwmwl ['kumul] 'cloud'   cymylau [kə'məlaɨ] 'pl.'
       cwmwd ['kumud] 'neighbourhood' cymydog [kə'mədɔg] 'neighbour'
       bwrlwm [burlum] 'gurgling'   byrlymu [bər'ləmɨ] 'bubble over'

An inspection of forms like these reveals that prefinal [u] is possible only when directly followed or supported by an identical vowel in the final nucleus. Once the final source of support is removed, [u] cannot appear in prefinal position, hence *[ku'mədɔg] is not a possible form. The examples like [29], although interesting in themselves, do not invalidate the reality of Vowel Mutation in Welsh: they show that phonological subregularities may interact with or impinge upon dominant generalisations. Keeping these subregularities in mind we can rightly conclude that in Welsh [u] is only possible in the last (pronounced) nucleus of a word. When we turn to the other vowel involved in Vowel Mutation, namely [ɨ] we have to reach a different conclusion. As the examples in [30] show, this vowel may genuinely resist Vowel Mutation and remain unaffected in prefinal position.

[30]   pur [pɨːr] 'pure'   puro ['pɨːrɔ] 'purify'
       hun [hɨn] 'self'   hunan ['hɨnan] 'pl.'
       llun [ɬɨːn] 'picture'   lluniau [ɬɨnjɛ] 'pl.'
       papur ['papɨr] 'paper'   papurau [pa'pɨrɛ] 'pl.'

These examples of forms resisting Vowel Mutation are very different from those in [29]: there is nothing that could be said to unite them or set them apart from forms conforming to Vowel Mutation. The tentative conclusion seems to be then that [ɨ] may but does not have to conform to Vowel Mutation. Alternatively we can say that [ɨ] displays two different types of phonological behaviour, as exemplified in [27a, 28] on the one hand and [30] on the other.

If we believe in the synchronic reality of Vowel Mutation in Welsh, then the fact that only some instances of [ɨ] are well behaved with respect to it must mean that the vowel [ɨ] masks two phonologically different objects. In the terminology adopted in this chapter the Welsh vowel [ɨ] must be (another candidate for) a double agent. We seem to have produced enough phonological evidence to justify the setting up of two different phonological units. As an additional bit of evidence let us note the effect the addition of a suffix containing [ɨ] has on the preceding vowel [a]:

[31]
a.   mab [maːb] 'son'   mebyd ['mɛːbɨd] 'youth'
      aeth [aiθ] 'he went'   euthum ['eiθɨm] 'I went'
      plant [plant] 'children'   plentyn ['plɛntɨn] 'child'
b.   glas [glaːs] 'green'   glasu ['glasɨ] 'become green'
      can [kaːn] 'song'   canu ['kaːnɨ] 'sing'

The above examples seem to indicate that of the two vowels pronounced uniformly as [ɨ] one is front and hence fronts the preceding vowel as in [31a]; the other would accordingly have to be back as in [31b]. What this means for the phonological structure of Welsh high vowels remains to be worked out. Here we are merely interested in showing that a single phonetic object may cover two distinct types of phonological behaviour.

8.6 Summary

This chapter has attempted to explore an idea which in a certain sense is the opposite of phonetic effect. The latter, it will be recalled, entails the claim that there may be phonetic properties which do not play any phonologically significant part. In other words, the specific phonetic configuration is more or less an accident and could very well be different: this accounts for the equivalence in German and other languages of the apical trill [r] and the uvular fricative [ʁ]. Very different phonic effects probably correspond to the same phonological reality.

The concept of the double agent which we introduced in the present chapter refers to what must be regarded as the directly opposite situation: distinct phonological objects are realised by means of the same phonetic configuration (sound). Consequently there is nothing in the sound itself which would indicate or give away its phonological status. We have explored, admittedly somewhat tentatively, a few cases where evidence can be found which supports the existence of such segments with double identity. The basic task facing a phonologist is to provide evidence for such a covert distinction for if it is a real distinction, then it must yield tangible consequences. What is the same segment phonetically may show different and distinct patterns of interactions or may condition or be conditioned by other regularities in perceptibly different ways. We have seen that some German voiceless plosives undergo contextually conditioned spirantisation while others do not. Some instances of [s] in Icelandic are located in the coda while others must necessarily occupy the onset, with concomitant differences in the length of the preceding vowels. Russian labial fricatives are devoiced like regular obstruents but themselves do not condition the voicing of other obstruents. In Polish the velar spirant in some words shows the same patterns of alternations as other velar obstruents, while in other cases it patterns with non-velars. Finally, in Welsh some instances of the vowel [ɨ] influence other vowels, while others remain inert.

It goes without saying that the suggestions made above may not in every case stand up to closer study, or may have to be adjusted in the light of more extensive data. What we have examined above are little more than morsels of the phonologies of the languages involved. Possibly alternative accounts can be found which will not recognise such ambiguous objects. However, any such alternative analysis will have to provide an account of the ambiguous patterns of behaviour which accompany their distribution.

Let us note finally that the existence of ambiguous segments should not come as much of a surprise if we consider the existence of empty positions, i.e. empty onsets, empty nuclei. Recognising distinct phonological segments which sound the same is not really different from recognising positions with no melody attached to them. Both cases amount to the claim that phonological regularities are to be found in but are not to be identified with phonetic matter.

8.7 Suggested further reading

German spirantisation is studied in Hall (1992, chapter 5), Brockhaus (1995a, chapter 5), and Wiese (1996, section 7.3.2).

Icelandic data can be verified in the sources mentioned earlier, and particularly in dictionaries providing phonetic transcriptions such as Blöndal (1924) or Bérkov and Böðvarsson (1962).

The behaviour of the Russian labio-dentals is examined in detail in Andersen (1969), Hayes (1984) and Cyran and Nilsson (1998).

Polish dorsal obstruents are described from a phonetic point of view by Wierzchowska (1971); they are compared with the English glottal spirant by Jassem (1972).

For Welsh vowels consult Thomas (1984) and Thorne (1993).

9
Words and feet: stress in Munster Irish

9.1 Introduction

One of the first problems we presented in chapter 1 was the alternation of the low vowels [ɑ – a] in Muskerry Irish. It seems fitting that we should turn again to a dialect of Irish in the last chapter. The dialect in question is that of the southern region, also called Munster, and we will be examining some problems connected with the placement of primary stress on its basis. Our main concern is not the stress intricacies of a given group of dialects. What will primarily concern us will be the theoretical machinery required for an insightful description of one particular stress system.

The choice of Munster Irish is dictated by the fact that its stress system is not of the fixed type found in languages such as French or Finnish, where relatively little of theoretical interest could be said. Nor is it of the extremely complex kind found in English or Russian where little could be said within a single chapter. We will see that the skeletal and melodic structures organised into onsets and rhymes as syllabic constituents are not capable of handling the job of describing Munster Irish stress, and consequently the machinery will be enriched by the inclusion of feet. As throughout this book we show that such an enrichment is not just possible, which it always is, but indispensable. In what follows we study the data to find out why rhymes will not do and why feet are necessary.

Word-stress in the dialect at hand has attracted considerable attention mostly in the context of the history of the language and dialect studies. In the earlier stages of the language, just like in its other dialects today, stress fell predominantly on the first syllable within a word. In the southern dialect today, as we will see directly, it can be found in different positions in a word. The question that was often asked in the past concerned the mechanism or mechanisms which brought about the change from the earlier initial stress to the present-day variety. In what follows we will disregard the history and concentrate instead on a synchronic account of word-stress, although a historical implication will emerge towards the end of the account. The basic question we will be asking is quite simple: where does stress fall in Munster Irish words? Since in Irish, as in many other languages, it is the vocalic nucleus that manifests the presence of stress, we will want to consider what relation there is, if any, between the various types of nuclei and stress. As nuclei form parts of rhymes, we will look at the structure of rhymes in an attempt to determine whether codas affect stress placement. In brief, we will try to identify what properties of Munster Irish must be taken into account in a full description of stress patterns in the dialect.

We will start by reviewing the basic data and considering some traditional findings; their partial inadequacy will serve as a starting point for a revised formulation. Before looking at the data, some comment about sounds and transcription is called for. As illustrated in chapter 1, Irish nuclei can be both branching and non-branching; the latter are, of course, short vowels, while the former comprise long vowels and diphthongs. In this Irish does not differ from languages like English or German. We noted earlier that Irish consonants are broadly divided into palatalised and velarised. As in our transcriptions in 1.2 we follow the IPA tradition of marking palatalisation by the symbol ^{j} after a consonant; in this we depart from the Irish tradition of indicating palatalisation by the diacritic '. Velarised consonants are left unmarked; stress, as everywhere in this book is marked by '.

9.2 Stress and nuclei

Words in Irish can contain one or more nuclei; when there is only one pronounced nucleus, it obviously carries word stress although its stressedness can only be seen in combination with other nuclei. The noun *cead* [k^{j}ad] 'permission' can be seen to be stressed when preceded by the definite article which is unstressed: *an cead* [ə 'k^{j}ad]. We will be concerned with the place of stress in longer words.

An initial observation about stress is that it is closely connected with the branching or non-branching nature of the nucleus. If a word contains short vowels only, the stress most frequently falls on the initial syllable. In [1a] we provide several examples of phonetically bisyllabic words and in [1b] of trisyllabic ones: all the nuclei are non-branching, i.e. the vowels are short and it is the first of them that receives stress.

[1]
a. solas ['soləs] 'light'
gearraim ['g^{j}arim^j] 'I cut'
bata ['batə] 'stick'
b. ocrach ['okərəx] 'hungry'
thuigeadar ['hig^{j}ədər] 'they understood'
farraige ['farəg^{j}ə] 'sea'

If a short or non-branching nucleus appears in the company of a branching one, it is the latter that attracts stress in most cases. In [2] we illustrate a single long vowel preceded or followed by a short one in bisyllabic words [a–b], and also the three possible positions for a branching nucleus in trisyllabic words [c–e].

[2]
a. gadaí [gɑˈdiː] 'thief'
   garsún [gɑrˈsuːn] 'boy'
   Carghas [kɑˈriːs] 'Lent'
b. eolas [ˈoːləs] 'knowledge'
   tógaim [ˈtoːgimʲ] 'I take'
   intinn [ˈiːnʲtʲinʲ] 'mind'
c. amadán [əməˈdɑːn] 'fool'
   tamaillín [tɑməˈlʲiːnʲ] 'a little while'
   seachnaím [ʃaxəˈniːmʲ] 'I avoid'
d. macánta [məˈkɑːntə] 'modest'
   fuinneoige [fiˈnʲoːgʲə] 'window, gen. sg.'
   tiomáinim [tʲəˈmɑːnʲimʲ] 'I drive'
e. Lúnasa [ˈluːnəsə] 'August'
   uaigneas [ˈuəgʲənʲəs] 'loneliness'
   buíochasach [ˈbeːxəsəx] 'grateful'

Given the choice of a short and a long vowel [2a–b], it is the long vowel that attracts stress; in the remaining cases a complex vowel is preceded by two short ones [2c], or is flanked by them [2d], or precedes them [2e], but in all cases it is the branching nucleus that is stressed. Thus, if one or two short vowels occur in the same word as a long vowel or a diphthong, the complex nucleus bears the stress.

Before proceeding to consider words containing more than one complex nucleus we need to note a subregularity affecting words which consist of short vowels only. A departure from the initial place of stress in words of this type is found when the second syllable contains a low vowel followed by a voiceless velar spirant, i.e. either [ax] or [ɑx]. In such cases stress goes to this second syllable. Some examples illustrating this follow in [3].

[3] bacach [bəˈkɑx] 'lame'
    bacacha [bəˈkɑxə] 'lame, pl.'
    cailleach [kəˈlʲax] 'hag'
    cuideachta [kəˈdʲaxtə] 'company'
    lagachar [ləˈgɑxər] 'weakness'
    beannachtach [bʲəˈnɑxtəx] 'blessed'

Let us look at the syllabic structure of these words. In view of what has been established about syllabification in preceding chapters, the claim that the sequence [ɑx] appears fully in the second syllable cannot be maintained. Consider a relatively uncontroversial representation of the word *bacacha* 'lame, pl.'

[4]
```
     O   R   O   R   O   R
     |   |   |   |   |   |
         N       N       N
         |       |       |
     x   x   x   x   x   x
     |   |   |   |   |   |
     b   ə   k   ɑ   x   ə
```

There can be no doubt that while the vowel [ɑ] appears in the second nucleus, the velar spirant [x] occupies the onset licensed by the third nucleus. In [4] the third nucleus contains a full vowel, i.e. one with a melodic content. Since word-final consonants are invariably onsets, the singular of the adjective, i.e. *bacach* [bə'kɑx] has exactly the syllable structure as in [4]; they differ not syllabically but melodically, namely in [4] the final nucleus contains a melody while in *bacach* it is empty. In both forms of the adjective the velar spirant appears as the onset of the syllable following the vowel [ɑ]. In some of the examples of [3], e.g. *cuideachta* [ki'dʲaxtə] 'company', the velar spirant would undoubtedly be placed in the coda position, but this, as the other examples show, is not a necessary requirement for stress to be placed on the second nucleus.

An inspection of the forms in [1 – 3] reveals another characteristic property: the vowel [ə] is never stressed in Irish. As in English, German and Russian, but unlike Welsh, schwa typically occurs in unstressed nuclei. Could we perhaps suggest that the second-syllable stress in [3] is simply due to the fact that the first syllable contains the unstressable vowel, hence stress moves to the first eligible nucleus? There is a group of words which might be used to support such a proposal. Consider some examples.

[5]   macalla [mə'kɑlə] 'echo'
        anseo [ən'so] 'here'
        cathain [kə'hin] 'when'
        anuraidh [ə'nirʲigʲ] 'last year'
        anocht [ə'noxt] 'tonight'
        abach [ə'bɑx] 'great damage'

All such words with stress falling on the second vowel, could be seen as being quite regular if we excluded the schwa vowel from serving as a potential stress-bearing unit. In such a case, stress would automatically fall on the next stressable vowel, which happens to be the second in a word. Although such a solution cannot be ruled out for some forms, there are others where it would be difficult to maintain. Consider, for example, the verbal noun endings *-ach* and *-acht*. When attached to

9.2 Stress and nuclei

a stem containing a branching nucleus, the verbal noun suffix displays the vowel [ə] and the branching nucleus of the stem is stressed, as in [6a]; if appended to a stem with a non-branching nucleus, the suffix vowel is stressed while the vowel in the stem emerges as [ə], as in [6b].

[6]
a. éist [eːʃtʲ] 'listen' éisteacht [ˈeːʃtʲəxt] 'vb. n.'
   réitigh [ˈreːtʲigʲ] 'solve' réiteach [ˈreːtʲəx] 'vb. n.'
b. fan [fɑn] 'wait' fanacht [fəˈnɑxt] 'vb. n.'
   ceannaigh [ˈkʲanəgʲ] 'buy' ceannach [kʲəˈnɑx] 'vb. n.'
   imigh [ˈimʲigʲ] 'go' imeacht [əˈmʲaxt] 'vb. n.'

If we were to assume that stress assignment is sensitive to the presence of schwa, we would have to conclude that the alternations [əxt – ɑxt] and [əx – ɑx] are an accident. Note that in the verbal nouns in [6a] stress falls on the first nucleus because it is branching rather than because the second nucleus appears as schwa. Conversely, it would seem, the second nucleus contains schwa precisely because it is not stressed – in other words, unstressed nuclei cannot support the vowel [ɑ]. The same can be observed in [6b]: here the vowel which appears as [ɑ] (or [a]) in the stem is unstressed in the verbal noun and results as schwa. It transpires, then, that Irish does not tolerate [ɑ] in unstressed position and replaces it by [ə]. Thus the alternations of the verbal noun suffixes – [əxt – ɑxt] and [əx – ɑx] – are quite systematic: the variants with [ɑ] appear only when stressed, while those with [ə] are unstressed. What needs to be accounted for is the mechanism of stress placement; for the moment we simply note that in a word consisting of short vowels the first is stressed unless the second contains the vowel [ɑ], in which case it is the second nucleus that attracts stress.

Let us turn now to words containing more than one complex nucleus and see how stress is assigned there. In [7] we have examples of words containing two branching nuclei:

[7] báistí [bɑːʃˈtʲiː] 'rain, gen. sg.'
    saighdiúir [saiˈdʲuːrʲ] 'soldier'
    páistiúil [pɑːʃˈtʲuːlʲ] 'childish'
    éirí [aiˈrʲiː] 'rise, vb. n.'
    Seáinín [ʃɑːˈnʲiːnʲ] 'Seán, dim.'

The evidence is quite unambiguous: in a sequence of two complex nuclei, it is the second that receives stress. The regularity remains unchanged if a simplex nucleus follows such a combination of two branching nuclei.

[8] saighdiúra [saiˈdʲuːrə] 'soldier, gen. sg.'
    bádóireacht [bɑːˈdoːrʲəxt] 'boating'
    tógálach [toːˈgɑːləx] 'contagious'

The second branching nucleus remains the focus of stress also when followed by another nucleus of the same type, i.e. in a sequence of three branching nuclei, the second or middle one is stressed.

[9]   saighdiúirí [sai'dʲuːrʲiː] 'soldier, nom. pl.'
        scrúdúchán [skruː'duːxaːn] 'examination'
        páircíní [paːrʲ'kʲiːnʲiːʲ] 'field, dim. nom. pl.'

Another variation emerges when a sequence of two branching nuclei is preceded by a non-branching one; in such a case the first of the branching nuclei or the second nucleus in the sequence receives stress.

[10]   cailíní [kɑ'lʲiːnʲiː] 'girl, nom. pl.'
        aistriúchán [aʃ'tʲrʲuːxaːn] 'translation'
        dochtúirí [dox'tuːrʲiː] 'doctor, nom. pl.'

There is yet another possibility, namely for two complex nuclei to be separated by a simplex one. In such a case the stress, somewhat surprisingly, goes to the first of them so that a word consisting of a complex nucleus followed by a simplex one and followed in turn by another complex one will receive initial stress.

[11]   iascairí ['iəskərʲiː] 'fisherman, nom. pl.'
        údarás ['uːdəraːs] 'authority'
        buachaillí ['buəxəlʲiː] 'boy, nom. pl.'
        féileacán ['feːlʲəkaːn] 'butterfly'
        méaracán ['mʲiarəkaːn] 'thimble'

The complexity of the regularity or regularities controlling stress assignment in Munster Irish is becoming clearer and clearer although we have not yet considered all the relevant possibilities. Words longer than those reviewed above do occur but for the most part they display the same patterns as trisyllabic words. Thus if any of the first three nuclei is branching while the remaining ones are non-branching, then the branching one is stressed.

[12]   máithreacha ['maːhirʲəxə] 'mother, nom. pl.'
        cathaoireacha [kɑ'hiːrʲəxə] 'chair, nom. pl.'
        strapadóireacht [strɑpə'doːrʲəxt] 'climbing'
        strapadóireachta [strɑpə'doːrʲəxtə] 'climbing, gen. sg.'

These results are unsurprising. Nor is there anything unusual when the second of two initial complex nuclei is stressed ([13a]) since this mirrors the situation in shorter words (see [8]); likewise the first of two final complex nuclei is stressed ([13b]) in accordance with what we have seen above (see [10]).

[13]
a. múinteoireachta [muːnʲˈtʲoːrəxtə] 'teaching, gen. sg.'
b. spealadóirí [spʲaləˈdoːrʲiː] 'scytheman, nom. pl.'
   amadántaíocht [əməˈdɑːntiːxt] 'foolishness'

The different arrangements of complex and simplex nuclei and the positioning of stress as presented so far have one thing in common: stress can fall on one of the first three nuclei only. We have seen no cases as yet where this regularity would be violated. In fact there is some rather striking support for this conclusion.

There is a sizeable number of words where the first three nuclei are all simplex and are followed by a branching one. Above we have seen cases where a single branching nucleus is invariably stressed if surrounded by non-branching ones, and we would expect that the same would be true here. In fact it is not. As the examples in [14] show, stress falls on the first short vowel in contravention of the regularity that if there is only one branching nucleus in a word it must be stressed.

[14] imleacán [ˈimʲəlʲəkɑːn] 'navel'
     gioblachán [ˈgʲubələxɑːn] 'ragamuffin'
     seilmidí [ˈʃelʲəmʲidʲiː] 'snail, pl.'
     patalachán [ˈpɑtələxɑːn] 'plump creature'
     carthanachtúil [ˈkarhənəxtuːlʲ] 'charitable'

All the examples show four nuclei of which the last is branching but stress is found on the initial short one. If stress in Munster Irish is restricted to the first three syllables only, then whatever follows these three syllables is irrelevant and has no influence on the position of stress. Particularly significant in this context are the two last examples since side by side with the forms given in [15] there exist alternative forms containing one syllable less, namely

[15] patachán [pɑtəˈxɑːn]
     carthanúil [kɑrhəˈnuːlʲ]

In these shortened forms, both containing three nuclei, it is the branching nucleus that is stressed, exactly as we would expect. We can tentatively conclude that stress in Munster Irish must go to one of the first three nuclei in the word.

With this reservation in mind we can look again at the different patterns illustrated in the preceding pages. The position of stress is conditioned by the skeletal and partly also by melodic structure of the nuclei present in a given word. These conditions can be summarised as in [16].

[16]
a.   the first nucleus is stressed if it is branching and followed by a non-branching nucleus or if the first three nuclei are non-branching
b.   the second nucleus is stressed if it is branching or if it contains an [ɑ] which does not precede or follow a branching nucleus
c.   the third nucleus is stressed if it is branching and preceded by non-branching nuclei

Condition [16a] accounts for the forms in [1, 2b, 2e, 6a, 11, 14]. Condition [16b] accounts for the stressed nuclei in [2a, 2d, 3, 6b, 7, 8, 9, 10, 13a]. Condition [16c] predicts the stress in [2c, 13b, 14, 15].

The three conditions of [16] constitute a significant improvement over the list-like account which accompanied our presentation of the data in [1 – 15]. This is due to the fact that they attempt to reduce the rather chaotic stress variation to a handful of general principles. Before we assess the efficacy of this particular attempt we must note that Irish, in a way common to numerous languages, admits a certain number of **lexical exceptions**. These are forms which depart from what is predicted by the general stress conditions and must have stress individually marked in the lexicon of the language. There is nothing unusual or surprising about the existence of lexical exceptions – this happens even in languages in which stress is quite regularly associated with a specific position. A few examples of such exceptional positioning of stress in Irish follow below.

[17]   lámhacán ['lɑːkɑːn] 'crawling'
        sladamóireacht ['slɑdəmoːrʲəxt] 'plundering'
        basadaer ['bɑsədeːr] 'match-maker'
        lapadán ['lɑpədɑːn] 'bare-footed child'

In all these exceptional forms stress is initial although the conditions summarised in [16] would put it either on the second or the third vowel. Apart from exceptions like these, the attested stress patterns conform to the conditions laid down above. This results in rich morphological alternations where stress appears to move over the different vowels of morpheme combinations. Consider the position of the stress and the nature of the nuclei in the following words:

[18]   gadaí [gɑ'diː] 'thief'   gadaithe ['gɑdəhi] 'nom. pl.'
        speala ['spʲalə] 'scythe, mom. pl.'   spealadóir [spʲalə'doːrʲ] 'scytheman'
        capall ['kɑpəl] 'horse'   capaillín [kɑpə'lʲiːnʲ] 'dim.'
        múinim ['muːnʲimʲ] 'I teach'   múinteoir [muːnʲ'tʲoːrʲ] 'teacher'
        ceannaigh ['kʲanəgʲ] 'buy, imper.'   ceannach [kʲə'nax] 'vb. n.'
        ceannaithe ['kʲanəhi] 'bought, part.' ceannaím [kʲa'niːmʲ] 'I buy'
        giobal ['gʲubəl] 'rag'   giobach [gʲu'bax] 'unkempt'
        giobalachán ['gʲubələxɑːn]   giobachán [gʲubə'xɑːn]
           'ragamuffin'   'something unkempt'

In the left-hand column we have initial stress, while the accent falls on the second or third vowel in the right-hand one. In all cases the placement of stress follows from one of the conditions in [16]. The existence of numerous alternations like those above strengthens the case for the predominantly regular nature of Munster Irish stress assignment. It is a different question, of course, whether the specific formulation is completely adequate, and whether we want to present it in precisely this way.

If by adequacy we understand agreement with recorded facts, then [16] passes the test: given a word with a specific arrangement of simplex and complex nuclei, stress will be appropriately ascribed to one of them. To question the adequacy of [16] we would need to find examples which stand in conflict with it, apart from lexical exceptions, of course.

The formulation of [16] is a different matter. First of all we must admit to a degree of disingenuousness or downright deception in the way the conditions are stated. There are three conditions but only in the sense that there are three possible sites for stress placement: the first, the second or the third nucleus. However, the conditions under which stress is assigned initially can hardly be said to constitute a single generalisation. Recall that *the first nucleus is stressed if it is branching and followed by a non-branching nucleus or if all three nuclei are non-branching*. This condition conflates two very different contexts: one referring to a sequence of a complex and a simplex nucleus and one to a series of three simplex ones. These two contexts combined by the conjunction 'or' are totally disjoint and have nothing in common; one could easily imagine a formulation whose second part would be a mirror image of the first: *the first nucleus is stressed if it is branching and followed by a non-branching nucleus or if it is non-branching and followed by a branching one*. This, of course, does not happen, but there is nothing in the formulation that rules it out, or makes it unlikely. In other words, given the actual situation as captured in [16a] and a completely arbitrary combination of contexts, a statement using disjunctions fares equally well in both cases. Crucially, the formulation fails to reveal any connection between the two contexts and this is exactly what a phonologically based generalisation should attempt to do. In other words, unless it is an accident that the initial vowel is stressed in just those contexts listed in [16a], it would be desirable for a description to reveal the nature of the connection between the contexts. Put briefly, why is the first nucleus stressed in both the contexts of [16a]? Exactly the same arguments could be brought against the disjunction contained in the two contexts of [16b]: the second nucleus is stressed if it branches or if it contains the non-branching [ɑ] and is further flanked by non-branching nuclei. What is there in the branching of the second nucleus that unites it with the non-branching of [ɑ]?

Conflated statements such as those in [16], regularly found in traditional phonetic descriptions, are superficially adequate in the sense that they are not contradicted by observed facts. They may serve as starting points for more detailed analyses or they may perhaps serve some didactic purposes. However, they fail phonologically because they reveal little of substance about the structure of the language – they amount to the unintended claim that stress results from accidents. Such reasoning leads us to look for an alternative account of Munster stress. The account below is not meant as the final word on the subject but rather as an attempt to see what an insightful analysis could look like. The Munster facts are quite intricate, as we have seen, and it should further be added that not all vagaries have been included in our presentation. It is hoped, however, that enough relevant facts have been taken into account to justify a rejection of the traditional description.

9.3 Stress and feet

The account which we reconstructed in the preceding pages is based on the arrangement of simplex and complex nuclei. Everything else has been assumed to be irrelevant; thus there is no evidence that onsets, either branching or non-branching, have any role to play in the principles which determine stress placement. In this Irish is not different from any other language whose stress pattern has been investigated in sufficient detail: no compelling argument has been offered indicating that onsets ever influence the placement of stress in a word. The consonantal coda presents a different situation as it commonly plays a part in stress regularities: a branching rhyme, i.e. one containing a coda, attracts stress while a non-branching one does not. English is a case in point where stress goes to the nucleus in the penultimate pronounced nucleus in a rhyme that branches, e.g. *veranda* [vəˈrændə], *utensil* [juːˈtensɪl], and otherwise goes to the antepenultimate pronounced nucleus, e.g. *cinnamon* [ˈsɪnəmən], *America* [əˈmerɪkə]. Irish is different from English in that the consonantal coda does not contribute to the way the stress is placed. This is shown by the existence of words where a simplex vowel is stressed although a branching rhyme is available in the word, e.g. *eitilt* [ˈetʲilʲtʲ] 'flying', *sagart* [ˈsɑgərt] 'priest'. In Irish, then, a branching rhyme is not – from the point of view of stress placement – equivalent to a branching nucleus: the [ilʲ] of *eitilt* [ˈetʲilʲtʲ] is not the same thing as the [iː] of *gadaí* [gɑˈdiː] 'thief'.

Another argument supporting the irrelevance of the consonantal coda to stress placement in Irish comes from words containing two complex nuclei, as illustrated in [7]. By [16b] it is the second of these complex nuclei that receives stress: *éirí* [aiˈrʲiː] 'rise, vb. n.', *báistí* [bɑːʃˈtʲiː] 'rain, gen. sg.' If branching rhymes were equivalent to branching nuclei, then we would expect a branching rhyme to be stressed when following a branching nucleus. This does not happen: in [7] we saw that the verbal noun suffix -*acht* attracts stress when attached to a stem containing a non-branching nucleus, e.g. *fanacht* [fə'nɑxt] 'wait, vb. n.' If this suffix is attached to a stem containing a branching nucleus, the suffix is unstressed and its vowel reduces to schwa, e.g. *dúisigh* ['duːʃigʲ] 'awake' – *dúiseacht* ['duːʃəxt] 'vb. n.' If [ɑx] were equivalent to [uː], then *dúiseacht* would be end-stressed, just like *éirí*, *báistí* etc. We must conclude that what plays a role in stress assignment in Irish is the branching or non-branching nature of nuclei rather than the branching or non-branching structure of rhymes.

Although stress is determined by nuclei alone, we have seen above that a description which just takes into consideration the different sequences of nuclei is highly unsatisfactory. This kind of description can be reduced to a few pseudo-general conditions like those in [16] but it fails to reveal any internal connection among them. In short, the description is atomistic and uninsightful. We need to look elsewhere for a mechanism which would yield a more satisfactory description. As a possible source for such a mechanism let us consider again stress placement in words like *éirí* [aiˈrʲiː] 'rise, vb. n.' on the one hand and *údarás* ['uːdərɑːs] 'authority' on the other.

Both these words contain two complex nuclei, but stress is assigned differently to each of them. Where the words contain nothing apart from the two complex nuclei, it is the second nucleus that is stressed, hence [aiˈrʲiː]; if, however, the first complex nucleus is followed by one with the reduced schwa vowel, stress goes to this first nucleus. It thus transpires that the reduced – and, as far as Irish is concerned, unstressable – vowel [ə] has a role to play in the assignment of stress to the word as a whole. In other words, what determines stress placement in Irish is not so much the mere presence of complex and simplex nuclei but their groupings or arrangements. Such combinations of nuclei are said to make up phonological feet.

The concept of the **foot** and foot or **pedal structure** is a much discussed issue in phonological theory and practice. It is not our purpose here to describe the different approaches to the foot or to present even a small part of the variation in foot structure that has been described in the literature. What we are primarily interested in is to argue that some sort of organisation above and beyond that afforded by segmental and syllabic organisation must be recognised. The system of Munster Irish stress seems to offer a relatively simple case where feet are necessary if a more adequate description is to be arrived at, more adequate, that is, than the list-like formulation of [16]. It should be kept in mind, however, that the particular characterisation of foot structure is dictated by the stress facts of Munster Irish and might need to be revised in the light of other evidence. As a final rider, or admission, let us note that we use the data of Munster stress to argue for the reality of foot structure in the Irish language and at the same time we try to gain an understanding of the existing stress patterns by invoking foot structure. It seems that a certain degree of reasoning bordering on the vicious circle is unavoidable in phonology (or linguistics at large): theoretical constructs such as *the segment, the onset, sharing* etc. are hypotheses about linguistic organisation. Their validity is confirmed to the extent that they allow us to describe more data or to describe data in a more satisfactory manner. In other words, to show that a construct such as foot structure is mistaken or superfluous, one needs to provide a more or equally insightful analysis of the same facts without this notion. For the moment we will assume that the way nuclei are combined into feet contributes to our understanding of word stress. Words break up into feet: in Irish the foot comprises nuclei and, as we have seen above, disregards codas.

Going back to the Munster stress pattern, recall again the word *údarás* ['uːdəraːs] 'authority' and the other examples in [11] where stress is initial if two complex nuclei are separated by a simplex one. This, we suggested above, clearly points to the fact that a complex nucleus followed by a simplex one constitutes a unity called a foot. [19] offers a possible nuclear and pedal structure for the word *údarás*; in the representations below we omit information which is irrelevant to feet, hence we bypass onsets and codas, as well as empty nuclei, which seem to play no role in Irish foot structure.

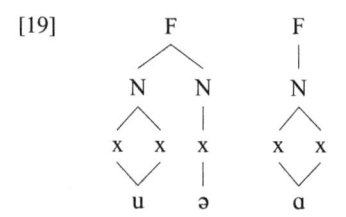

[19]
$$\begin{array}{cc} F & F \\ \bigwedge & | \\ N\ \ N & N \\ \bigwedge\ \ | & \bigwedge \\ x\ \ x\ \ x & x\ \ x \\ \vee\ \ | & \vee \\ u\ \ \ \ \ \ \ \ \ \ə & ɑ \end{array}$$

The word *údarás* is seen to embrace two feet of which the first one is the focus of word stress. More precisely, it is the first nucleus of the first foot that is stressed; the leftmost nucleus of a foot will be referred to as **the head of the foot**. Thus the head of the first foot in this word constitutes the location of word stress. We see, then, that for purposes of stress placement, the first foot in [19] is selected over a foot consisting of just a branching nucleus. What distinguishes the two feet is the fact that the first contains three nuclear positions (or slots) and the second just two. A three-position foot can be regarded as a **super** or **maximal foot**; thus we can say that the head of the maximal foot is the domain of word stress.

Consider now non-maximal feet, sometimes called **degenerate feet**. The most typical cases of such feet can be found in words consisting of:

[20]
a. a single branching nucleus, e.g. *beo* [bʲoː] 'alive', *bua* [buə] 'victory'
b. a sequence of two non-branching nuclei, e.g. *fada* ['fɑdə] 'long', *ollamh* ['oləv] 'professor'
c. a single non-branching nucleus, e.g. *ba* [bɑ] 'cow, nom. pl.', *teas* [tʲas] 'heat', *locht* [loxt] 'fault'

Such degenerate feet have the structures in [21]:

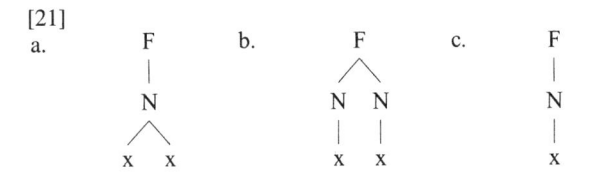

[21]
a.   F   b.   F   c.   F
       | /\ |
       N   N N   N
      /\ | | |
     x x   x x   x

These foot types in conjunction with the maximal foot in [19] constitute the foot inventory as found in Munster Irish. Feet are combined to make up words. Obviously if words consist of single feet, their heads will become the focus of stress assignment. We are fundamentally interested in different foot combinations within words and the consequences of these combinations for the position of word stress.

We have seen in examples [7] and [9], reproduced as [21a–b], that a word consisting of two or three branching nuclei stresses the second of them.

[22]
a. báistí [bɑːʃˈtʲiː] 'rain, gen. sg.'
   saighdiúir [saiˈdʲuːrʲ] 'soldier'
   páistiúil [pɑːʃˈtʲuːlʲ] 'childish'
   éirí [aiˈrʲiː] 'rise, vb. n.'
   Seáinín [ʃɑːˈnʲiːnʲ] 'Seán, dim.'
b. saighdiúirí [saiˈdʲuːrʲiː] 'soldier, nom. pl.'
   scrúdúchán [skruːˈduːxɑːn] 'examination'
   páircíní [pɑːrʲˈkʲiːnʲiːʲ] 'field, dim. nom. pl.'

The foot structure of these words is depicted in [23].

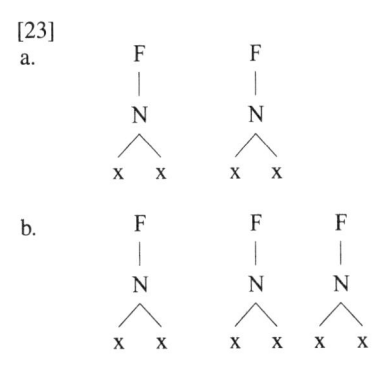

[23]
a.   F   F
        | |
        N   N
       /\   /\
      x x   x x

b.   F   F   F
        | | |
        N   N   N
       /\   /\   /\
      x x   x x   x x

In such cases, as can be seen, it is the second foot that attracts stress. This, we would like to argue, is the general situation in Irish. That is, unless pre-empted by a maximal foot, the second foot in a word receives primary stress. Let us study the remaining examples which we used in the first part of this chapter to illustrate the different stress patterns.

If a non-branching nucleus precedes one or two branching ones, then the non-branching one must form a foot of its own, since it cannot combine with the branching one either to form a maximal foot or to form any of the degenerate types. Examples of two-feet words are supplied in [24a], while the sequences of single non-branching followed by two branching nuclei in [10] are repeated here as [24b].

[24]
a. gadaí [gɑˈdiː] 'thief'
cailín [kaˈlʲiːnʲ] 'girl'
dochtúir [doxˈtuːrʲ] 'doctor'
b. cailíní [kɑˈlʲiːnʲiː] 'girl, nom. pl.'
aistriúchán [aʃˈtʲrʲuːxɑːn] 'translation'
dochtúirí [doxˈtuːrʲiː] 'doctor, nom. pl.'

The foot structures corresponding to [24a–b] look like the following:

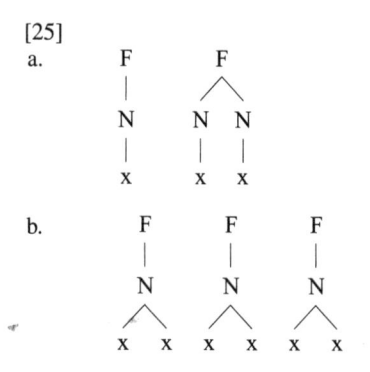

[25]
a.
```
      F         F
      |        / \
      N       N   N
      |       |   |
      x       x   x
```
b.
```
      F         F         F
      |         |         |
      N         N         N
     / \       / \       / \
    x   x     x   x     x   x
```

As before, it is the second foot that receives primary stress. At this juncture it is important to underline that the number of nuclei preceding the second foot is not really relevant – in the examples just presented, there is only one non-branching nucleus in the first foot. It is perfectly possible for two such nuclei to appear and for the stress to still go to the second foot. Consider the words in [26].

[26] bacachán [bakəˈxɑːn] 'a lame person'
strapadóireacht [strɑpəˈdoːrʲəxt] 'climbing'
beannaitheoir [bʲanəˈhoːrʲ] 'sanctifier'

Here the first two nuclei form a foot, as does the final branching nucleus; thus the words constitute a combination of [21b] and [21a] in this order:

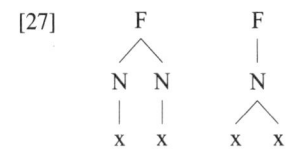

[27]
```
       F           F
      / \          |
     N   N         N
     |   |        / \
     x   x       x   x
```

As before, the second foot carries the word stress.

Let us turn now to cases that seemed initially quite puzzling, namely those where stress goes to the second nucleus if it contains the vowel [ɑ] (see [6] which is reproduced below as [28]).

[28]
a. éist [eːʃtʲ] 'listen'   éisteacht ['eːʃtʲəxt] 'vb. n.'
    réitigh ['reːtʲigʲ] 'solve'   réiteach ['reːtʲəx] 'vb. n.'
b. fan [fɑn] 'wait'   fanacht [fə'nɑxt] 'vb. n.'
    ceannaigh ['kʲanəgʲ] 'buy'   ceannach [kʲə'nɑx] 'vb. n.'
    imigh ['imʲigʲ] 'go'   imeacht [ə'mʲaxt] 'vb. n.'

The right-hand column words in [28a] comprise a branching nucleus followed by a simplex one, a combination that constitutes a maximal foot. Since the head of the maximal foot is automatically the place where word stress falls, the initial stress in these words is exactly what we have come to expect. It is the right-hand column words in [28b] that require special attention.

The left-hand column words show that the first (or only) stem vowel contains a full, i.e. unreduced vowel. In the verbal noun, with the shift of stress, the vowel [ɑ/a] is realised as schwa. However, the replacement of the full vowel by the reduced one is a result of the absence of stress, i.e. unstressed nuclei fail to support the full melody. Thus we can say that the verbal noun forms contain a sequence of two full nuclei of which the unstressed one is not licensed in the representation, its place being taken by the ubiquitous vowel schwa. Since the second nucleus is stressed, this can only mean that it belongs to the second foot of the word, i.e. the vowels rather than making up a branching foot [21b] are assigned to two separate non-branching feet of the type [21c]:

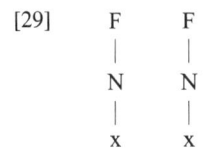

[29]
```
     F   F
     |   |
     N   N
     |   |
     x   x
```

The assumption about the bi-pedal structure of such words allows us to unify stress placement in words containing branching nuclei, non-branching nuclei and also combinations of the two types. Within this interpretation, the stress patterns illustrated by [30] all fall out from the fact that the second foot of the word is singled out as the proper domain of stress placement in the absence of a maximal or super foot.

[30] gadaí [gɑˈdiː] 'thief'
      fanacht [fəˈnɑxt] 'wait, vb. n.'
      báistí [bɑːʃˈtʲiː] 'rain, gen. sg.'
      strapadóir [strɑpəˈdoːrʲ] 'climber'
      cailíní [kaˈlʲiːnʲiː] 'girl, nom. pl.'
      scrúdúchán [skruːˈduːxɑːn] 'examination'

It is worth keeping in mind that the bi-pedal structure of words like *fanacht* in [28b] is an assumption that would call for more justification. Short of delving extensively into the phonology of Irish this cannot be attempted here, hence the conclusion must be regarded as somewhat tentative. However, cross-linguistically it appears to be true that in languages which license different sets of nuclei in stressed and unstressed positions, consecutive full vowels tend to belong to separate feet. In English words such as *bamboo* [bæmˈbuː] or *syntax* [ˈsɪntæks] must be viewed as bi-pedal, a fact that accounts for the presence of a full vowel in the unstressed syllable – note that the two words cannot be pronounced as *[bəmˈbuː] or *[ˈsɪntəks].

Let us finally look at the cases of initial stress in words containing a branching nucleus. Recall the relevant examples.

[31] imleacán [ˈimʲəlʲəkɑːn] 'navel'
      gioblachán [ˈgʲubələxɑːn] 'ragamuffin'
      seilmidí [ˈʃelʲəmʲidʲiː] 'snail, pl.'
      patalachán [ˈpɑtələxɑːn] 'plump creature'
      carthanachtúil [ˈkɑrhənəxtuːlʲ] 'charitable'

To see why stress is initial here we need to observe that the first three nuclei are all non-branching, hence they correspond to three skeletal positions. This is exactly what is found in the maximal foot which, as we have seen, overrides all other considerations. Thus the presence of a maximal foot automatically marks it as the domain for word-stress placement. The maximal or super foot is responsible for initial and non-initial stress in the following types of words:

[32] eolas [ˈoːləs] 'knowledge'
      fuinneoige [fiˈnʲoːgʲə] 'window, gen. sg.'
      tógálach [toːˈgɑːləx] 'contagious'
      údarás [ˈuːdərɑːs] 'authority'
      strapadóireacht [strɑpəˈdoːrʲəxt] 'climbing'
      imleacán [ˈimʲəlʲəkɑːn] 'navel'
      laprachánaí [ˈlɑpərəxɑːniː] 'toddler'

There is a minor technical difficulty with a maximal foot comprising three non-branching nuclei, as in *imleacán* ['iməlʲəkɑːn] above. The maximal foot as illustrated above (see [19]) embraces two nuclei: a branching one followed by a non-branching one. Thus a maximal foot is a binary structure just like the other objects in the inventory of foot types [21]. A maximal foot comprising three individual nuclei would amount to the recognition of a ternary foot, a step that would increase considerably the number of available structures and as such is not particularly desirable. Although we note the emergence of this theoretical difficulty, the crucial issue from the point of view of Munster stress is that a structure comprising three nuclear slots is special in that it attracts stress irrespective of the structure of the environment. If this is the case, then the question suggests itself of what happens when two maximal feet appear within a single word. Examples of this type are not easy to come by but a few can be found. Although the evidence is not completely unambiguous, at least in some varieties of Munster Irish it is the second such super foot that attracts stress. Some examples are offered in [33].

[33]   eadargála [adərə'gɑːlə] 'mediation, gen. sg.'
       slánaitheora [slɑːnə'hoːrə] 'saviour, gen. sg.'
       údarásach [uːdə'rɑːsəx] 'authoritative'

These examples are significant for two reasons. On the positive side, they confirm the reality of the special status of the second foot. In view of what has been said above our description of Munster Irish stress reduces to two generalisations:

[34]
a.   the maximal foot, if single, is the stress centre of the word
b.   otherwise, the second foot is the stress centre of the word

To what extent these two statements could be further improved on or conflated is not germane at the moment. What we have established is that apart from the case when a word contains a single occurrence of a maximal foot, it is always the second foot that predominates, or gains the upper hand. It matters little whether the feet involved are non-branching, binary-branching or ternary-branching. In this sense the essence of the historical process of stress shift that we referred to briefly at the outset consists in shifting the centre of the prominence of the word from the first foot (as was the case in Old Irish and is still the case in other dialects of Modern Irish) to the second foot. Although a relatively simple modification when considered in isolation, this development, as we have seen, has produced a great variety in the attested stress patterns and much apparent irregularity. With the notion of the foot, however, the apparent stress richness is greatly impoverished, while most of the irregularities turn out to be illusory.

The negative reason why the examples with stress falling on the second maximal foot are important is that they again confirm the futility of operating with nuclei only. Recall that in summing up the traditional or nucleus-based approach we pointed out that one of the few firm conclusions about it is that the stress must fall on one of the first three nuclei. The example *eadargála* [adərə'gɑːlə] 'mediation, gen. sg.' shows that this is not true. The noun in the nominative case has initial stress, i.e. *eadargáil* ['adərəgɑːlʲ], exactly as predicted by the first of our two generalisations [34a]. In the genitive, however, the addition of the inflectional vocalic ending creates a sequence of two maximal feet, which means that the second of them receives stress, as per [35b], even if the stress finds itself on the fourth nucleus. In effect, it is feet not nuclei that determine the position of stress in the language.

9.4 Summary

The fairly complex data illustrating the stress pattern of Munster Irish have been used to demonstrate the need for more structured representations than those found in the preceding chapters. In addition to structures embracing the skeletal, melodic and syllabic levels we seem to need yet another level. The foot level in the Munster case emerges out of the structure of nuclei; in other languages it entails the structure of the rhyme. We have looked at the Irish facts with a view to justifying and providing evidence for this additional level of representation.

As in other sections of the book it has been pointed out here that competing descriptions of the same set of facts can be constructed with a larger or smaller degree of inventiveness (usually smaller). The coverage of all available facts is a prerequisite – no description failing to meet this requirement should even be considered. On the other hand, descriptions may inadvertently omit data or interesting connections; it frequently happens that an insightful interpretation will indicate where new or relevant data may be sought.

Given alternative descriptions it is crucial that the selection of the best one be made in a principled way. In this chapter we have suggested yet again that the elements of a description should form a coherent unity, with individual cases or clauses falling out of a general regularity or principle. Whether the phenomenon is stress in Munster, spirantisation in Icelandic or any other, an attempt should made to bring out the basic phonological mechanisms at work. In this a search for adequate generalisations must go hand in hand with a search for restrictive theoretical machinery.

9.5 Suggested further reading

Munster stress has been described in numerous studies. Here are some of them: Loth (1913), Sjoestedt (1931), Sjoestedt-Jonval (1938), Ó Cuív (1944), Blankenhorn (1981), Ó Sé (1989), Green (1996), Rowicka (1996), Gussmann (1997).

For possibilities of the use of feet in stress descriptions see Halle and Vergnaud (1987), Giegerich (1992), Hayes (1995), Kager (1995), Halle and Idsardi (1995). Especially useful are the theoretical and descriptive contributions in van der Hulst (1999).

Conclusion

The recurring theme in this book has been the realisation that things are not the way they look. We started by considering sounds and came to the conclusion that what are called sounds in everyday speech need to be broken up into separate levels or tiers. These embrace the tier of temporal positions, called the skeleton, and the tier of phonetic properties, called the melody. Furthermore, we saw on several occasions that the melody itself is a composite of units which act independently of other units within the melody.

The ordinary notion of the word has likewise turned out to require a reinterpretation in linguistic terms. We have seen that word-like units which function as separate entities for phonological purposes often comprise only parts of traditional (orthographic) words. What we need for phonology are domains which may but do not have to be coterminous with such words.

The difference between the ordinary and the linguistic usage of terms emerges most dramatically in the case of the syllable. While in everyday speech a word is said to be broken up into a number of consecutive syllables, we have seen that phonologically the situation is much more complex. The existence of empty nuclei and empty onsets introduces a basic divide between what ordinary intuitions prompt and what is required as a result of linguistic analysis. Similarly, membership in onsets or codas is not something which can be ascertained on the basis of an inspection of a phonetic sequence, but must result from a language-specific study within a framework which should be ready to accommodate any language.

Phonological regularities may hold for the units of one particular tier independently of other tiers but they may also have consequences for other tiers. They affect adjacent units, although the adjacency may refer to a given tier only, while the interacting units will not be adjacent at every tier, e.g. consecutive nuclei may interact although at the melodic level they will not be adjacent, being separated by, say, a coda–onset sequence. We have also seen that the domains of certain phonological regularities may require reference to a category called the foot, formed out of rhymal projections.

Throughout the book we have tacitly assumed that the core phonological structure is universal. This embraces the division into tiers, the recognition of syllabic constituents, the existence of empty categories, the restricted possibilities for the skeletal and melodic composition of syllabic constituents, and the adjacency of units involved in phonological processing, to mention just some of the more salient properties. What is language-specific must be drawn out of the inventory of universal possibilities coupled with a degree of idiosyncratic information, such as the existence or not of branching nuclei or specific melodies.

In this book we have been mostly concerned with identifying phonological regularities and finding an adequate theoretical apparatus for their formulation. As the title suggests we were primarily occupied with analysis. Theories were only developed when called for by the data. Needless to say, different or additional data would have enriched the theoretical results arrived at here. Possibly this would mean that some of the conclusions would be undermined or discarded. This is nothing surprising – progress in phonology can only come about by broadening the data and the range of languages studied. But data are relevant only in so far as they lead to novel theoretical discoveries, which at the same time allow us to reach a better understanding of old or familiar facts.

Appendix The phonetic alphabet of the International Phonetic Association

THE INTERNATIONAL PHONETIC ALPHABET (revised to 1993, updated 1996)

CONSONANTS (PULMONIC)

	Bilabial	Labiodental	Dental	Alveolar	Post alveolar	Retroflex	Palatal	Velar	Uvular	Pharyngeal	Glottal
Plosive	p b			t d		ʈ ɖ	c ɟ	k ɡ	q ɢ		ʔ
Nasal	m	ɱ		n		ɳ	ɲ	ŋ	ɴ		
Trill	B			r					ʀ		
Tap or Flap				ɾ		ɽ					
Fricative	ɸ β	f v	θ ð	s z	ʃ ʒ	ʂ ʐ	ç ʝ	x ɣ	χ ʁ	ħ ʕ	h ɦ
Lateral fricative				ɬ ɮ							
Approximant		ʋ		ɹ		ɻ	j	ɰ			
Lateral approximant				l		ɭ	ʎ	L			

Where symbols appear in pairs, the one to the right represents a voiced consonant. Shaded areas denote articulations judged impossible.

CONSONANTS (NON-PULMONIC)

Clicks	Voiced implosives	Ejectives
ʘ Bilabial	ɓ Bilabial	ʼ Examples:
ǀ Dental	ɗ Dental/alveolar	pʼ Bilabial
ǃ (Post)alveolar	ʄ Palatal	tʼ Dental/alveolar
ǂ Palatoalveolar	ɠ Velar	kʼ Velar
ǁ Alveolar lateral	ʛ Uvular	sʼ Alveolar fricative

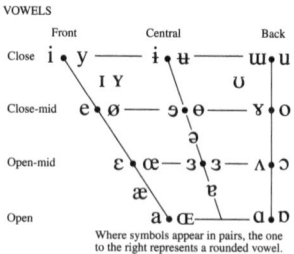

OTHER SYMBOLS

ʍ Voiceless labial-velar fricative   ɕ ʑ Alveolo-palatal fricatives
w Voiced labial-velar approximant   ɺ Alveolar lateral flap
ɥ Voiced labial-palatal approximant   ɧ Simultaneous ʃ and x
H Voiceless epiglottal fricative
ʢ Voiced epiglottal fricative   Affricates and double articulations can be represented by two symbols joined by a tie bar if necessary. k͡p t͡s
ʡ Epiglottal plosive

VOWELS

Front   Central   Back
Close   i • y — ɨ • ʉ — ɯ • u
         ɪ ʏ   ʊ
Close-mid   e • ø — ɘ • ɵ — ɤ • o
                    ə
Open-mid   ɛ • œ — ɜ • ɞ — ʌ • ɔ
              æ   ɐ
Open   a • ɶ ——— ɑ • ɒ

Where symbols appear in pairs, the one to the right represents a rounded vowel.

SUPRASEGMENTALS

ˈ Primary stress
ˌ Secondary stress   ˌfoʊnəˈtɪʃən
ː Long   eː
ˑ Half-long   eˑ
˘ Extra-short   ĕ
| Minor (foot) group
‖ Major (intonation) group
. Syllable break   ɹi.ækt
‿ Linking (absence of a break)

DIACRITICS   Diacritics may be placed above a symbol with a descender, e.g. ŋ̊

̥ Voiceless	n̥ d̥	̤ Breathy voiced	b̤ a̤	̪ Dental	t̪ d̪
̬ Voiced	s̬ t̬	̰ Creaky voiced	b̰ a̰	̺ Apical	t̺ d̺
ʰ Aspirated	tʰ dʰ	̼ Linguolabial	t̼ d̼	̻ Laminal	t̻ d̻
̹ More rounded	ɔ̹	ʷ Labialized	tʷ dʷ	̃ Nasalized	ẽ
̜ Less rounded	ɔ̜	ʲ Palatalized	tʲ dʲ	ⁿ Nasal release	dⁿ
̟ Advanced	u̟	ˠ Velarized	tˠ dˠ	ˡ Lateral release	dˡ
̠ Retracted	e̠	ˤ Pharyngealized	tˤ dˤ	̚ No audible release	d̚
̈ Centralized	ë	̴ Velarized or pharyngealized	ɫ		
̽ Mid-centralized	ẽ̽	̝ Raised	e̝	(ɹ̝ = voiced alveolar fricative)	
̩ Syllabic	n̩	̞ Lowered	e̞	(β̞ = voiced bilabial approximant)	
̯ Non-syllabic	e̯	̘ Advanced Tongue Root	e̘		
˞ Rhoticity	ɚ a˞	̙ Retracted Tongue Root	e̙		

TONES AND WORD ACCENTS

LEVEL   CONTOUR
e̋ or ˥ Extra high   ě or ˩˥ Rising
é   ˦ High   ê   ˥˩ Falling
ē   ˧ Mid   e᷄   ˦˥ High rising
è   ˨ Low   e᷅   ˩˨ Low rising
ȅ   ˩ Extra low   e᷈   ˧˦˧ Rising-Falling
↓ Downstep   ↗ Global rise
↑ Upstep   ↘ Global fall

References

Andersen, Henning (1969) The phonological status of the Russian 'labial fricatives'. *Journal of Linguistics* 5: 121–7.
   (1986) (ed.) *Sandhi phenomena in the languages of Europe*. Berlin: de Gruyter.
Anderson, Stephen R. (1974) *The organization of phonology*. New York: Academic Press.
   (1984) A metrical interpretation of some traditional claims about quantity and stress. In Aronoff and Oehrle, 83–106.
   (1985) *Phonology in the twentieth century: theories of rules and theories of representations*. Chicago: University of Chicago Press.
Árnason, Kristján (1980) *Quantity in historical phonology: Icelandic and related cases*. Cambridge: Cambridge University Press.
   (1986) The segmental and suprasegmental status of preaspiration in Modern Icelandic. *Nordic Journal of Linguistics* 9: 1–23.
   (1998) Vowel shortness in Icelandic. In Wolfgang Kehrein and Richard Wiese (eds.), *Phonology and morphology of the Germanic languages*, 3–25. Tübingen: Niemeyer.
Aronoff, Mark and Mary-Louise Kean (1980) (eds.) *Juncture*. Saratoga, CA: Anma Libri.
Aronoff, Mark and Richard T. Oehrle (1984) (eds.) *Language sound structure: studies in phonology presented to Morris Halle by his teacher and students*. Cambridge, MA: MIT Press.
Benediktsson, Hreinn (1963) The non-uniqueness of phonemic solutions: quantity and stress in Icelandic. *Phonetica* 10: 133–53.
Bérkov, Valeríj P. and Árni Böðvarsson (1962) *Íslenzk-rússnesk orðabók*. Moskva: Gosudarstvennoje Izdatel'stvo Inostrannych i Nacional' nych Slovarej.
Bethin, Christina Y. (1992) *Polish syllables: the role of prosody in phonology and morphology*. Columbus, OH: Slavica.
Bickmore, Lee S. (1995) Accounting for compensatory lengthening in the CV and moraic frameworks. In Durand, 119–48.
Blankenhorn, Victoria S. (1981) Pitch, quantity and stress in Munster Irish. *Éigse* 18: 225–50.
Blevins, Juliette (1995) The syllable in phonological theory. In Goldsmith, 206–44.
Blöndal, Sigfús (1924) *Íslensk-dönsk orðabók*. Reprinted 1980, Reykjavík: Íslensk-Danskur Orðabókarsjóður.
Bloomfield, Leonard (1933) *Language*. London: Allen and Unwin.
Booij, Geert (1995) *The phonology of Dutch*. Oxford: Oxford University Press.
Brockhaus, Wiebke (1995a) *Final devoicing in the phonology of German*. Tübingen: Niemeyer.

(1995b) Skeletal and suprasegmental structure within Government Phonology. In Durand, 180–221.

Campbell, Alistair (1959) *Old English grammar*. Oxford: Clarendon.

Charette, Monik (1991) *Conditions on phonological government*. Cambridge: Cambridge University Press.

Charette, Monik and Aslı Göksel (1998) Licensing constraints and vowel harmony in Turkic language. In Cyran, 65–88.

Chomsky, Noam and Morris Halle (1968) *The sound pattern of English*. New York: Harper and Row.

Clements, George N. and Samuel J. Keyser (1983) *CV phonology: a generative theory of the syllable*. Cambridge, MA: MIT Press.

Clements, George N. and Engin Sezer (1982) Vowel and consonant disharmony in Turkish. In van der Hulst and Smith, 213–55.

Cyran, Eugeniusz (1998) (ed.) *Structure and interpretation: studies in phonology*. Lublin: Folium.

Cyran, Eugeniusz and Morgan Nilsson (1998) The Slavic [w>v] shift: a case for phonological strength. In Cyran, 89–100.

Dressler, Wolfgang U. (1985) On the definite Austrian and Italian articles. In Gussmann 1985b, 35–47.

Durand, Jacques (1986) French liaison, floating segments and other matters in a Dependency framework. In Jacques Durand (ed.), *Dependency and non-linear phonology*, 161–201. London: Croom Helm.

(1995) (ed.) *Frontiers of phonology: atoms, structures, derivations*. London: Longman.

Einarsson, Stefán (1945) *Icelandic: grammar texts glossary*. Baltimore: Johns Hopkins Press.

Fischer-Jørgensen, Eli (1975) *Trends in phonological theory: a historical introduction*. Copenhagen: Akademisk Vorlag.

Fromkin, Victoria A. (1971) The non-anomalous nature of anomalous utterances. *Language* 47: 27–52.

Fudge, Erik (1972) (ed.) *Phonology: selected readings*. Harmondsworth: Penguin.

Giegerich, Heinz J. (1985) *Metrical phonology and phonological structure: German and English*. Cambridge: Cambridge University Press.

(1992) *English Phonology: an introduction*. Cambridge: Cambridge University Press.

(1999) *Lexical strata in English: morphological causes, phonological effects*. Cambridge: Cambridge University Press.

Gimson, Alfred C. and Allan Cruttenden (1994) *Gimson's Pronunciation of English*. London: Edward Arnold.

Gíslason, Indriði and Höskuldur Þráinsson (1993) *Handbók um íslenskan framburð*. Reykjavík: Rannsóknarstofnun Kennaraháskóla Íslands.

Goldsmith, John A. (1990) *Autosegmental and metrical phonology*. Oxford: Blackwell.

(1995) (ed.) *The handbook of phonological theory*. Oxford: Blackwell.

Green, Antony D. (1996) Stress placement in Munster Irish. In *Papers from the 32nd regional meeting of the Chicago Linguistic Society*, 77–91. Chicago: Chicago Linguistic Society.

Guðfinnsson, Björn (1946) *Mállýzkur I*. Reykjavík: Ísafoldarprenstsmiðja.

Gussmann, Edmund (1980) *Studies in abstract phonology*. Cambridge, MA: MIT Press.

(1985a) The morphology of a phonological rule: Icelandic vowel length. In Gussmann, Edmund 1985b, 75–94.
(1985b) (ed.), *Phono-Morphology: studies in the interaction of phonology and morphology*. Lublin: Redakcja Wydawnictw Katolickiego Uniwersytetu Lubelskiego.
(1991) Schwa and syllabic sonorants in a non-linear phonology of English. *Anglica Wratislaviensia* 18: 25–39.
(1997) Putting your best foot forward: stress in Munster Irish. In Josephson Folke (ed.), *Celts and Vikings: Proceedings of the Fourth Symposium of Societas Celtologica Nordica*, 103–33. Göteborg: Göteborgs Universitet.
(1998) Domains, relations, and the English agma. In Cyran, 101–26.
(1999) Preaspiration in Icelandic: unity in diversity. *Anglica Wratislaviensia* 35: 163–81.
(2000) Icelandic preaspiration as a testing ground for phonological theories. In Gudrún Thórhallsdóttir (ed.), *The Nordic languages and modern linguistics 10*, 93–103. Reykjavík: Institute of Linguistics.
Hall, Tracy A. (1992) *Syllable structure and syllable-related processes in German*. Tübingen: Niemeyer.
Halle, Morris and William Idsardi (1995) General properties of stress and metrical structure. In Goldsmith, 403–43.
Halle, Morris and Jean-Roger Vergnaud (1987) *An essay on stress*. Cambridge, MA: MIT Press.
Handbook of the International Phonetic Association (1999). Cambridge: Cambridge University Press.
Harris, John (1994) *English sound structure*. Oxford: Blackwell.
(1997) Licensing inheritance: an integrated theory of neutralisation. *Phonology* 14: 315–70.
Harris, John and Edmund Gussmann (1998) Final codas: why the west was wrong. In Cyran, 139–62.
Haugen, Einar (1958) The phonemics of Modern Icelandic. *Language* 34: 55–88. Reprinted in Evelyn S. Firchow, Kaaren Grimstad, Nils Hasselmo and Wayne A. O'Neil (eds.), *Studies by Einar Haugen*, 355–89. The Hague: Mouton.
Hayes, Bruce (1984) The phonetics and phonology of Russian voicing assimilation. In Aronoff and Oehrle, 318–28.
(1986) Inalterability in CV phonology. *Language* 62: 321–51.
(1995) *Metrical stress theory: principles and case studies*. Chicago: University of Chicago Press.
Hogg, Richard M. (1992) *A grammar of Old English*, Volume I: *Phonology*. Oxford: Blackwell.
Hooper, Joan B. (1972) The syllable in phonological theory. *Language* 48: 525–40.
(1976) *An introduction to Natural Generative Phonology*. New York: Academic Press.
Jassem, Wiktor (1972) *Fonetyka języka angielskiego*. Warszawa: Państwowe Wydawnictwo Naukowe.
Jones, Daniel (1939) Concrete and abstract sounds. In E. Blancquaert and W. Pee (eds.), *Proceedings of the third International Congress of Phonetic Studies*, 1–7. Ghent: Laboratory of Phonetics of the University of Ghent.

(1975) *An outline of English phonetics*. 9th edition. Cambridge: Cambridge University Press.

(1997) *English pronouncing dictionary*. 15th edition, edited by Peter Roach and James Hartman. Cambridge: Cambridge University Press.

Kager, René (1995) The metrical theory of word stress. In Goldsmith, 367–402.

Kardela, Henryk and Bogdan Szymanek (1996) (eds.) *A festschrift for Edmund Gussmann from his friends and colleagues*. Lublin: University Press of the Catholic University of Lublin.

Kaye, Jonathan (1990) 'Coda' licensing. *Phonology* 7: 301–30.

(1995) Derivations and interfaces. In Durand, 289–332.

(1996) Do you believe in magic? The story of s+C sequences. In Kardela and Szymanek, 155–76.

Kaye, Jonathan, Jean Lowenstamm and Jean-Roger Vergnaud (1990) Constituent structure and government in phonology. *Phonology* 7: 193–231.

Kenstowicz, Michael (1994) *Phonology in generative grammar*. Oxford: Blackwell.

Keyser, Samuel J. and Paul Kiparsky (1984) Syllable structure in Finnish phonology. In Aronoff and Oehrle, 7–31.

Kilbury, James (1976) *The development of morphophonemic theory*. Amsterdam: John Benjamins.

Kress, Bruno (1982) *Isländische Grammatik*. Leipzig: Verlag Enzyklopädie.

Lass, Roger (1984) *Phonology: an introduction to basic concepts*. Cambridge: Cambridge University Press.

Loth, Joseph (1913) L'accent dans le gaelique du Munster. *Revue de Phonétique* 3: 317–43.

Meillet, Antoine (1970) *General characteristics of the Germanic languages*. Coral Gables, FL: University of Miami Press.

Mester, R. Armin (1986) *Studies in tier structure*. Amherst, MA: Graduate Linguistics Student Association.

Mitchell, Bruce and Fred C. Robinson (1992) *A guide to Old English*. 5th Edition. Oxford: Blackwell.

Morozova, Aune G. (1972) *Učebnik finskogo jazyka*. Petrozavodsk: Izdatel'stvo 'Karelija'.

Ó Cuív, Brian (1944) *The Irish of West Muskerry, Co. Cork: a phonetic study*. Dublin: Dublin Institute for Advanced Studies.

Ó Sé, Diarmuid (1989) Contributions to the study of word stress in Irish. *Ériu* 40: 147–78.

Ó Siadhail, Mícheál (1989) *Modern Irish: grammatical structure and dialectal variation*. Cambridge: Cambridge University Press.

Ó Siadhail Mícheál and Arndt Wigger (1975) *Córas fuaimeanna na Gaeilge*. Dublin: Institiúid Ard-Léinn Bhaile Átha Cliath.

Orešnik, Janez and Magnús Pétursson (1977) Quantity in Modern Icelandic. *Arkiv för Nordisk Filologii* 92: 155–71.

Perlmutter, David (1995) Phonological quantity and multiple association. In Goldsmith, 307–17.

Pigott, Glyne L. (1991) Apocope and the licensing of empty-headed syllables. *Linguistic Review* 8: 287–318.

(1999) At the right edge of words. *Linguistic Review* 16: 143–85.

Prince, Alan S. (1984) Phonology with tiers. In Aronoff and Oehrle, 234–44.

Rowicka, Grażyna (1996) 2 + 2 = 3. Stress in Munster Irish. In Kardela and Szymanek, 217–37.
Rubach, Jerzy (1990) Final devoicing and cyclic syllabification in German. *Linguistic Inquiry* 21: 79–94.
Sapir, Edward (1925) Sound patterns in language. *Language* 1: 37–51. Reprinted in Fudge 1972: 101–14.
Schein, Barry and Donca Steriade (1986) On geminates. *Linguistic Inquiry* 17: 691–744.
Selkirk, Elisabeth O. (1982) The syllable. In van der Hulst and Smith, 337–83.
Sezer, Engin (1986) An autosegmental analysis of compensatory lengthening in Turkish. In Leo Wetzels and Engin Sezer (eds.), *Studies in compensatory lengthening*, 227–50. Dordrecht: Foris.
Shvedova, N. J. (1980) (ed.) *Russkaja grammatika*, Volume I. Moskva: Izdatel'stvo Nauka.
Sjoestedt, Marie L. (1931) *Phonétique d'un parler irlandais de Kerry*. Paris: Librairie Ernest Leroux.
Sjoestedt-Jonval, Marie L. (1938) *Description d'un parler irlandais de Kerry*. Paris: Librairie Ancienne Honoré Champion.
Stanley, Richard (1973) Boundaries in phonology. In Stephen R. Anderson and Paul Kiparsky (eds.), *A festschrift for Morris Halle*, 185–206. New York: Holt, Rinehart and Winston.
Stong-Jensen, Margaret (1992) Syncope as syllabification in Icelandic. In J. Louis-Jensen and J. H. W. Poulsen (eds.), *The Nordic languages and modern linguistics 7*, 605–14. Tórshaven: Føroya Fróðskaparfelag.
Thomas, Alan R. (1984) A lowering rule for vowels and its ramifications, in a dialect of north Welsh. In Martin J. Ball and Glyn E. Jones (eds.), *Welsh phonology: selected readings*, 105–24. Cardiff: University of Wales Press.
Thorne, David (1993) *A comprehensive grammar of Welsh*. Oxford: Blackwell.
Thráinsson, Höskuldur (1978) On the phonology of Icelandic preaspiration. *Nordic Journal of Linguistics* 1: 3–54.
Trask, R. L. (1996) A dictionary of phonetics and phonology. London: Routledge.
Vachek, Josef (1964) Notes on the phonematic value of the modern English [ŋ]-sound. In D. Abercrombie, D. B. Fry, P. A. D. MacCarthy, N. C. Scott, and J. L. M. Trim (eds.), *In honour of Daniel Jones*, 191–205. London: Longman.
  (1976) The problem of the phonematic status of the Modern English [ŋ] sound. In Josef Vachek, *Selected writings in English and general linguistics*, 224–33. Prague: Academia.
van der Hulst, Harry (1999) (ed.) *Word prosodic systems in the languages of Europe*. Berlin: Mouton de Gruyter.
van der Hulst, Harry and Norval Smith (eds.) (1982) *The structure of phonological representations* (part 2). Dordrecht: Foris.
van der Hulst, Harry and Jeroen van de Weijer (1995) Vowel harmony. In Goldsmith, 495–534.
van der Hulst, Harry and Nancy A. Ritter (1999) (eds.) *The syllable: views and facts*. Berlin: Mouton de Gruyter.
Vennemann, Theo (1972) On the theory of syllabic phonology. *Linguistische Berichte* 18: 1–18.
  (1988) *Preference laws for syllable structure and the explanation of sound change*. Berlin: Mouton de Gruyter.

Wells, John C. (1982) *Accents of English*, Volumes I–III. Cambridge: Cambridge University Press.
— (1990) *Longman Pronunciation Dictionary*. London: Longman.
Whitney, Arthur H. (1959) *Teach yourself Finnish*. London: English Universities Press.
Wierzchowska, Bożena (1971) *Wymowa polska*. Warszawa: Państwowe Zakłady Wydawnictw Szkolnych.
Wiese, Richard (1996) *The phonology of German*. Oxford: Oxford University Press.

Index

alternations 9, 11, 13, 56, 60, 87, 89, 99, 100, 108, 126, 129, 131, 139, 142, 144, 146, 163, 204, 209
assimilation *see* sharing
association condition 23, 24, 42–3

codas 76–8, 91–117
   coda–onset combination 77–8, 88, 95, 96–9, 101, 109, 160–1, 168, 171, 173, 175–7, 178–81, 183–4, 188, 191, 224
complement, rhymal *see* codas
concatenation 48
consitutents, syllabic *see* onset, rhymes, nuclei
constraint 35, 36, 103, 106, 135, 139, 186

diphthong 2, 20–3, 26
   short 27, 133, 158
distribution 5, 15, 31, 37
domain 45, 49–54, 58–9, 63–4, 99, 189–91, 224
Dutch
   place sharing 82–4, 105–6

effect, phonetic 61, 64, 186, 203
English
   affricates 31–40, 80
   aspiration 4–6, 17
   coronals 21, 23, 31–40
   diphthongs 2, 20–3
   dark and *clear l* 11–12
   fake geminates 26–7
   fricatives 12–17, 31–40, 80–1
   inflectional morphology 31–40
   intrusive r 42–3
   linking r 40–3
   nasal sharing 79–82, 102–5
   nasals 45–54
   onsets 72–6
   place sharing 81–2
   plosives 4–6
   quantity of vowels 20, 22
   rhymes 76–8
   s-clusters 74
   strong and weak forms 39–40, 124–5
   syllabic sonorants 69, 129–30
   tense–lax opposition 20

triphthongs 20, 73
velar nasal 20–1, 23, 46–54
voice sharing 33–4
voiceless sonorants 6
vowel reduction 124–30, 154
vowels 2, 20–3
yod 113–15
erasure 152
exceptionality 32, 58
   lexical 212
exclusiveness, mutual 32

Finnish
   vowel simplifications 24–6
   geminates 26
foot 215
   degenerate 216
   head of 261
   maximal 216–22
fortition 146
French
   absence of aspiration 5
   h-aspiré 69–72
   h-muet 70–2
   liaison 71–2
   vowel elision 70–1

geminates 13, 15, 26, 134
   fake 26–7
   partial 51
German
   backness sharing 61–2
   dorsal spirants 59–63
   final devoicing 145–54, 155, 186–7
   place sharing 84–6, 105–6
   r-sounds 64
   spirantisation 187, 204
   spirants 61–3
Germanic
   compensatory lengthening 28–9
   nuclear simplifications 23–4

heterosyllabicity 94, 112
homophony, morphological 36

homorganicity 50, 74–6, 79–82, 83, 84–5, 87–9, 98–9, 107, 132

Icelandic
  aspiration of plosives 5, 54–5, 134
  codas 163–7, 185
  consonants 158
  diphthongs 158
  onsets 163–7, 185
  open syllable lengthening 159–61, 184, 188
  preaspiration 54–59, 134
  short diphthongs 27, 158
  spirantisation 135–9
  voiceless sonorants 6, 55
  voicelessness of plosives 5, 54
  vowels 157–8
Irish
  codas 92–5
  foot structure 217–22
  low vowels 7–11, 17
  palatalisation of consonants 7
  velarisation of consonants 7
  word stress 205–22
Italian
  vowel length 108–10
  article, variants of 110–13

lengthening, compensatory 28–30
lenition 137, 146
licensing 41, 101, 106, 147–8, 153, 163, 181

melody 9, 22–3, 26–7, 31, 42, 45, 66, 68, 71, 91, 118, 224
  floating 90

neutralisation 147
nuclei 67–70, 91
  atonic 141
  branching 68
  complex 21
  empty 33–4, 38–40, 76, 85, 87–90, 91, 95, 97–8, 101, 104, 106, 112, 113, 115, 138, 149–50, 152–3, 155, 162, 165, 169, 175, 184, 189, 224
  non-branching 68
  simplifications of, 23–6
  tonic 141

Old English
  compensatory lengthening 28–9, 30
  fricatives 12–17, 17
  vowels 23–4
onset 67–70, 91, 107–8, 116
  branching 68, 73–6, 107, 114–15, 164–7
  empty 67, 69–72, 89–90, 91, 224

  non-branching 68, 73–6, 107
optionality 29

phonotactics 96
Polish
  dorsal obstruents 197–200, 204
  frontness sharing 198–200
  nasal sharing 86–9, 105–6, 132
  nasal vowels 130–4, 155
  place sharing 132
  stress 86
positions, skeletal *see* skeleton
productivity 31
pseudo-morpheme 54

rhymes 76–8, 80–2, 91, 161, 214
Russian
  absence of aspiration 5
  final devoicing 193
  frontness sharing 140–2
  labial fricatives 193–7, 204
  voice assimilation 193–4
  vowel reduction 139–45

sandhi 64
sharing 33, 51, 61–2, 79–82, 82–4, 84–6, 101–6, 118, 140–1, 198–200
skeleton 19, 22–3, 26–7, 31, 42, 45, 66, 68, 71, 91, 118, 224
slot, skeletal *see* skeleton
spreading 194
syllabification 91–2, 93, 107, 113, 116, 136
syllable 66, 89, 224
  closed 76, 99, 100, 160–1
  open 67, 160–1

Turkish
  compensatory lengthening 29–30
  Frontness Harmony 120–2, 154
  Rounding Harmony 122–3, 154
  vowels 119
tautosyllabicity 94
tiers *see* melody, skeleton, onsets, rhymes

vowel harmony 119

Welsh
  vowels 200–3, 204
  vowel mutation 201–3
words 1, 45, 49, 57, 63–4
  attested 3
  function 16, 124
  major class 16
  potential 3, 46